Financialisation and Poverty Alleviation in Ghana

Studies in Critical Social Sciences

Series Editor
David Fasenfest
(*Wayne State University*)

VOLUME 209

New Scholarship in Political Economy

Series Editors
David Fasenfest
(*Wayne State University*)
Alfredo Saad-Filho
(*King's College London*)

Editorial Board
Kevin B. Anderson (*University of California, Santa Barbara*)
Tom Brass (*formerly of SPS, University of Cambridge*)
Raju Das (*York University*)
Ben Fine ((*emeritus*) SOAS *University of London*)
Jayati Ghosh (*Jawaharlal Nehru University*)
Elizabeth Hill (*University of Sydney*)
Dan Krier (*Iowa State University*)
Lauren Langman (*Loyola University Chicago*)
Valentine Moghadam (*Northeastern University*)
David N. Smith (*University of Kansas*)
Susanne Soederberg (*Queen's University*)
Aylin Topal (*Middle East Technical University*)
Fiona Tregenna (*University of Johannesburg*)
Matt Vidal (*Loughborough University London*)
Michelle Williams (*University of the Witwatersrand*)

VOLUME 14

The titles published in this series are listed at *brill.com/nspe*

Financialisation and Poverty Alleviation in Ghana

Myths and Realities

By

Francis Boateng Frimpong

BRILL

LEIDEN | BOSTON

Cover illustration: Bust of Karl Marx, 1939, by S.D. Merkurov, at the Fallen Monument Park (Muzeon Park of Arts) in Moscow, Russia. Photo courtesy of Alfredo Saad-Filho.

Library of Congress Cataloging-in-Publication Data

Names: Frimpong, Francis Boateng, author.
Title: Financialisation and poverty alleviation in Ghana : myths and realities / by Francis Boateng Frimpong.
Description: Leiden ; Boston : Brill, [2022] | Series: Studies in critical social sciences, 2666-2205 ; volume 209 | Includes index.
Identifiers: LCCN 2021047781 (print) | LCCN 202104778 (ebook) | ISBN 9789004499973 (hardback) | ISBN 9789004500020 (ebook)
Subjects: LCSH: Ghana–Economic policy–20th century. | Ghana–Economic conditions–1957-1979.
Classification: LCC HC1060 .F755 2022 (print) | LCC HC1060 (ebook) | DDC 338.09667–dc23
LC record available at https://lccn.loc.gov/2021047781
LC ebook record available at https://lccn.loc.gov/2021047782

Typeface for the Latin, Greek, and Cyrillic scripts: "Brill". See and download: brill.com/brill-typeface.

ISSN 2666-2205
ISBN 978-90-04-49997-3 (hardback)
ISBN 978-90-04-50002-0 (e-book)

Copyright 2022 by Francis Boateng Frimpong. Published by Koninklijke Brill NV, Leiden, The Netherlands.
Koninklijke Brill NV incorporates the imprints Brill, Brill Nijhoff, Brill Hotei, Brill Schöningh, Brill Fink, Brill mentis, Vandenhoeck & Ruprecht, Böhlau Verlag and V&R Unipress.
All rights reserved. No part of this publication may be reproduced, translated, stored in a retrieval system, or transmitted in any form or by any means, electronic, mechanical, photocopying, recording or otherwise, without prior written permission from the publisher.
Authorization to photocopy items for internal or personal use is granted by Koninklijke Brill NV provided that the appropriate fees are paid directly to The Copyright Clearance Center, 222 Rosewood Drive, Suite 910, Danvers, MA 01923, USA. Fees are subject to change.

This book is printed on acid-free paper and produced in a sustainable manner.

Contents

Foreword IX
   Vassilis K. Fouskas
Acknowledgements XI
List of Figures and Tables XII
Abbreviations XV
About *Financialisation and Poverty Alleviation in Ghana* XVI

1 **Introduction** 1
  1 The Historical Background of Finance and Growth 3
  2 Scope and Limitations of the Book 10
  3 Structure of the Book 13

2 **Neoliberalisation and Financialisation**
  The Debate 18
  1 Introduction 18
  2 The Rise of Neoliberal Capitalism 18
  3 Theoretical Debates and Historical Precedents of Financialisation 30
  4 From Stagnation to Financialisation 32
  5 French Regulation School Theory of Financialisation 38
  6 Post-Keynesianism and Financialisation 40
  7 Trans-nationalisation and Liberalisation of Finance 45
  8 Financialisation and Poverty Alleviation: Banking the Unbanked 48
  9 Conclusion 53

3 **Finance-Growth-Nexus**
  Theoretical and Empirical Literature 55
  1 Introduction 55
  2 The Rise of Finance and the Financialisation of Everything 55
  3 The Financial Profit Conundrum – Profit in Marxist Economics 61
  4 Real Commodity Accumulation and Fictitious Accumulation 65
  5 Contemporary Heterodox Perspectives on Finance-led Growth Debate 69
    5.1 *Banks, Financial Markets and Economic Growth: The Dilemma* 70
  6 Economic Functions of Financial Intermediaries 76
    6.1 *Empirical Evidence on Finance and Growth* 77

    6.2   *Cross-country Studies of the Finance-Growth Nexus* 77
    6.3   *Contemporary Literature on Econometric Models for Ghana* 79
7   Dynamics of Financial Development, Income Distribution, Economic Growth and Poverty Reduction in Ghana 80
8   Poverty and the Pandemic: The Case of Ghana 83
    8.1   *The Economics of It All* 84
9   Conclusion 91

4 The Case of Ghana 93
1   Introduction 93
2   Country Profile and Overview of Recent Economic Performance 93
3   The Political Economy of Ghana: From State-led Accumulation to Neoliberalism 97
    3.1   *Political and Economic Developments from Independence (1957) to 1982* 98
    3.2   *Political and Economic Developments 1983–2019* 102
4   Neoliberalism in Ghana 103
    4.1   *Neoliberalism and Housing Provision in Ghana* 112
5   Financial Sector Reforms in Ghana – A Historical Perspective 117
    5.1   *Pre-structural Adjustment Financial Reforms 1957–1982* 117
    5.2   *Post-liberalised Reforms* 118
    5.3   *Relaxation of Bank Entry Restrictions, and Abolishment of Secondary Reserve Requirements 2005–2006* 120
    5.4   *Recapitalising Banks* 120
6   Financialisation in Sub-Saharan Africa: Accounting for the Ghanaian Paradox 121
    6.1   *Under-financed* 122
    6.2   *... Yet Financialising* 129
    6.3   *Reverse of Net Capital Flows – A Subordinate/Inferior Financialisation* 135
7   Conclusion 142

5 Dimensions of Capital Structure and Liquidity Management in Ghana 144
1   Introduction 144
2   Theories of Capital Structure 145
    2.1   *Capital Structure: Traditionalists' View* 145
    2.2   *Value-irrelevance Theory by Modigliani-Miller* 146

         2.3   *Capital Structure: Trade-off Theory*   147
         2.4   *Capital Structure: Pecking-order Theory*   147
   3   Financialisation and Capital Structure Accumulation in Ghana   148
   4   Classification of Capital Accumulation Process in Ghana   149
   5   Contradictions in Political-Economic Arrangements in Ghana   152
         5.1   *Financing Challenges*   152
         5.2   *Government Policies*   164
               5.2.1   Corruption   165
               5.2.2   State of Infrastructural Development   167
   6   Conclusion   169

6   **The Issue of Poverty**   171
   1   Introduction   171
   2   Poverty Measurement Conundrum   176
   3   Absolute Poverty   189
         3.1   *Poverty in Administrative Regions*   189
   4   Relative Poverty   192
         4.1   *Using Non-monetary Deprivation*   193
   5   The Paradox of Sub-Saharan Africa's Middle Class   194
         5.1   *The Two Competing Narratives on Africa*   199
   6   Neoliberal Globalisation and Poverty   200
   7   Conclusion   207

7   **Financialisation and Households**
   From Theory to the Context of Ghana   209
   1   Introduction   209
   2   Theory of Consumption Function: Household Debt and the Life Cycle and Permanent Income Hypotheses   209
   3   The Political Economy of Household Finance   212
   4   Payment Systems in Ghana: A Route towards Financialisation   217
         4.1   *Background-Mobile Money Services in Ghana*   217
         4.2   *The Role of Mobile Money in Financial Inclusion in Ghana*   223
   5   Financialisation, Financial Inclusion and Mobile Money   227
   6   Conclusion   232

8   **Conclusion**   234
   1   Summing Up the Argument   234
   2   The Content of Financialisation in Ghana   238
         2.1   *Banking Sector*   238

        2.2   *Industrial Enterprises*   238
        2.3   *Households*   239
   3 Policy Recommendations   240

References   243
Index   265

Foreword

Vassilis K. Fouskas

One set of mainstream neo-liberal economic theories have several illusions. One of them is that they believe that the world can become, so to speak, "flat", especially when free market rules prevail. The free market will be in a position to deliver, distribute and re-distribute economic prosperity, wealth and equality embracing all humankind from Chile to Russia and from Scotland to Nigeria and India. Another set of the same neo-liberal stock is more careful. It argues more forcefully than the first one that the market, in order to deliver equality and drive people out of poverty, needs to compound strict rules and legal-institutional frameworks, also by way of completely de-politicising its functions. Effectively, the attempt here is to exclude social struggle and politics from economic decision-making, so that the market rule becomes the only rule – this is the famous German-Austrian notion of "social market economy", at times also referred to as "ordoliberalism". Alas, none of these two sets of orthodoxy delivered any of these promises since the 1970s, when their political programmes found expression through the policies of Pinochet in Chile, Margaret Thatcher in the UK and Ronald Reagan in the USA.

But there is also the international aspect of neo-liberalism which, conventionally, came to be called "globalisation" – some also prefer the term "financialisation", as finance was the first economic sector that became truly globalised after the official end of the Bretton Woods system in August 1971. Frimpong, using the works of Peter Gowan, Giovanni Arrighi and other political economists that subscribe to the core-periphery dichotomy, argues that neo-liberal globalisation spread from the Anglo-American core to the rest of the world in a manner that damaged the countries of the periphery. Other than making the world "flat" delivering prosperity and alleviating poverty, the opening up of the economies of the periphery to global financial operations worsened the everyday lives of people in sub-Saharan Africa while transferring funds back to the financial systems of the core. By focusing on the case of Ghana, Frimpong shows that although Ghana's economy is financialised, none or very little of this finance trickles down to the real economic sector.

Financialisation takes the form of subordinate financialisation and massive transfers of value occur undermining domestic capital accumulation and developmental policies. Thus, in 2010 an estimated 240 million people in sub-Saharan Africa (around 30% of the population) were well below poverty levels and, effectively, hungry. The numbers are the same in 2020 and the pandemic made the situation worse. The Central African Republic is ranked the poorest state in the world with a GDP per capita of no more than $656. Hundreds of millions of people lack access to clean water, live without electricity and 1/3 of the population is under-nourished. To top it all, less than 20% of women have access to education and 1 in every 16 women die during childbirth or pregnancy – the respective numbers on North America are 1 in 4,000 women.

Effectively, as the aim of neo-liberal globalisation/financialisation is to increase the financial profit and transfer it back to the core financial systems, the entire operation ended up "banking the unbanked", Frimpong argues, further damaging the poor. As global finance tried to include in its operation of extracting profits from the poor, the poor became poorer rather than richer (chapter 2). In this respect, and because of "financial expropriation" as argued by Costas Lapavitsas, the financialisation of household and everyday life worsened instead of ameliorating the lives of individuals in Ghana (chapter 7). Further, Frimpong takes issue with the inadequate official definitions of "relative" and "absolute" "poverty" considering them as one of the obstacles to the solution of the problem in Ghana and more broadly. Overall, that is how much "flat" our world has become in the era of globalisation/financialisation. Frimpong delivers an unmistakable, yet measured and scholarly, verdict on all this in chapter 6.

But has growth not occurred since Ghana's independence? Frimpong asks. It has, but this growth was slow and not good enough. Funds were diverted to unproductive economic sectors, whereas government elites have been rife with corruption and incompetence. Thus, not only external but also domestic factors contribute to the current malaise of the country and, indeed, of the entire sub-Saharan Africa (chapter 4). In the end, Frimpong's argument is that growth has been sluggish and poor, yet without development.

One of the most remarkable aspects of this work is that it is both empirically and theoretically informed. It is a work that should be read in the great tradition of "world systems theory", propounded by Immanuel Wallerstein, Andre Gunder Frank, Christopher Chase-Dunn and Giovanni Arrighi (chapter 2). No accident that most of these theorists began their initial investigation by way of focusing on "third world" countries, either in Africa or Latin America. Frimpong, recognising the theoretical, historical and empirical value of this tradition adopts the same path, yet renewing and revitalising this tradition taking into account new heterodox, Marxian and post-Keynesian contributions. Frimpong's work is a very significant contribution to the scholarly development of African studies in the UK and internationally and its findings and criticisms to mainstream neoliberal economic theories should be read and debated widely.

Acknowledgements

The success of this book has been possible due to the huge support of a number of people. First and foremost, my deepest appreciation goes to my mentor, Professor Vassilis Fouskas, for his guidance, scrutiny and immense support throughout. It was an honour and privilege working with him. I would also like to acknowledge and appreciate comments and suggestions of Dr Ejike Udeogu. My sincere thanks also go to my friends, Dr Godfried Adaba and Dr Abraham Adu for their friendly support and encouragement. My utmost appreciation goes to my very special friend, Leah Mwainyekule, whom without, this book would have never been possible. She spent weeks editing, proofreading, and commenting on everything, with the goal of making the final product of high standard. I will forever be indebted to her. My final gratitude goes to my family for their support and love throughout my professional journey. I thank my mum and dad, who, however, did not live to see the fruits of their labour.

Figures and Tables

Figures

1. Brent Crude oil six months price to July 2020   87
2. Gold prices 12 months to July 2020   89
3. Real GDP growth rate (%) 2000–2018   95
4. GDP composition by sector 2002–2016   96
5. Inflation rates in Ghana 1965–1995   104
6. Broad money relative to GDP 2004–2018 – selected countries   125
7. Stock market capitalisation relative to GDP – selected countries (2000–2017)   125
8. Total credit to private non-financial sector – selected countries (2000–2016)   126
9. Deposit money bank assets and central bank assets relative to GDP Ghana (1973–2016)   127
10. 15 years of age and over with bank account at a formal financial institution – selected countries 2011–2017   128
11. Commercial/universal bank branches per 1000km^2 in Ghana (2004- 2017)   129
12. Deposit money bank assets relative to GDP (Ghana) 1975–2015   130
13. Deposit money bank assets relative to GDP – selected countries 1973–2015   130
14. Percentage of foreign bank assets relative to total bank assets in Ghana 2005–2012   131
15. Universal banks profit before tax margin (2011–2017)   132
16. Return on equity for Ghana, the UK and the US banks   133
17. Trade balance, current transfers and capital flows to Ghana (in millions US$)   139
18. Various sources of finance for long term investment   153
19. Percentage of working capital that is financed by external sources   154
20. Percentage of working capital across firm size   155
21. Financial constraints and loan conditions in Ghana, SSA, and lower middle-income countries   156
22. Financial constraints across firms based on size of firm   156
23. Monetary policy rate, inflation (end of the year), and 91-day treasury bill rates 2000–2016   157
24. Graft Index of corruption: Ghana, Sub-Saharan Africa and low middle-income countries   165
25. Exchange rate of the Ghana cedi against the pound, the dollar and the euro 2013–2017   167

26	The evolution of extreme poverty rates by region 1981–2010	172
27	The number of poor by region (million) 1981–2010	174
28	Regional share of the world's extreme poor population (%) 1981–2010	174
29	Proportion of population in absolute poverty ($1.90 per day in 2011 PPP)	175
30	Global extreme poverty rate and headcount, 1990–2015	175
31	Projections to 2030 of global extreme poverty	177
32	Poverty incidence by locality 2005–2017 (poverty line = GHc 1,314)	184
33	Extreme poverty incidence by locality 2005–2017 (poverty line = GHc 792.05)	186
34	Poverty incidence by region 2005–2017 (poverty line = GHc 1,314)	190
35	Distribution of African population by classes	196
36	Trade balance for Ghana (1995–2017 in $billion)	201
37	Exports relative to GDP for Ghana (1995–2017 in $billion)	202
38	Mobile Money float balance 2012–2017	218
39	Mobile Money transactions in Ghana 2012–2017	221
40	Comparison between bank accounts and Mobile Money accounts in Ghana 2013–2017	223
41	Mobile phone ownership and access, by demographic groups (percentage of each demographic group who owns and can access a mobile phone)	227
42	The amount (commission) paid in fees for transferring GHc 10	229

Tables

1	Selected key economic indicators, 2000–2017	95
2	Basic indicators of economic performance (percentage annual average growth) 1960–1995	103
3	List of universal banks in Ghana as of June 2018	123
4	Trade balance, current transfers and net capital flows to Ghana (in millions US$) 2003–2014	138
5	Sector distribution of foreign direct investment (in millions US$) 2010–2012	140
6	Universal bank lending and deposit annual percentage rates as of 31st January 2018	159
7	Composition of bank loans and advances (percentage) 2013–2017	163
8	Selected infrastructure indicators for Ghana, Sub-Saharan Africa and low middle-income countries	168
9	Poverty incidence and poverty gap by localities- 2005–2017 (poverty line = Ghc 1,314)	185

10   Extreme poverty incidence and poverty gap by locality 2005–2017 (extreme poverty line = GHc 792.05)   188
11   Poverty incidence and poverty gap by region (%) 2006–2017 (poverty line = GHc 1,314)   191
12   Mobile Money transactions 2012- 2017   220
13   Retail payment instruments in Ghana   222
14   Households with a bank account or contributing to a saving scheme by locality and gender   225
15   Reasons for not having a bank account or contributing to a saving scheme by locality and gender   226

Abbreviations

DMB	Deposit Money Bank
ERP	Economic Recovery Programme
FDI	Foreign Direct Investment
FIH	Financial Instability Hypothesis
FINSAP	Financial Institution Sector Adjustment Programme
FINSSP	Financial Sector Strategic Plan
GAMA	Greater Accra Metropolitan Area
GDP	Gross Domestic Product
Ghc	New Ghanaian Cedi
GLSS	Ghana Living Standard Survey
GSS	Ghana Statistical Service
HIPC	Highly Indebted Poor Countries
IMF	International Monetary Fund
IPL	International Poverty Line
MFI	Microfinance Industry
MM	Mobile Money
MNCS	Multinational Corporations
NLC	National Liberation Council
NPART	Non-Performance Asset Recovery Trust
PHC	Population and Housing Census
PNDC	Provisional National Defence Council
PPP	Purchasing Power Parity
PwC	PricewaterhouseCoopers
RCBS	Rural and Community Banks
SAP	Structural Adjustment Programme
SMES	Small and Medium Scale Enterprises
SSA	Sub-Saharan Africa
SVO	Shareholders Value Orientation
UNCTAD	United Nations Conference on Trade and Development

About *Financialisation and Poverty Alleviation in Ghana*

Financial inclusion policy as a way of empowering the poor makes poverty a financial problem in Ghana – the financialisation of poverty. Francis Boateng Frimpong tackles this question with theoretical sophistication and vivid empirical detail. This is an original addition to our understanding of how-and-why neoliberal restructuring and its financialisation dimension work in a low middle-income country, the first country in Sub-Saharan Africa to achieve the *Millennium Development Goal 1*, which is the target of halving extreme poverty. Frimpong has authoritatively produced this important political economy contribution about the impact of the exponential growth of finance on poverty alleviation in Ghana. Highly recommended.
 – *Bülent Gökay, Professor of International Relations, Keele University*

This book provides original theoretically sophisticated, historically sensitive and empirically grounded analysis. The political economy history of Ghana is narrated in a way that makes the reader understand what the country went through, and where it is headed. The author has done justice in his narration.
 – *Abraham Adu, University of Aberdeen*

The book offers a comprehensive assessment of the nature and distinctive features of financialisation in the periphery, with a focus on Ghana. This book provides academics, professionals and policy makers with the understanding of policy response towards the alleviation of the overarching poverty in Ghana. Crucially, espousing an indispensable hypothetical approach to financialisation, the uniqueness of Ghana and its common features with the core. It is a must-read for supporters of both Keynesian and Marxism.
 – *Emmanuel Affum-Osei, Kwame Nkrumah University of Science and Technology*

All aspects of this book are fascinating to read. However, the one that fascinated me the most was the in-depth analysis on baking the unbanked, specifically the use of mobile money and how it still benefits the capitalists despite promises of relieving the poor. Frimpong's analyses throughout are a very interesting read for researchers, students, and even Marx and Keynes enthusiasts. It is a must read.
 – *Leah Mwainyekule, University of Hull*

A book on this historically specific geographical setting contributes theoretically to studies on financialisation in general, helping to determine its prominent features better. It is a good source of information for researchers who want to explore the history of the political economy of Sub-Saharan Africa, and in particular, Ghana.

– *Mato Magobe, The Open University of Tanzania*

CHAPTER 1

Introduction

This chapter lays out the theoretical concepts upon which the thesis of this book rests. The historical, theoretical and empirical evidence backing up this can be found in the chapters that follow.

Ghana has been hailed as one of the success stories in the sub-Saharan Africa subregion. The first country to gain independence from colonial rule in 1957 and the first to build a stable multi-party democracy in the 1990s. However, Ghana's post-independence achievements in improving life expectancy, infant mortality and literacy rates occurred during the period up to the mid-1970s. Since then, progress has generally slowed and in some cases, reversed. The leading causes of this chronic underdevelopment have been a subject of debate over many years.

A nation blessed with abundant natural and human resources, Ghana's slow economic development has been one of the most baffling paradoxes. Inexplicably, there is no agreement concerning the key factors obstructing economic progress in Ghana. However, there is no doubt that the country has experienced many obstacles, internally as well as externally, which undermined sustainable economic development. Some of these obstacles were self-inflicted and others because of its subordinate/peripheral status in the modern world-system.[1] Thus, the development crisis could be understood to reflect the country's history, geography, domestic policies as well as global geopolitics. The confluence of these factors has left the country stuck in chronic poverty.

The recent stable political-economic arrangements cast doubt on some of the previous findings that have investigated the weak economic development in Ghana (Quartey 2008; Adusei 2013). This draws attention to the fact that the major obstructing factor(s) slowing down economic progress have not been identified and addressed. This book is then set to investigate those impeding factors integral in the inconsistencies in the contemporary political-economic arrangement that have resulted in somewhat economic growth without sufficient development in Ghana.

---

1 The internal factors include the inconsistent political-economic arrangements adopted post-independence, the political instability, inept government, corruption, unfavourable weather (especially in the early 1980s), and lack of social capital. The external factors include imperialism and antagonistic international relations (see, for instance, Emmanuel 1972; Arrighi 2002).

The policy response of the Washington Consensus[2] to Ghana's problem was to provide the needed financial assistance on condition of strict austerity plus deregulation. The implementation of these measures led to the reduction of the workforce in the public sector, abolishing government subsidies, public sector wage freeze and rising unemployment in the economy. Moreover, the neoliberal globalisation policies of trade and financial liberalisation, deregulation and privatisation of state companies has resulted in severe socio-economic dislocation, poverty and inequality at the macroeconomic level.

The recent government developmental agenda is to emulate the success story of the East Asian miracle, which saw them growing faster than all the regions in the world. The transition from poverty to prosperity will require Ghana to turn back on the old economy, which has been dependent on the neoliberal market mechanism, aid, and the production and export of primary commodities. The institutional restructuring, modernising the agricultural sector to enhance productivity and growth and investment in manufacturing and industry will enable sustained economic development that will improve the standard of living of the people.

The economic success stories of the East Asian miracle, where the region's GDP per capita increased significantly, accompanied by a drastic decrease in poverty, have frequently been attributed to neoliberal economic policies. However, Chang (2010) argues that the development trajectories of these countries demonstrate the significance of strategic, rather than unrestricted integration with the global economy. Korea and Taiwan all embarked on state-owned enterprises more broadly. Singapore embraced free trade more extensively than other Asian countries and also relied on FDI for its economic development. However, it doesn't conform to many aspects of neoliberal doctrines. For instance, Singapore provides extensive support in the form of subsidies to attract Multinational Corporations (MNCs) into sectors that are considered strategic for national development. State infrastructure development and targeted academic and vocational courses at particular sectors and industries have been used widely. Singapore is a global leader in State Owned-Enterprises. The State Housing Development Board, for instance, provides about 85% of all housing units, and the government owns and controls almost all land in the country.

China and India's integration into the global economy was based on nationalistic inward-looking vision rather than global outward-looking dreams.

---

2 The Washington Consensus is the market-based economic policy prescriptions supported by prominent financial institutions such as the International Monetary Fund, the World Bank, and the US Treasury.

China adopted high tariffs to protect its strategic industries, in particular, the manufacturing base of the economy. The average Chinese tariff was about 30% in the 1990s. Nevertheless, the country attracts more FDI but still imposes foreign ownership ceiling and local content requirements, which mandate foreign firms to acquire a certain proportion of their inputs from domestic businesses and suppliers.

Furthermore, neoliberals wrongly attribute India's economic success to globalisation and financial liberalisation the country adopted in the 1990s. However, India's economic growth started in the 1980s, and even after the country's trade and financial liberalisation, industry tariffs remain stubbornly high at around 25%. Thus, there is no evidence to suggest that the Indian economy would have been better off had it adopted a neoliberal free trade policy at independence in 1947. Contrary to the neoliberal assertion, India embarked on severe restrictions on FDI, in particular, entry restrictions, foreign ownership and several performance requirements such as local content requirements.

The argument in this book is that neoliberal policy response to the crisis in Ghana did not succeed in reversing the economic decline both in medium and long-term. In fact, quite the opposite; rather than undoing economic decline, the policy prescriptions weakened the country's ability to diversify its economy into industrialisation, particularly the manufacturing sector. Neoliberal policies implemented in the 1980s undermined instead of resolving capital accumulation constraints in the country. This is because the policies intentionally or unintentionally encouraged factors that destabilised the possibility of the real productive assets to earn commensurate returns to facilitate the flow of capital to these sectors to ensure the survival of industrial enterprises. Rising profit in the financial sector incentivised managers to divert funds into financial assets at the expense of productive investment. Thus, the pace of real capital accumulation has been disappointing in the era of neoliberalisation/ financialisation due to rising financial profit.

1 The Historical Background of Finance and Growth

The relationship between development in the financial system and economic development has received much attention throughout the modern history of economics. For example, Smith's (1776) central principle was the increasing returns on investment, which he argued helps to induce capital accumulation and economic well-being through the division of labour. Smith asserted that the growth of profits accrued from the division of labour will further accelerate capital accumulation, the foundation of the wealth of a nation.

Marx (2019[1867]) was concerned with the internal contradictions of the capitalist mode of production and argued that there is a tendency for capital to accumulate and become concentrated in the hands of a tiny minority, with no natural limit to the process. Marx contended that the inherent class struggle in the capitalist system would, in the end, destabilise the capitalist mode of production. Bagehot (1873) emphasised the significance of the financial system (investment banks) in economic development and outlined the importance of banks in inducing innovation and growth by providing credit for productive investments.

Joseph Schumpeter (1911) postulated that financial deepening is essential in accelerating economic growth (development). He argued that for production to materialise, it requires bank credit and that one can only become an entrepreneur by previously becoming a debtor. Schumpeter's bank-based hypothesis argued that the entrepreneur requires credit-purchasing power before any goods can be produced. The entrepreneur is, therefore, a debtor in the capitalist system. Keynes (2018[1936]) also stressed the significance of bank credit in economic growth but supported active and direct government control of investment. Robbinson (1952, 86) on the other hand, argued that development in the financial system follows economic growth, and expressed this causality argument by stressing that *'where enterprise leads, finance follows.'*

The endogenous growth studies have argued that financial sector deepening impacts positively on economic growth and development. They argue that active government participation in the financial sector has a regressive effect on the equilibrium growth rate (King and Levine 1993). These arguments can be considered as an antidote to Modigliani and Miller's (1958) irrelevance hypothesis.[3] Despite the severe drawbacks of the 'irrelevance theory', advocates of the theory suggest that there is no relationship between finance and growth. Lucas (1988) contends that economists severely overstress the significance of the financial system in the growth debate. This presents the conundrum of the finance-growth-poverty nexus. This suggests that the channels through which financial development impacts growth are not well understood. Stockhammer (2004), Crotty (2005), Lapavitsas (2013), and Storm (2018) have argued that financial sector development adversely affects the performance of the real sector of the economy. They postulate that contemporary managerial activities are geared towards maximising the share price of their companies and distributing a huge part of the company's profits to shareholders as dividends. This book aims to investigate the relationship between financial sector

---

3 A detailed analysis of Modigliani and Miller's (1958) hypothesis is found in chapter 5.

development and sustainable economic development from the perspective of the effects of financial liberalisation on capital structure and poverty.

Ghana's economy is characterised by dualism – with capital intensive in the mining and quarrying sub-sector (including oil) which demonstrates a developed modern economy and an underdeveloped informal/agricultural sector in which the overwhelming majority of the population remain dependent. The existence of this 'great divide' with a large underdeveloped informal sector and more affluent formal sector identifies Ghana as an example of *'uneven and combined development'*.[4]

The dominant role of governments in the financial sector was highlighted by many Sub-Saharan Africa (SSA) countries in their development agenda post-independence. State banks were established with directed credit allocation to sectors seen as essential to national development. Foreign banks and domestic private banks were restricted, and large reserve requirements were implemented.

In line with the post-war developmental agenda, Ghana adopted active government intervention in the economic process of mobilising capital, which was deemed important for driving economic development. The Keynesian hypothesis drove this active government participation that market economy is prone to mistakes and errors, which could lead to severe depressions without government stimulus in variations in private investments. Nevertheless, the concerted efforts to bring about sustainable economic development did not yield the needed fruits for many SSA countries. The confluence of the late 1970s global stagflation, global recession, and the bushfires that destroyed many foods and cash crops in Ghana forced many to believe that active government participation in the economic process may be inferior to an alternative market-based policy, which was being promoted by Hayek and the *Mont Pelerin Society*.[5] Thus, a retreat from the Keynesian economic model, the active state intervention, and the welfare policies.

---

4   This refers to the tenacious differences in levels and rates of economic development across sectors in an economy. A term used by Trotsky (2010) when investigating the developmental possibilities for industrialisation in the Russian Empire – Results and Prospects- it is a concept in Marxian Political Economy aimed to describe the dynamics of human history involving the interaction of capitalist laws of motion and starting world market conditions whose national units are highly heterogeneous. A more recent contribution has been given by Justine Rosenberg (2013) in his debate on *the 'philosophical premises' of uneven and combined development*.

5   This is a post-war international classical liberal association consisted of economists, philosophers, historians and other intellectuals intending to promote a free-market and open society.

Developmental agenda in the 1970s turned to economic liberalisation pioneered by McKinnon (2010) and Shaw (1973). They maintain that periphery countries require economic liberalisation to be able to develop. This tradition, together with Hayek and Friedman's epistemological claim that the market is omniscient, persuaded many periphery countries to adopt these free-market ideologies willingly or were forced to accept it by the Washington Consensus.

Fortunately, following the liberalisation and deregulation of the economy, Ghana experienced sustained economic growth. For example, from 1983 to 1990, the economic growth averaged 5%, and between 2000 and 2015, the average growth was 8% (Ghana Statistical Service 1999; 2018). Paradoxically, these economic growth rates in Ghana have benefited only a tiny minority, whereas for the overwhelming majority of the population, the growth has only been available on credit. Thus, while the country gets richer, most citizens are no better off. Low and middle-income segments took on more debt to finance everyday life activities such as food shopping, health, education and housing encouraged by the deregulation in the financial market. For instance, between 2013 and 2017, GDP per capita increased by 11%, the national poverty rate fell sharply between 1990 and 2012/13 from 51% to 24.3%. However, poverty incidence declined marginally to 23.2% between 2012/13 and 2016/17, with extreme poverty incidences worsening in five out of the ten regions in the country. Ironically, national inequality measured by the Gini coefficient rose from 41.9% in 2005 to 42.3% in 2013, and further increased to 43.0% in 2017[6] (Bank of Ghana 2018; Ghana Statistical Service 2018). The worsening inequality over the period illustrates that few people benefit from growth rates in the country with a sharp rural-urban divide.

The Ghanaian economy, having undertaken Structural Adjustment Programmes (SAP) initiated by the International Monetary Fund (IMF) and the World Bank in 1983, welcomed the various waves of financial sector reforms. These reforms – Financial Sector Adjustment Programme (FINSAP1 in 1983, and FINSAP2 in 1990) resulted in liberalisation and deregulation of interest rates and exchange rates, eradication of state-directed lending, recapitalisation of banks and restructuring of distress banks by off-loading non-performing loans to the public sector and loans guaranteed by the state, and most importantly, encouraging foreign bank entry. The structural transformation of the banking industry was significant as new banks entered the market with rapid growth in bank branches. The competition of banks resulted in new

---

6   The Gini coefficient measures the degree of inequality in income (consumption) in a country. A numerical value of 0 indicates perfect equality, while 100 represents absolute inequality.

products offering, which included electronic banking, asset-backed lending, mortgage financing, and the recent surge in Mobile Money services (MM).[7]

The liberalisation and deregulation of the financial markets coupled with the monetary and fiscal discipline fostered the growth of capital movements, where domestic legal and illegal capital flight were compensated by foreign capital inflow. The capital inflows into the mining and quarrying sub-sector (including oil) are in the form of Foreign Direct Investment (FDI), while finance and communication sub-sectors attract mostly portfolio inflows in search of undervalued assets and high domestic interest rates.

The various waves of reforms have resulted in exponential growth in the financial market, making it undoubtedly the most vibrant sector in the country. The growing dominance of the financial sector has drawn attention to the rise of finance and its implications for sustainable economic development in the country. The recognition of financialisation in Ghana is, however, limited. Initial examples emphasise the linkages and the nature of the integration of the Ghanaian economy with the global financial markets (Quartey and Prah 2008; Esso 2010). More recently, Adu et al. (2013) and Adusei (2013) presented their assessments of the financial sector as the driving force of the Ghanaian economy. However, their examinations were inadequate on the impact of the financial sector development on productive investment, especially on Small and Medium Scale Enterprises (SMEs) and the overall welfare of the population. That is, the changing conduct of the capitalist agents – banks, industrial enterprises and households within a changing world market was ignored. In light of these, this book will examine the effect of financialisation on firms' capital structure and its impact on sustainable economic development, in particular poverty indicators. The investigation will illuminate the inconsistencies of the political-economic arrangement on Ghana's capability to develop.

The perennial underdevelopment and the inadequacies of the previous studies to identify and address the key factors undermining economic development in Ghana have been derived primarily from the focus and in some cases, the methodologies espoused. Kotz (2013) remarks that although past studies have recognised lack of sufficient profit as a critical factor obstructing the capitalist accumulation process, many scholars failed to acknowledge the significance of the political-economic arrangement in the expectation of the rate of profit.

---

7 A detailed analysis of this is in chapter 6- *Financialisation, financial inclusion and mobile money.*

Many past studies have been criticised for being instigated solely on the hypotheses of empirical investigations that are commonly guided on episodic events or in a specific era, which may not have historical connotations that might also influence economic development in a country. For instance, the scholarly work of McKinnon (2010[1973]) and Shaw (1973) hypothesises that transformed economic policy of the growing underdevelopment of periphery countries and the bank-based state participation economic policies covered just 25 years.[8] This, thereby, failed to account for the historical elements that some of the periphery countries might have experienced. Consequently, episodic, and solely empirical investigations are deemed insufficient in relation to distinctive events such as historical developments that could have a lasting influence on the countries examined.

This book will, therefore, be designed to probe the contradictions of the contemporary political-economic arrangement, together with historical developments that are undermining sustainable economic development in Ghana.

In view of the increasing financialisation, it is essential to ascertain how financialisation becomes transplanted and the impacts on poverty in Ghana. This book seeks to discover the existence of financialisation and how it is emerging in the periphery and more importantly, the impact of financialisation on poverty reduction programmes in Ghana. The main objective is to test the relationship between increasing financialisation and trends in poverty using household data, which is a crucial variable in measuring poverty as a social condition. That is, the impact of the growth of finance and credit infrastructures in Ghana in the era of neoliberal capitalism on poverty alleviation in the country.

Studies of financialisation away from the core countries are essential to ascertain the uniqueness and discrepancies in various geographical settings. The historical and social characteristics of economic processes embedded in Marxist political economy necessitate the uniqueness of the ascendency of finance in different national settings. Peck and Theodore (2007) argue that it is only through a comparative investigation of particular social backgrounds that are susceptible to develop their hypothetical reproductive features, can new theoretical contributions be made to the study of financialisation. Consequently, given Ghana's peculiar historical trajectory and integration into the global economy, it is important to examine the rise of finance, or as it is generally characterised, 'the increasing role of financial motives, financial

---

8 See Price (1974) for a critique of McKinnon's (1973), and Shaw's (1973) hypotheses.

markets, financial actors and financial institutions in the operation of the domestic and the international economies' (Epstein 2005, 3) in Ghana.

Most of the previous studies that have investigated the impacts of the inconsistency in the political-economic arrangements on economic development have done so by investigating their impact on the core countries as well as the emerging or semi-periphery economies. There is little focus on the periphery countries, in particular, SSA (excluding South Africa).[9] The few studies on Africa, for instance, Roy-Mukherjee (2015), and Udeogu (2018)[10] did not incorporate the changing conduct of the capitalist agents – banks, industrial enterprises and households. Given the geography and variations between financial and economic structures in these economies and Ghana, it will be inaccurate to rely on the conclusions drawn from these studies to account for the experiences in Ghana.

This book argues that as an international phenomenon, financialisation *must* reproduce the hierarchies of imperial relations,[11] ensuing in the unique nature of financialisation in Ghana. Even though integrating the essential trends as observed in the core countries, financialisation in the periphery will produce unique features. The book, therefore, offers a comprehensive assessment of the nature and distinctive features of financialisation in the periphery, with a focus on Ghana. Crucially, espousing an indispensable hypothetical approach to financialisation, the uniqueness of Ghana and its common features with the core will be exposed. The sectoral meaning of financialisation – banks, industrial enterprises and households will be examined, giving a robust insight into the transformation of the Ghanaian economy in the last four decades. Furthermore, investigation of this historically specific geographical setting will contribute theoretically to studies on financialisation in general, helping to determine its prominent features better.

Previous studies also contrast the interests of predatory finance against those of the real economy and focus on capital flow from the core to the periphery. However, this book examines the existence of financialisation and

---

9   For the emerging economies, see, for instance, Palma (2013), and Chandrasekhar and Ghosh (2013). For the core countries, notably the US., see, for instance, Stockhammer (2004); Krippner (2005; 2011); Crotty (2005); Orhangazi (2008); Davis and Kim (2015); and Kiely (2018). See Lapavitsas (2013); Fouskas and Dimoulas (2013); Fouskas and Gökay (2018) to name a few that focused primarily on the European Union. All these authors discussed the consequences of neoliberal ideologies on real sector investment.

10 Roy-Mukherjee (2015) discussed the socio-economic causes integral in the Arab uprisings and the spread of neoliberalism in North Africa. Udeogu (2018) focused his discussion on the Nigerian economy.

11 This refers to the hierarchies of the world order- the core-periphery relations.

how it is emerging in the periphery. This requires an international theory of financialisation and the understanding of the *core-periphery*[12] relations of that theory.

This book brings a new perspective to the debate on financialisation and poverty to the understanding of how financialisation affects capital structure and poverty. We argue that financialisation in the periphery takes a *subordinate/inferior* form because of imperialism, dependency and the nature of finance in Africa.[13] This has crucial implications for investment, economic growth, employment, inequality and poverty. This work provides very useful evidence for the development of sensitive policy interventions to help reduce poverty in SSA. It deviates from the orthodox economics approach of examining Ghana's predicaments solely based on factors internal to the economy, but instead places it in connexion with the world system and imposes historical evidence on theoretical logic, an approach typically known as the *Marxist method of analysis*.[14]

2   Scope and Limitations of the Book

This book focuses on the contradiction of political-economic arrangement on Ghana's ability to develop. Nevertheless, focusing on Ghana alone restricts the generalisation of the investigation findings. However, it does not take away/obstruct the validity of the outcomes. Arestis and Demetriades (1997) and Ang (2008) discovered that cross-sectional studies do not explain the main underlying factors concerning a specific country. The cross-section studies put countries with different identities together, thereby concealing the uniqueness and its historical trajectory that account for the social formation of each country. Therefore, to better understand and explain the main factors concerning a

---

12   This book adopts the *Core-Periphery* relation, which is based on Immanuel Wallerstein's world-system theory. Core countries are the Advanced Western/Capitalist Economies, while the periphery countries are the less developed countries. Semi-periphery countries are the industrialising/emerging economies that are positioned between the core and periphery economies.

13   Financialisation in the periphery has specific characteristics reflecting the dominant role of the core. Lapavitsas (2013) asserts that there has been no return to formal imperialism, but financialisation in the periphery countries has had a subordinate character deriving from the hierarchical and exploitative nature of interaction in the world market.

14   Mandel (1969) defines this approach as the integration of dialectical rationalism with the empirical grasping of facts; i.e. a critical, materialistic, dialectical interpretation of history.

INTRODUCTION

country's underdevelopment, it is essential to study an individual country in juxtaposition with the world system than cross-section for the sake of generalisation, which will have limited specificity and policy relevance.

The second limitation of the book is the focus purely on the framework of the political-economic arrangements and the historical elements as the main factors undermining sustainable development of the Ghanaian economy. The study deliberately put less emphasis on administrative, nepotism, ecological and other indeterminate constraints, not because they are not necessary, but rather most of these factors have mainly been deliberated without success to the problem of underdevelopment. Besides, if the contradictions of the political-economic arrangement are tackled first, then administrative competency for gallant actions could be a viable entry point for any effective reforms that could stimulate economic progress in the country. As noted by Smith (1776), the growing commerce and manufacturing bring together an order, good governance, liberty and security of the population. Thus, rising employment and incomes of the population will reduce inequality and poverty as well as decrease nepotism and corruption, which will induce shared economic prosperity for all.

For the empirical analysis, data for the period from 1965 to 2020 were used to circumvent structural breaks as well as the availability of data for such period. Moreover, although reliable sources of data were used, questions could be raised about the validity of these sources.[15] Thus, the findings from the empirical sources may contain some elements of errors, regardless of the careful considerations. To improve the validity of the data source, attempts are made, where possible, to substantiate data from various sources to limit the extent of data anomaly. These sources of primary information, which largely rely on surveys and semi-structured interviews, were augmented by academic literature on the relationship between the financial sector on the one hand, and industrial enterprises and households on the other. However, despite these attempts to improve reliability and validity, it does not entirely eradicate the findings from any data anomaly.

Thus, the threat posed to the findings of this book (albeit non-generalisation) is the pure focus on Ghana and the possible unreliability of the

---

15 Most data used in this thesis were collected from official sources – the World Bank database, the Federal Reserve Economic Data (FRED), the PENN World data, the IMF World Economic Outlook database, Bank of Ghana, Ghana Statistical Service. Ghana Investment Promotion Council. United Nations Conference on Trade and Development (UNCTAD) and the World Bank Enterprise Survey for Ghana (2013).

empirical data sources. Nevertheless, this study has many advantages, albeit a few shortcomings.

Different methodological choices have framed the theoretical and empirical work carried out throughout in this book. The aim is to contribute to an in-depth understanding of financialisation and to fill the gap on how financialisation affects firms' capital structure and poverty in Ghana.

This study is grounded on the principle that particular methods of investigation are not inexorably connected to a specific methodology. This permits the option for different methods, through the alteration of their practice and understanding, to be combined in the study (Downward and Mearman 2007). With such a mixed-method approach, Sayer (1999) argues that the main test is to balance the selected methods with a suitable level of abstraction and with the material under study; this is the key challenge in this study.

This book makes original contributions to both the theoretical and the empirical understandings of financialisation. We attempt to empirically grasp the developments/patterns and forms of financialisation across the core countries and corroborate the phenomenon as it is emerging in Ghana, with specific emphasis on the impact of financialisation on firms' capital structure and poverty. The design of a middle-range theory requires a theorisation of banks, industrial enterprises and households, and their changing behaviour/conduct with each other within the economy. The empirical examination and preciseness of the concrete exhibitions of financialisation in Ghana require a multiplicity of data sources and deductive techniques that are available at the international, regional and national levels, and the incorporation of various sectoral vantage points. For these reasons, a mixed-method approach, unified within the contradiction of a critical political economy, is most suitable.

Different methods of empirical analysis are used in this book. National account data are analysed to document and evaluate the theory of financialisation, as outlined in chapter 4 and its subordinate/inferior nature examined in chapters 4 and 6. Also, inter and intraclass relations are analysed in chapter 5 to grasp and present financialisation as it manifests in the shape and form that it does in the Ghanaian economy. The empirical data used in this analysis is from 1965–2020.

The reason to have profound structural and political changes as historical marks of study is initiated in the succeeding financial transformation of the Ghanaian economy, with the opening to the global economy and national financial sector adjustment programmes. However, it will be wrong to be inflexible and rigidly follow this periodisation as many of the processes identified had their historical origin years or even decades before 1965. Furthermore, the innate economic structures from SAP explain much of the political and

INTRODUCTION 13

economic routes acquired subsequently. The study will, thus, incorporate historical examinations that go back from 1965 whenever it proves relevant to clarify ensuing economic developments.

3 Structure of the Book

The book is organised into two sections with eight chapters. The first section comprises two chapters – the introduction in chapter 1, which presents the background to the book and discusses the methodological choices that framed the work. The theoretical debates on neoliberalisation and financialisation are presented in chapter 2. This chapter examines the rise of neoliberal capitalism and the emergence of the associated financialisation. It documents the shift from the *Keynesian-Fordist* mass-production mass-consumption economic principles and management to the mid-1970s neoliberal era and the contradictions of neoliberal capitalism. The rest of the chapter focuses on the theoretical debates of financialisation by examining the historical background of the emergence of financialisation.

Four strands mark the literature, which attempts to explain the prominence of financialisation. These are stagnation of production theory; French Regulation school theory; post-Keynesian and the rise of the rentier; and the trans-nationalisation and liberalisation of finance. These strands in the literature focus on the performance of the core countries, particularly the United States and the United Kingdom. All the arguments deliberately deal with the issue of global instead of solely national accumulation. However, lacking are the more fine-grained analyses of the changing behaviour/conduct of the agents of capitalism (industrial enterprise, banks and households) both within countries and across borders, and their specification within a changing world market. Consequently, the discussions fail to analyse the uniqueness of the rise of finance in the periphery, in particular, sub-Saharan Africa.

Since the evidence provided does not account for the emergence of financialisation across the world market, this book argues that the tendencies of financialisation should not be limited to a few archetypical financialised economies. Consequently, the book sets out a testable hypothesis that financialisation should be observed as a worldwide phenomenon. However, it is not expected that countries will experience a similar fashion across the world. The chapter ends with financialisation and poverty alleviation: banking the unbanked, which explores the essential vehicles (microfinance and financial inclusion) used to transplant financialisation of households in developing countries.

The second section offers a theoretical and empirical investigation of the Ghanaian economy starting with chapter 3, which investigates the long-standing debate of finance-growth nexus. It starts with the rise of finance and the financialisation of everything by examining the collateralisation of everything that could be collateralised. The financial profit conundrum is explained by examining Marx's profit upon alienation, in particular financial profit extracted from individuals and profit derived from trading financial assets. Chapter 3 further provides a clear distinction between real commodity accumulation and fictitious accumulation, and the balance of power between them. The contemporary heterodox perspective on the finance-growth debate is also examined in this chapter by providing the supply-leading hypothesis relative to demand following theory. This chapter ends with the impact of COVID-19 on Ghana's economic performance. The argument here is that globalisation/financialisation did not alleviate poverty in Ghana and current deglobalisation trends amidst the global pandemic would increase poverty levels as Ghana's rural society is not conducive to digitisation and social distancing.

Chapter 4 is the case study of Ghana, which details the political and economic developments that have shaped economic and financial sectors since independence in 1957. The chapter starts with the reasons that forced Ghana to adopt neoliberal's Structural Adjustment Programme (SAP) and details the paradox of financialisation in Ghana – under-financed, yet financialising. Chapter 4 presents the country's profile from independence in 1957 to 2017. The chapter also discusses the evolution of the financial sector and investigates the effects of banking reforms on the economy. Section 2 in that chapter presents recent economic performance, including some key economic indicators since 2000. Section 3 is divided into two sub-sections and examines the political economy of Ghana from 1957 to 1982, the trajectory of state-led accumulation to neoliberalism.

Sub-section 3.2 covers the political and economic developments from 1983–2019. This sub-section explains the reason why Ghana adopted the Structural Adjustment Programme (SAP) and the transition into multi-party democracy in 1992. The consequences of neoliberalism are investigated in section 4. The various waves of financial sector reforms pre- and post-adjustments periods are presented in section 5. Section 6 presents the distinctive features and the commonality of financialisation in the core and the periphery. This section analyses why the Ghanaian economy is under-financed yet financialising. Section 7 concludes with the empirical study of net capital flow from Ghana and other periphery countries to the core countries, notably the US.

Chapter 5 provides an overview of financialisation and firms' capital structure. A critical issue that faces firms in their external financing decision is the proportion of debt and equity to be used. These external financing options illustrate the capital structure of a firm. A wrong financing decision can endanger an economy due to the significant role played by firms in the provision of jobs to the people, paying wages and thereby reducing poverty, which is a vital issue facing most periphery countries, in particular Ghana. It follows that making the right and accurate financial decision can stimulate economic growth and development. This is relevant to private as well as public sector enterprises that can access external financing.

Given the transformation of the financial sector in the era of neoliberalism and its associated debts and financial crises, capital structure and firms financing decisions is of paramount importance. The chapter further examines the empirical challenges facing firms in Ghana that have contributed to the perennial underdevelopment of the country's real economy over the years. Notably, it presents the various consequences related to the contradictions of the political-economic arrangement that have undermined Ghana's real capital accumulation process over many years. This chapter presents graphically/visually the impeding factors undermining economic development with data from the World Bank Enterprise Survey (2013).

Chapter 6 presents the issue of poverty and its measurement conundrum. This chapter considers issues surrounding the definition of poverty, how poverty is measured at both national and international levels and highlights the drawbacks associated with some of these measurements. It investigates absolute and relative poverty issues as well as the paradox of sub-Saharan Africa's middle class. The argument here is that, if decades of economic growth have been shared growth, the evidence should be a rising middle class on the continent. The passionate debate about the impact of neoliberal globalisation on poverty ends the chapter.

Chapter 7 provides the theoretical and empirical evidence of financialisation and households, and the ascendency of financial inclusion and mobile money. Two main objectives drive chapter 7: The first is to establish the theoretical bases by reviewing the literature on household finance and to assess the importance of political economy in addressing household finance/debt. The second provides an empirical assessment of financialisation of households in Ghana using Bank of Ghana and National Communication Authority data on financial inclusion policy. This policy is pioneered by the World Bank and the IMF to measure/assess the transformation of households' finance.

Section 2 examines household debt through Modigliani's *Life Cycle* and Friedman's *Permanent Income Hypotheses*. The theories assume that a rational household will smooth out consumption over time by taking on debts. Section 3 investigates the political economy of household finance and argues that household assets and liabilities are managed by financial agents, financial actors and financial institutions with their idiosyncratic interests. Section 4 provides an overview of the payment systems in Ghana. The chapter ends with financialisation, financial inclusion and Mobile Money, providing the specificities of financialisation in Ghana.

The book ends with chapter 8, which contains the summary of the main findings, and draws on the general conclusion and policy implications. I present that the hegemony of finance has been a distinctive component of contemporary capitalism. The chapter provides the specificities of financialisation in Ghana and offers some tentative theoretical contributions to a more substantial theoretical approach to investigation on financialisation in the periphery countries. I argued that the failure of the traditional banking system to provide for the needs of all classes in the economy resulted in the financial exclusion of the unbanked, underserved and those living in rural areas. The push for financial inclusion through Mobile Money (MM) and the demonetisation and cashless society by the Bank of Ghana has been argued in this book as the prominence of financialisation of households. These activities have created new avenues for extracting profit, and therefore the privatisation of the payment systems in Ghana. The argument in this book is that neoliberal policy prescriptions to the crisis in Ghana did not succeed in reversing the economic decline permanently. Quite the opposite, rather than undoing decline, the policy prescriptions weakened the country's ability to diversify its economy into industrialisation, particularly manufacturing.

The chapter ends with policy recommendations and suggestions for future research. It has been suggested in this book that State-owned banks should not be privatised for the sake of banking reforming. With the right supervision and operating environment, these banks could compete and provide the needed capital for industrial enterprises to perform efficiently. The government can also set up community banks to provide the needed capital to SMEs to ease the credit constraints. Furthermore, universal banks should be encouraged/incentivised to offer medium to long-term financing to industrial enterprises/capitalists at affordable rates and with minimum collateral. Besides, government deficits should be financed from other sources to enable banks to invest in the real sector of the economy. Banks are too reliant on short-term government gilts, which undermine their ability to explore other investment avenues. Reforms to Africa Growth and Opportunity Act (AGOA) started two decades ago, could help boost manufacturing-based employment in many regions and towns where the incidence of poverty has been rising, particularly rural savannah.

However, this alone will not be enough; investment in agriculture, a sector that employs the overwhelming majority of the labour force in the country will increase output and income for farmers. Irrigation, useful transport links, storage facilities, training and education of farmers on modern ways of farming could reduce chronic hunger, rural isolation and vulnerability of the rural people. Investment well-tuned to local needs and conditions should be able to benefit the hunger-disease-poverty nexus and set many people free from the bondage of poverty. It is essential that the poor should be involved in decision-making that affects them than has been assumed for them. Previous poverty alleviation programmes have been unsuccessful because organisers have failed to listen to the needs of the local communities who have lived experience.

CHAPTER 2

Neoliberalisation and Financialisation
The Debate

1 Introduction

In this chapter, we document the rise of neoliberal capitalism and the emergence of the associated financialisation. The chapter starts with the shift from the *Keynesian-Fordist* mass-production mass-consumption economic principles and management to the mid-1970s neoliberal era, and the contradictions of neoliberal capitalism. The rest of the chapter focuses on the theoretical debates of financialisation by examining the historical background of the emergence of financialisation. Four strands mark the literature, which attempts to explain the prominence of financialisation. These are stagnation of production theory; French Regulation school theory; post-Keynesian and the rise of the rentier; and the trans-nationalisation and liberalisation of finance.

2 The Rise of Neoliberal Capitalism

The last four decades have witnessed the dynamic transformation of financial markets and their dominance in the world market. This is probably the most in-depth and most extensive change in the history of capitalism in recent eras. Finance, profiting from its impalpability and technological innovations, of late, has upheld itself as the hegemony of neoliberalism/globalisation/financialisation.

Changes in capitalism have both long-term structural and short-term precipitate causes. This means that to have a clear sense of the emergence of neoliberalism,[1] it is imperative to first look at a broad picture regarding the configuration of the world economy from a long-term historical perspective. That is, how the world economy was organised before neoliberalism, its contradictions and trends, as well as the kind of shifts that were taking place in the late 1960s

---

1 Neoliberalism could be summed up as replacing the government role of guiding and regulating economic activity with market-based policies through privatisation of state-owned enterprises and public services, eliminating state social programmes and the dominant role of capital with the help from the state.

and early 1970s. Transformation of this extent and complexity do not emerge by accident. Therefore, it is relevant to investigate by what means and paths the new economic alignment was pulled from.

It has been argued by Harvey (2005) that this newfound ideology was pulled from the shades of relative obscurity, a particular policy that went under the name of neoliberalism and changed it into the dominant guiding principle of economic thought and management. For Harvey, the elections that brought Margaret Thatcher in the UK, and Reagan in the USA to power in 1979 and 1980, respectively with a mandate to control trade union power, tame inflation, deregulate industries and unleash the powers of domestic and international finance changed the world around us for good. Margaret Thatcher, Ronald Reagan and the likes of Paul Volker seized this minority argument that has long been in dissemination and transformed it into a dominant economic thought and management. This newfound ideology (neoliberalism) – its origins, rise and consequences for poverty as a social condition, is the primary concern of this book. A standard view in the political economy is that the rise of neoliberalism is elucidated by the increasing role and power of finance in the political economy (Kiely 2005; 2018; Lapavitsas 2013; Storm 2018).

It is important to acknowledge that neoliberal capitalism emerged from the crisis of regulated capitalism that has existed post-second world war and therefore to some extent neoliberal capitalism was in response to the challenges faced by regulated capitalism. Therefore, to grasp the distinctive features of neoliberalism, it is vital to start with the background of the preceding system. As Kotz (2015) argues, both regulated and neoliberal capitalism are complex entities with several characteristics. They both possess dominant economic ideas and the main institutions that govern them.

The capitalism that transpired from the great depression in 1929 in most of the core countries was in sharp contrast to the pre-war forms of capitalism. The state took on a more active and interventionist role – the state grew more prominent in the performance of the economy. Although there were some variations reflecting the particular history of each country, the common features among them include a peaceful, rule-based collective bargaining relationship between capital and labour.[2]

The use of fiscal and monetary policies was to tame the business cycle (the periodic short-run fluctuations in the economy) and the government actively

---

[2] Varieties of capitalism are the institutional foundation of organising a capitalist economy- the coordinated market economy models and the liberal market economy models (See, Hall and Soskice 2001). Ordoliberal as the coordinated market economy model and neoliberal as the liberal market economy model.

intervened in the private sector and controlled over the financial sector. The term *'regulated capitalism'* according to Kotz (2015) seems an apt one for that period. He lauds regulated capitalism for being a success. No major depression occurred despite the business cycle not being fully eliminated. The core countries showed the fastest growth of any long period – 1948–1973. The focus was to achieve full employment, economic growth and social welfare for the population. Income inequality in the core countries, especially in the US declined with the income share of the bottom 20% rising from 4.9% to 5.5%, while the wealthiest 5% saw a reduction in their share of income to 15.5% from 17.1%. Thus, the income gap was not widening but slightly closing.

A similar pattern occurred in the distribution of wealth. During this period, Mader, Mertens, and Van der Zwan (2020) argued that poverty was viewed as a lack of access to quality employment and consequently, policy intervention was to address this. OXFAM (2014) report that global wealth inequality during the neoliberal era – post-1980s increased noticeably with the top 1% of the population having more than twice as much wealth as the 6.9 billion people, yet only 4 cents in every dollar of tax revenue comes from taxes on wealth. The concentration of wealth is in the hands of a very small group of people whose fortune and power grew exponentially during neoliberal restructuring. Meanwhile, the majority of the world population are still living in extreme poverty with many others on the poverty line and just one hospital bill or failed harvest away from falling back into the poverty line.

While the richest continue to see trillions of dollars in wealth, they also benefit from some of the lowest tax. This has affected government tax revenues, and hence austerity has become a key part of neoliberal capitalism with reducing spending on vital services such as healthcare, education, and other public goods. The report concludes that the 22 richest men in the world have more wealth than all the women in Africa. Piketty (2013) and Milanovic (2016) present a comprehensive assessment of the growing income inequality in the era of neoliberal financialisation in the core as well as the peripheral regions and states. For instance, the UK's Gini coefficient just before the neoliberal restructuring in 1977 was 0.24 compared to 0.34 in 2012. Thirty-five years of neoliberal capitalism have resulted in rising inequality. It is therefore safe to argue that neoliberalism increases inequality with the richest individuals and corporations benefiting at the expense of ordinary men and women.

State regulations of banks during this *'Golden Age of Capitalism'* – 1948–1973 meant that there was little to no financial speculation in the period in the core countries. Banks and other financial institutions performed their traditional role of supporting industries with long-term fixed-rate lending and households with home mortgage loans and holding them to maturity as described by

Schumpeter (1982, 74).[3] Thus, the banker in Schumpeter's view stands between those who wish to form new combinations and the possessors of productive means. The banker then becomes a phenomenon of development, nurturing the process of accumulation and steering the pace and nature of economic growth and technological progress (Mazzucato and Wray 2015). As argued by Kotz (2010), during this period, there were no significant financial panics or crises, and there were no bank failures in the core countries. These roles played by bank-based financial systems – where banks and industrial enterprises form long-term relationships, have inside knowledge and are in a position to exercise strategic influence on firms, impose rationality on their decisions and prioritise the repayment of their debt.

The business cycle of the *Golden Age* peaked in 1973 marked the end of the sustained and shared economic prosperity. The accelerated inflation coupled with high unemployment compromised the peaceful relation between capital and labour to break down; the average rate of profit began a long decline in the core countries. A general sense emerged that things were getting out of control, while the effort to re-establish economic stability using Keynesian tools failed (Kotz 2010; Kiely 2018; Storm 2018). In response to this crisis of post-war regulated capitalism, the institutional form of capitalism along with the central economic ideas changed with surprising rapidity.

During this period of regulated capitalism, new capitalist institutions also emerged at the global level. The Bretton Woods system[4] of fixed exchange rates among the major trading currencies, with the US dollar, backed by gold at a fixed rate, served as the major trading and reserved currency used to govern the global financial and economic systems. The most notable outcomes of the Bretton Woods Conference were the formation of global institutions such as the United Nations, the International Monetary Fund (IMF), the World Bank, and the Bank for International Settlements in Basle. The International Monetary Fund (IMF) was established to manage and allow nation-states the right to exercise significant control over cross-border capital movements (Kiely 2005; 2018; Kotz 2015). These international institutions were managed and stabilised international relations. It is essential to acknowledge that although

---

[3] Schumpeter (1982:74) called the banker '*the ephor of the exchange economy*'- someone who creates credit to finance new investments and innovations.
[4] The Bretton Woods conference, in 1944, established the rules for commercial and financial relations among the world's major industrial states. The Bretton Woods system prevailed from 1944 to 1971 and coincided with the *Golden Age of Capitalism*. It is important to recognise that the Bretton Woods system was a hegemonic system, dominated by the global hegemon, the USA, and worked mainly in favour of the United States.

these capitalist institutions operated supposedly on the global scale, many countries in the periphery especially in Sub-Saharan Africa (SSA) were under colonial rule and did as the colonial masters said. Until 1957 when Ghana gained its independence, its apparatus was under the control of the British government. Therefore, the regulated and embedded capitalism did not have roots in Sub-Saharan Africa as a sovereign continent, and it is, therefore, significant to assess the origin of contemporary capitalism and its impact on the political-economic arrangement on the continent and the implication for poverty alleviation.

Neoliberalism, according to Harvey (2005) and Kotz (2015), is associated with the trilogy of liberalisation, privatisation, and stabilisation.[5] However, neoliberal capitalism involves a broader set of ideological and institutional changes than the trilogy outlined. The policies connected to this trilogy were the vehicles used to convert reformist institutions under the regulated capitalism into radical revolutionary institutions of neoliberalism. Kotz (2013) argues that neoliberal capitalism did resolve the problems that undermined regulated capitalism in the early 1970s; however, he cautions that neoliberal restructuring steered a period of economic expansion with high financial profits, while at the same time planting the seeds of the global financial and economic crisis that broke out in 2008.[6] He concludes that the neoliberal model was fully incorporated at the international level of cross-country trade and capital flows, where the role of the IMF and the World Bank changed, and new neoliberal global institutions were constructed. As we shall see later, the IMF and the World Bank were the vehicles that transplanted neoliberalism in sub-Saharan Africa (SSA).

It could be argued that neoliberal restructuring was aimed at all the institutions that had bolstered the bargaining power of labour and other popular groups. Kiely (2018) argues that it dismantled the progress made by organised labour in the core and ended *labour-friendly and development-friendly regimes*. By doing so, it restored effective control to capital. The result was a reverse of the falling rate of profit, which began a long-term rise in the early 1980s in the

---

5 Liberalisation refers to freeing up markets and firms from regulation (that had sustained capitalism during the Golden Age). Privatisation involves but not exclusive to selling off state-owned enterprises but also contracting out public services to private firms. Stabilisation covers the cut in government social programme and tight fiscal and monetary policies.
6 See David Harvey (2005). *A Brief History of Neoliberalism*- (Chile's experience) – The first experiment of neoliberal state formation according to Harvey, was in Chile, after general Pinochet's coup on the 'little September 11th' 1973, which was followed by economic expansion and later financial crisis.

US and Europe (Kotz and McDonough 2010). It is essential to recognise that profit in the real sector of the economy has been in decline while financial sector profits are on the rise.

The collapse of the Bretton Woods system enabled the rise of the neoliberal project. This was after the US ended the convertibility of the dollar to gold in the early 1970s, a move that brought about the free-floating of exchange rates, stimulating international capital flows (Harvey 2005; Fouskas and Gökay 2012). These combined factors in the 1970s (stagflation, the falling rate of profits, the fall of the Bretton Woods system and the development of sophisticated mathematical tools for valuing financial assets) gave the political opportunity to try a new economic project that has been prepared and been promoted by the elite, the media, think tanks, and business forums. Thus, neoliberalisation is neither an accident nor produced by the economic conditions of the 1970s. This was constructed through lobby groups, corporate-sponsored foundations and research institutions. International grouping emerged, which was associated with imperialism (Miller and Dinan 2008). In short, there were grounds to believe that the regulated capitalism – bank-based (Keynesian) system is inferior to an alternative market-based (Hayekian) system. As Friedman argued, 'only a crisis – actual or perceived – produces real change. When that crisis occurs, the actions that are taken depend on the ideas that are lying around. That, I believe, is our basic function: to develop alternatives to existing policies, to keep them alive and available until the politically impossible becomes the politically inevitable'.[7] Thus, for Friedman, citizens are more likely to change their minds and ready to accept alternatives when the old ways of doing things are not providing the needed outcomes.

Friedrich Hayek, Milton Friedman and the *Mont Pelerin Society* pioneered the view of this supremacy of a market-based (neoliberal) policy by claiming that '*the market*' is an omniscient way of knowing, the one that profoundly goes beyond the capability of any individual thinking as well as the state (Friedman 1999; Hayek 2014). For them, the principles and the mechanism of the *market* should be implemented in all realms of life. This would be accomplished by the financialisation of everything[8] in everyday life because market discipline and rationality could be achieved through financial logic and constraints on economic agents. In short, the Hayekian legacy endorses and promotes neoliberal

---

7 *Milton Friedman in His Own Words* – https://bfi.uchicago.edu/news/post/milton-friedman-his-own-words.
8 This is used in this book to represent the shift in financial intermediation from banks to financial markets, as well as the emergence of financial market logic into sectors where it was previously non-existent.

narratives and discourse. This advocates that authority-even sovereignty be ceded to markets (financial markets in this context) because the market is seen as an impartial and unequivocal referee, gathering and signalling information that is essential to economic decision making and harmonising these decisions. Thus, and as a judge, objectively enforcing market discipline and market rationality on economic agents will lead to efficient outcomes for the society (Storm 2018). In other words, the market represents the only proper form of knowledge, and all other modes of reflection constitute bias and opaque judgment. Individual values and preferences are mere opinions, but collectively, the market transforms these into prices and objective facts.

The collapse of the Bretton Woods system permitted relatively free movement of goods, services, and capital across national borders. This encourages cross-border integration of the production process. As the global production system emerged, so did the financial system. (Kotz 2013) argues that the global financial system became interdependent and intermeshed with the production system. The global integration of the production and financial systems was propelled by technological changes in transport, communication and data processing, but could not have developed without the institutional changes that allowed unregulated cross-border economic transactions. The globalisation of the production and financial systems meant that competition increased on a global scale. This forced many domestic Small and Medium-scale Enterprises (SMEs) into bankruptcy in many periphery countries.

This global competition also encouraged both horizontal and vertical mergers and conglomerates. A wave of innovation occurred in financial services to produce not only for the more sophisticated global interconnections, but also for new kinds of financial markets based on securitisation derivatives, and all types of futures trading (Kiely 2018; Storm 2018). Neoliberalisation has meant, in short, the financialisation of everything. This deepened the hold of finance over all other areas of the economy, as well as over the state apparatus and daily life, that is power shift away from production to finance (Harvey 2005, 32). Harvey makes the following observation:

> Since the 1980s it has not been uncommon for corporations to report losses in production offset by gains from financial operations (everything from credit and insurance operations to speculating in the volatile currency and futures markets).

Thus, the large non-financial corporations have become more intertwined with financial orientation from credit and insurance operations to speculating in risky currency and futures trading. Acquisition and mergers across sectors conjugated production, real-estate and financial orientation as a new form of a diversified conglomerate. Hence, the power shift from production to finance means that gains in real production have little impact on real per capita incomes, but the concentration in financial services provides benefits to per capita income. Consequently, the abutment of financial institutions and the virtue of the financial system is significant to the collectivity/well-being of neoliberal restructuring. Harvey argues that in the event of any incongruity between Wall Street and Main Street, that is the financial sector and the real sector, the former will be favoured. Accordingly, in the neoliberal era, while the financial sector performs better the rest of the economy performs badly.

Another feature of neoliberal capitalism is the dominant neoliberal ideology. Kotz and McDonough (2010), Lapavitsas (2013) and more recently Kiely (2018) and Storm (2018) assert that neoliberal thought is characterised by the glorification and justification of individual choice, market relations, and private property; a view of the state as inherently an enemy of individual freedom and economic efficiency; and an extreme individualist conception of society.

Neoliberal capitalism asserts that an unregulated market system is optimal and that government intervention to correct market failures only worsens the situation and destabilises the private sector. Kotz (2010) and Dardot and Lawal (2014) remark that it will be difficult to underestimate the important role played by neoliberal ideas in glorifying the policies and institutional transformations that took place in this period, both at the international level and the nation-state. Thus, in the era of neoliberalisation, the state/government can only do wrong. This exemplifies Margaret Thatcher's point, that ordinary citizens will always spend the pound in their pockets better than the state/government.

However, while individual freedom in the market is guaranteed, so is the responsibility and accountability for their action and inactions, decision-making and well-being. This belief extends to all walks of life such as education, healthcare and pension. The successes or failures of an individual are measured in terms of entrepreneurial virtues or personal failings. The state is assumed not to be responsible for the successes or failures of the individuals. Failures are attributed to individual decision-making, not the lack of state provision. MacLeavy (2011) asserts that this has led to the 'race-to-the-bottom or beggar-thy-neighbour' policies in which responsibility for the provision of political priorities is loosened further and further downwards until what ensues is a new form of citizenship in which societal rights and responsibilities transform personal deficiencies such as unemployment into the failure of the individual rather than society. This Western-styled neoliberal individualism has spread to the periphery countries where the poor and vulnerable individuals of society who are least capable of bearing the liability have been left behind to fend for themselves.

In contrast, Tickell and Peck (2003), and Dardot and Lawal (2014) believe that neoliberalism is a process of mobilising state power in the contradictory expansion and reproduction of market-like rules. They refute neoliberals' argument of minimal state intervention and argue that neoliberalism involves the shifting of state intervention to new forms of governance supported by market competitiveness, flexible labour policies and commodification regimes such as carbon trading, fiscal austerity, and public spending on supply-side inputs. D. Hall (2009, 2) extends this by arguing that during the great recession – recent (2008) global financial crisis, the total value of the re-nationalisation of banks and insurance firms in the core countries was approximately equivalent to reversing about half of all privatisations in the world over the last three decades. He further adds that the UK government liability to the debts of Northern Rock alone is more than the combined total value of all the Private Finance Initiative (PFI) and Public-Private Partnership (PPP) schemes in the UK and the rest of the EU over the last 17 years. Fine (2012) questions why the world-leading neoliberals (the USA and UK) introduce socialism for bankers/capitalists and capitalism/neoliberalism for the rest of us. This suggests that private sector companies can walk away whenever profits dry up leaving the public to pick up the pieces. Therefore, it is safe to argue that neoliberalism nationalises risks but privatises rewards.

The recent coronavirus pandemic has also revealed the ugly side of neoliberalism and the need for active participation of the government in the management of the economy. The UK Institute for Government reports that public borrowing during the COVID-19 pandemic will be £317.4 billion above the government plans. The majority of this is due to specific policy decisions to shield private businesses from the worst of the crisis. The Institute estimates two-thirds (64.5%) of the extra borrowing was to support the private sector. Although the report focused on the 20/21 financial year, it acknowledges that there is significant uncertainty about the future of COVID-19 and its long-term impact. In March 2020, the Chancellor of Exchequer, Rishi Sunak announced a £12 billion package to fund public services, businesses and individuals in response to the rising cases of COVID-19. In normal neoliberal times, this would have been a considerable rise in state spending, but this amount has been dwarfed by the recent government intervention announced by the chancellor to support businesses.[9]

---

9   Institute for Government: https://www.instituteforgovernment.org.uk/sites/default/files/publications/cost-of-covid19.pdf (accessed at 20/01/2021).

Thus, the spread, effects and impacts of neoliberalism differ from that of post-war capitalism. Unlike neoliberalism, the capitalism that arose post-World War II spread quickly in the advanced capitalist economies, including Continental Western Europe and Japan, and the peripheral continents and countries of Asia, Africa, and Latin America. Although there were differences in how countries adopted this, the dominant policy was active state intervention in the economy.

For instance, in continental Western Europe, the term social democracy was referred to as state intervention in the economy with state welfare programmes and stronger trade union powers. The European welfare system was more generous than what was happening in the USA. Japan on the other hand did not have a robust welfare state and influential labour unions but rather promoted a high degree of state intervention. Developing countries adopted state powers to promote extensive economic development. This reformist's approach to economic management differs significantly from the revolutionaries/radical approach of contemporary capitalism.

As Keynes argued in his book *The General Theory of Employment Interest and Money*, the state could run a budget deficit, if necessary, to maintain aggregate demand and full employment. Government spending should rise to compensate for any decline in private investment. This is in contrast to the uneven spread of neoliberalism from its epicentres – the United States and the United Kingdom – and reverberated quickly to other parts of the world, notably the former communist countries of Eastern Europe, Central Europe, and other developing nations whose external debt problems forced them to accept the IMF neoliberal restructuring. The distribution of neoliberal restructuring was very minimal in Japan and other Western European nations such as Sweden, Denmark, Germany and others.

Kotz (2015) sums up the core institutions that revolutionary transformed with the expansion of neoliberalism to include the global economy, which was governed by the Bretton Woods system. This system encouraged international trade in goods and the power for states to regulate capital movements in several ways. The formation of the IMF and the World Bank saw countries needing approval (in particular, from the IMF) for any change in their relative currency, which was tied to the dollar in a fixed exchange rate. The breakdown of the Bretton Woods system in 1971 propelled neoliberal capitalism and its associated financialisation (which is discussed later in this chapter) to flourish.

Another institution that changed radically is the role of government in the economy. The relation between state and the economy transforms from active state intervention to privatisation and contracting out public functions, reduction or abolish of government demand-side economic management, deregulation of basic industries, deregulation of the financial sector. Furthermore, the capital-labour relation was distorted. The collective negotiation that existed between capital and labour was eroded with rapidity. Labour unions/power declined, and the state had a hostile stance towards trade unions. This affected union membership and density, besides, wage rates and working conditions started deteriorating as part of neoliberal restructuring.

Last, but not least, is the revolution in the corporate sector. Unrestrained forms of competitive practices, collusion and other price wars are present. However, the most visible and significant change in neoliberal capitalism is the relation between financial and non-financial corporations. Under neoliberal capitalism, financial institutions, albeit deregulation, have shifted their activities from advancing credit to the real sector of the economy to pursuing risky and speculative activities. This new role of the financial institutions and the consequences are discussed in chapter 3.

Alongside neoliberal capitalism is ordoliberalism, which Dardot and Laval (2014), and Storey (2019) describe as *'the German form of neoliberalism'*. This emerged as a distinct school of thought post-War era with competition within the framework of the market economy as the central principle of the ordoliberal philosophy.[10] However, what sets ordoliberals apart from neoliberals is what Foucault, Davidson, and Burchell (2008) describes as permanent vigilance and active state intervention to foster and protect individuals and firms. Röpke (1982) argues that the state must not be a bystander but as a referee actively intervening and enforcing rules of the game by imposing penalties for anti-competitive behaviour. Thus, the driving principle of ordoliberalism is the watchful state intervention and nurturing the competitive market environment. By contrast, neoliberals argue that state intervention distorts markets, and that market competition will arise naturally as long as the government intervention is limited. Ordoliberals argue that markets on their own will not operate freely as described by the neoliberals.

Another feature of ordoliberalism is what Woodruff (2016) argues as the 'proper assignment of liability to market actors. He remarks that as a competitive market economy rewards risk-taking entrepreneurs for their effort and innovation, it should also punish those who fail the tests of the market for their errors/mistakes. Thus, ordoliberal underpin legal as well as moral principles.

---

10   Storey (2019) argues that *pure ordoliberalism* has been less influential in Germany and European economic policy than often assumed. See Fouskas and Gökay (2018) examination of how ordoliberalism was transplanted at the European level.

However, the social market economy – ordoliberalism bears some features of neoliberal economic thought and practices.

In line with the overall neoliberal outlook, Foucault, Davidson, and Burchell (2008) and Bonefeld (2012) argue that the ordoliberal project is to *embed entrepreneurialism* as a character trait into the society as a whole. Therefore, individuals take responsibility for their welfare, and where individuals are inadequately enterprising, their dignity is seen as undermined through their reliance on the state. This prompted Hayek to argue that the core ordoliberal projects do not deviate so much from the broader neoliberal principles. (Storey 2019) then queries the form of state intervention ordoliberals envisage in carrying out their tasks.

V.K. Fouskas (2018) sums up the neoliberal-ordoliberal arguments as the two forms of imperialism and authoritarianism because they are not stand-alone domestic policies. However, these two forms of separable, but not separate stylised public policies, dominate different public policies in different contexts. Neoliberalism is a dominant public policy doctrine in Anglo-American, which support/advocate supply-side economics and supply-side intervention, what Fouskas and Gökay (2018) term a class policy in its best. They argue that neoliberal capitalism is more relaxed, less authoritarian and more politicised than the German-Austrian model of ordoliberalism. The ordoliberal theory requires a strong state, which is disciplinarian and legalistic to ensure socio-economic order and market competition to work. Unlike the neoliberal model where politicians have some leverage over the central bank, monetary decision-making in ordoliberal theory is free from political influences. This ensures sound money and fiscal discipline, as argued by Bonefeld (2012, 108). Thus, the ordoliberal model involves strict technocrats, quantitative economics where rules and norms are made without any questioning from politicians and other social agencies, hence the phrase 'There Is No Alternative' (TINA). However, along with other authors such as Harvey (2005) and Kotz (2010), this book accepts that Anglo-American neoliberalism has come to dominate as the global crisis manager since the early1980.

Emphasising the hostility of neoliberalism, Palma (2009) and Kear (2013) argue that financialisation underwrites neoliberal narratives and discourses, which promote individuals taking responsibility for their own welfare through private insurance, risk-taking, active investment and the accumulation of private property to benefit themselves within the controls imposed by financial markets and financial norms. The next section presents the debates on financialisation.

3   Theoretical Debates and Historical Precedents of Financialisation

The transformation of the behaviour/conduct and role of industrial enterprises, banks, and households constitute the foundation of financialisation. Investigating these relationships theoretically and empirically, and therefore ascertaining a more in-depth content of financialised capitalism and how it manifests itself in the periphery and Ghana, is the task of this book. The concepts and the methods deployed for the purpose are derived from Marxist Political Economy as well as Post-Keynesians traditions.

The term financialisation has been widely used in political economy and other disciplines such as sociology and geography. Its prominence reflects the ascendancy of finance for more than four decades. Lapavitsas (2013, 3) argues that the financial sector had become increasingly more significant in the 1950s and 1960s, although it was working within the regulatory framework of the Bretton Woods system. He asserts that the decades following the late 1970s experienced an extraordinary expansion of financial markets, which resulted in the rapid growth of financial profits, permeation of economy and society by financial relations, and the domination of political, social and economic policies by the financial sector. The productive sector in the core countries during the same time experienced slow growth performance with profit rates below the levels witnessed during the era of regulated capitalism, stagnant growth in real wages and rising high unemployment. That is an asymmetry emerged between the sphere of production and the ballooning sphere of circulation.

What is clear is that as the literature on financialisation matures, the multidimensionality of it becomes evident. The literature offers both contradictory as well as a complementary nature of accounts drawn from diverse disciplines and sub-disciplines. This may be due to a corollary of disciplinary methodology. What is espoused herein, therefore, includes a subjective account of the relative emphasis given by different writers in their assessments of the emergence and manifestation of financialisation. Even within political economy, it is important to distinguish between Keynesian and post-Keynesian accounts of financialisation, which places more emphasis on the ascendancy of the rentier due to the neoliberal economic policy adopted by the state, and Marxist accounts of financialisation which tend to emphasise its material roots. That is, even within the same discipline, they often overlap in the accepted elements of the phenomenon, but disparity may exist over the causality and emphasis.

Financialisation is a revolving term, which is difficult to define (Orhangazi 2008; Lapavitsas 2013). However, the frequent occurrence in all definitions has been the rise of fictitious finance at the expense of the real economic sector. For instance, Palley (2013) sees financialisation as a process whereby financial institutions and markets gain more significant influences over economic policy. Krippner (2005, 174) defines financialisation as a pattern of accumulation in which profits accrue mainly from financial channels rather than trade and commodity production. Tabb (2013) views financialisation as the dominance of the financial sector in the totality of economic activity; such that financial markets dictate non-financial corporation and household behaviours and significantly shapes the whole economy. Stockhammer (2012b) describes financialisation as the broad aggregate change in the relationship between the financial sector and the real economic sector. For these authors, financialisation is such broad, interconnected, but a distinct phenomenon as the globalisation of financial markets, the rise of financial investments and incomes accrue from such investment. Thus, political economists and other disciplines have captured the exponential growth of financial markets and financial intermediaries in the concept of financialisation.

For this book, financialisation will designate the dominance of the financial sector in both scale and complexity and becoming more important as a share of national output, such that the financial market dictates the behaviour of industrial enterprises (firms) and households. Thus, the changing conduct of banks (financial market), industrial enterprises[11] and households in a changing world market.

The next section examines the historical background of the emergence of financialisation in the neoliberal era. Four key strands stand out in the literature, which tries to construe the emergence of financialisation.[12] These are stagnation of production; French Regulation School theory of financialisation; post-Keynesians and the rise of the rentier, and the trans-nationalisation and liberalisation of finance.

---

11   For the purpose of this book, banks will proxy for financial markets. This is because banks remain the core of the financial system in Ghana. Industrial enterprises represent all non-financial corporations.
12   Financialisation and globalisation will be used as identical concepts similar to the work of Fouskas and Gökay (2012; 2018) and Lapavitsas (2013). This is because the key characteristics of globalisation relate to finance. These encompass global lending, global financial institutions engaging in global operations, and capital markets attaining internal reach. Thus, central to globalisation is the ascendency of finance, which is the core of financialisation.

4 From Stagnation to Financialisation

The work of Paul Alexander Baran and Sweezy (1968) on '*Monopoly Capital*' is central to this tenet-'stagnation to financialisation'. The central theme of the work is the generation and absorption of surplus under conditions of monopoly capital.[13] Baran and Sweezy see themselves as updating Marx's work in light of the emergence of *monopoly capital* in contemporary capitalism. The authors claim that classical works on *monopoly capital* have failed to integrate the monopoly factor into the mechanisms of the capitalist system. They distinguish between the two stages of capitalism.

The first stage in this two stage-model is the competitive phase of capitalism, where small firms compete on innovation and cost to survive. Each firm accounts for a negligible portion of the total market produce and thus had little power to influence market conditions. Market outputs are prices determined by the market forces. Firms with a large amount of capital enjoy a competitive advantage through increased productivity that allows them to force other firms that are not competitive out of business, or are taken over by their competitors.

This competitive struggle for survival, takeovers and mergers led to oligopoly and monopoly stages of capitalism. Thus, the authors contend that giant corporations have substituted the small and competitive markets as the dominant form of capitalism with the ability to set prices and regulate production and investment. Marx and particularly Engels had acknowledged this defining moment in the capitalist accumulation, with Engels contending that the birth of the modern corporation or the joint-stock company heralds the demise of perfect competition. Although Marx and Engels observed this crucial turning point in capitalism, they wrongly thought that socialism was on the way. Baran and Sweezy argued that to understand contemporary capitalism, it is crucial to abandon the competitive model and put monopoly at the centre of the analytical effort.

Since oligopolies and monopolies can control output and price, profits will rise as the system develops. This means that the period of falling profit will be replaced by rising surplus-value.[14] Baran and Sweezy (1968) contend that in the monopoly stage of capitalism, price is no longer the weapon for capitalists to compete. Monopolies and oligopolies realised that price-cutting and price

---

13 For the concept of economic surplus, see Paul A. Baran (1957). *The Political Economy of Growth*, New York: Monthly Review Press.

14 Baran and Sweezy (1968, 76) define rising surplus as 'the difference between the total output and the social costs of producing the output.'

war are self-defeating, then engaged in a new form of non-price competition – marketing and sales techniques.

As capitalism matured and was accompanied by the explosion of oligopolies and monopolies, the exploitation of labour intensified, which results in an ever-increasing surplus value. This means that avenues should be found to absorb this ever-increasing surplus in either production or consumption. Other than that, it will lead to stagnation of the productive sector. Although Keynesians' and post-Keynesians' view of the emergence of financialisation differs from (Baran and Sweezy) Marxists, this evidence supports Keynes's analysis of deficient aggregate demand, and this has been acknowledged by Baran and Sweezy (1968) in *Monopoly Capital* (p.143).

The ever-expanding surplus value that cannot be easily absorbed through consumption and investment by the productive sector or wasteful activities associated with trade, led to a shift in investment from the real economic sector to the financial sector. Steindl's work – *Maturity and Stagnation in American Capitalism*, which was first published in 1952 investigating the causes of the great depression, presented that the expansion of monopolisation increased profit margins in matured corporations. Monopoly (high) prices led to weakening demand and built-up excess capacity. Consequently, the rate of investment growth slowed as large corporations chose to reduce capacity utilisation instead of cutting prices. This led to stagnation, slow growth and mass unemployment and underemployment as a wide-ranging economic trend. Foster (2014) advanced Sweezy and the *Monthly Review* analyses by arguing that financialisation resulting from the stagnation tendency of monopoly capitalism led in turn to neoliberalism. He argues that 'what we have come to call neoliberalism can be seen as the ideological counterpart of monopoly-finance capitalism' (9).

The thesis of monopoly capital rests on the critical issue of surplus absorption as the main contradiction at this stage of accumulation. Foster, McChesney, and Jonna (2011) argue that the internationalisation of capital is still a continuing concentration and centralisation of capital with fewer firms on the world stage accounting for substantial parts of both domestic and international economies. They revealed that the top 200 corporations in the US accounted for just 13% of gross profit in 1950, but this figure has increased to 30% at the time of the great recession of 2007–09. On the global scale, the top 500 corporations accounted for 20% of total global sales revenue in 1960 but received 40 market shares by 2007.

Magdoff and Sweezy (1988) argue that ever since the monopoly stage of capitalism took over the world, it has only resulted in compelling a greater part of the world population into poverty and spreading all the profit amongst very few people and countries. Other prominent supporters of monopoly capital included Amin (1970) in his book *Accumulation of a World State*, and Mandel (1969) in his *Marxist Economic Theory*. More recent advocates of the tradition could be traced to the publication in 2016 of a special edition of *Monthly Review* titled *Monopoly Capital a Half-Century On*, which brought together great economics minds such as Amin, Prabhat Patnaik, Jan Toporowski, and Costas Lapavitsas, among others.

However, it is important to recognise that theorists of monopoly capital tradition from the 1980s shifted from the core debate about the status of concentration and centralisation of capital to the commencement of economic stagnation in the mid-1970s, and the emergence of financialisation as a countervailing element, thus lifting the economy. Magdoff and Sweezy (1988) and Sweezy (1994) contended that the monopoly stage of capitalism and stagnation had resulted in a new form of contradictions in the capitalist system called *the financialisation of the capital accumulation process*.

The *Monthly Review School* theory of monopoly capital offers a ready analysis of the periodic events of the late 1970s and the consequent occurrence of financialisation. They hint at the epochal transformation of capitalism and propose a systemic or aggregate change of economy and society, which are consistent with Marxist theoretical predilections. By the 1970s, surplus absorption had grown into difficulty, the situation had exploded, and the threat of stagnation hung over the countries in the core. Consequently, capital began to seek refuge in the sphere of circulation and, above all, in the sphere of speculative activities of finance (Baran and Sweezy 1968; Lapavitsas 2013; Kiely 2018).

Lapavitsas remarks that financialisation has occurred as a crucial mode of sucking up the investible surplus that flooded the realm of production by directing it to the sphere of finance. For him, slowing down the rate of growth, the growth of giant MNCs and financialisation are the three periodic events of capitalist accumulation in the twentieth century. These three events are complexly interrelated, as the growth of monopolist Multinational Corporations (MNCs) led to the surplus value that cannot be easily re-absorbed through investment by the productive sector resulting in stagnation – the stagnation led to financialisation.

Baran and Sweezy, and the *Monthly Review School's* approach to financialisation has many remarkable strengths. The two models of capitalism – from competitive capitalism to monopoly capitalism and the emergence of financialisation to absorb surplus value. Here financialisation is seen as a flight of capital from malfunctioning productive sector into fictitious finance.

Despite the remarkable work of these scholars, they have not critically examined the causes of financialisation at the level of capitalist enterprises and financial institutions, other than updating the Marxist argument of monopolisation (Lapavitsas 2013). The closest that the *Monthly Review* current has been, is that financial asset tends to become inflated as non-financial institutions channel surplus-value to finance and creating a speculative bubble. Besides, if these giant corporation capitals have been seeking an escape route from stagnation by engaging in financial speculation activities, it could be argued that there are good economic reasons for the monopolies and bankers to change their behaviour/conduct, which has to be specified accordingly. The tendency towards monopolisation is significant in this regard, but as Lapavitsas (2013) puts it, also too general to account for the specific character of the economic transformation commencing in the mid-1970s.

Another weakness of Baran and Sweezy and the *Monthly Review*'s current claim is that the emergence of financialisation signals a periodic shift in the balance between the sphere of production and circulation, in favour of circulation. Lapavitsas (2013, 18) argues this is a departure from the theory of financialisation and suggests that analysis of financialisation ought to incorporate the agents of the capitalist economy – industrial enterprises, banks and households. He concludes that 'for if financialisation is not specifically related to the operations of the capitalist agents, its content will remain ambiguous.' However, unfortunately, the examination of the *Monthly Review* current and other Marxists outputs that treat financialisation as the escape of capital from the stagnation of production do not offer this critical analysis. This book provides a specific thorough investigation of the changing conduct of industrial enterprises, banks and households in Ghana.

Although the concept of the monopoly stage of capitalism was very influential in the early 1970s, the number of critics also grew. It became very common in late 1970 to downplay the notion of concentration and centralisation of production and monopoly profit. (Weeks 2014, 332:165) for instance, argues that the notion of historical stages of capitalist development has no existence beyond the works of Baran and Sweezy. Critics argued that the internationalisation of capital has essentially eradicated the essence of monopoly capital (Brenner 2006).

Another strand of analysis within Marxist Political Economy emphasising the role of productive stagnation is drawn from the work of Fernand Braudel (1981). Braudel argues that structural cycles of the *'longue duree'* mark the expansion and contraction of hegemonic powers. The declining phase of production – the *autumn* is associated with a rise of finance. Arrighi develops the concept of a systemic cycle of accumulation. He presents a structuralist model of the development of the capitalist world system. Arrighi (1994; 2007) adopted Braudel's framework to classify four systemic social cycles of accumulation, or century-long periods of hegemony based on combinations of economic power with territorial state power, each epoch involving increasing scope, higher intensity, and shorter duration. Each of these cycles begins in one of territorial state a productive advantage and places it in the centre of the world system and the position of hegemonic power.

Arrighi (2007) asserts that the capitalist world economy contains a hegemonic power that develops in a cyclical pattern. As the prowess in production and trade of one hegemonic declines, the sphere of finance grows, and another hegemonic succeeds the declining hegemony. Financialisation, according to Arrighi, thus represented a sign of *autumn*[15] in the cyclical trajectory of hegemonic power. One hegemony's *autumn* is another hegemony's *spring*. The hegemony historical path has traversed Italy (Genoa), the Dutch, Britain, and the US. Arrighi and his collaborators argue that the crisis of the 1970s signaled a decline of the US hegemony and posits a future emergence of new loci of power, particularly in East Asia. In each instance, the ascendant power has occurred partly as a consequence of abetting itself of the financial resources of the declining hegemony.

Although Arrighi's historical systemic cycles of accumulation give some insight into the emergence of financialisation, a degree of caution is necessary. The theory is at odds with contemporary realities. First, the rise of finance in the US has not been accompanied by a flight of capital to a new rising centre of power, but as we shall see later, an inflow of capital from the rest of the world, particularly from the periphery countries to the US. This prompted Panitch and Gindin (2004) to argue that Arrighi confuses Asian countries' ownership of US treasury bills with a structural shift in the distribution of power.

Arrighi's thesis, like Baran and Sweezy, associates the emergence of financialisation with declining productive dynamism, and thus fading hegemonic power. However, it does not elucidate the mechanism and pattern through which profit derives from finance. To demonstrate both the nature and the sources of financial profit, it is important to critically examine the activities of the agents whose conduct defines financialisation – industrial enterprises, banks and households. Orhangazi (2011) remark that the category of financial profit is hard to establish and that it is not an accident that the nature and sources of financial profit hardly exist in either classical, political economy, or Marxist economics. They maintain that once the theoretical analysis goes beyond the primary state that surplus is available which seeks investment in

---

15 A term coined by Braudel and frequently used by Arrighi to represent a declining hegemony.

finance, the sources and nature of financial profit in terms of the aggregate flows of value in the contemporary capitalist economy is ignored.

Another major drawback of Arrighi's theory of financialisation is a replacement of the current hegemony – the US. In *'The Long Twentieth Century,'* he suggested that Japan might inherit the mantle as the next hegemony, an idea shared by Boyer (2000). However, in *Adam Smith in Beijing*, Arrighi proposed China to be the next hegemony based on flexible accumulation and outsourcing. Neither of these suggestions work well in contemporary capitalism.

Lapavitsas (2013), and Fouskas and Gökay (2012) argue that the US has been a net borrower in recent decades with much of the money coming from Japan and China. The *autumn* of US hegemony whether due to financialisation or not has rather resulted in an inflow of capital to the US and conspicuously, from some of the poorest countries in the periphery. Lapavitsas (2009a; 2013) argues that this is due to the role of the US dollar as quasi world money, and this has imposed costs on the periphery countries. This is an aspect of *subordinate/ inferior* financialisation, which will be discussed later in the context of Ghana and sub-Saharan Africa.[16]

Certainly, the focus of the work of Arrighi, Baran and Sweezy, has been on the performance of the core countries, particularly the United States and the UK. All the arguments deliberately deal with the issue of global instead of solely national accumulation. However, lacking are the more fine-grained analysis of the changing behaviour/conduct of the agents of capitalism (industrial enterprises, banks and households) both within countries and across borders, and their specification within a changing world market. Consequently, the discussions fail to analyse the uniqueness of the rise of finance in the periphery, in particular, Sub-Saharan Africa.

Since the evidence provided from the review does not account for the emergence of financialisation across the world market, this book argues that the tendencies of financialisation should not be limited to a few archetypical financialised economies. Consequently, the book sets out a testable hypothesis that financialisation should be observed as a worldwide phenomenon. However, it is not expected that countries will experience a similar fashion across the world. Instead, as argued by Powell (2013), the fundamental tendencies of financialisation will manifest themselves unevenly across countries, and the impact will depend on the domestic institutional arrangements and the hierarchical nature of each nation's insertion into global processes of

---

16   See chapter 4, section 6, *Financialisation in Sub-Saharan Africa - Accounting for the Ghanaian Paradox*.

accumulation. Another tenet that explains the emergence of financialisation is the French Regulation School.

5   French Regulation School Theory of Financialisation

The Regulation theory sets out yet another scholarly argument from which to analyse heterodox approaches to financialised capitalism. This theory is influential in the debate of finance-led-growth regimes. It looks at how institutional frameworks, which are the manifestations of social relations, stabilise a particular accumulation, how they enter into crisis, and how they renew themselves (Boyer and Saillard 2005).

The Regulation school approach to financialisation came in part from the search for a replacement 'regime of accumulation' to *Fordism*, which they argue ended in the 1970s. Chesnais (2001) had suggested a new regime of accumulation with financial dominance. In his later writing, Chesnais (2006) ponders whether a new finance-dominated regime is developing after the weakening in productive accumulation and destruction of the capital-labour comprise seemingly embodied in the Fordist growth regime. Regulation School uses the post-war mass production, rising wages accompanied by rising productivity as *Fordism*, and the crisis of the 1970s weakens the element characteristics of the period of *Fordism*. Thus, a new regime of financial accumulation might emerge. Lordon (2000) suggests that financialisation regime of accumulation was replacing the loss of material basis of Fordism regulation.

Boyer (2000) argues whether finance-led growth is a viable alternative to Fordism. He argues that since the demise of the Fordist regime of accumulation, a search has begun to investigate a possible successor of mass production and mass consumption. Boyer proposed a vision of the future of capitalist growth, which he viewed as becoming increasingly influential in the late 1990s. Cross countries acquisition and capital movement, pressures on corporate governance, diffusion of equity among a more substantial proportion of the population; in his view, all these changes pointed to the emergence of finance-led accumulation regime. This he labelled as a new mode of regulation *'new economy'* – the new regime is characterised by labour-market flexibility, price stability, developing high-tech sectors, booming stock markets and credit to sustain the rapid growth of consumption, and permanent optimism of the expectations in firms.

The ability and how each country adopts and carries out this model would be a critical factor in the nation's macroeconomic performance (Aglietta 2008). Boyer opines that household behaviour has undergone a significant shake-up with the Fordist post-War. Undoubtedly, wages and salaries continue to be a crucial component of reward for labour; however, Boyer identifies two new mechanisms emerging.

On the one hand, under pressure for shareholder value, the wage bill has to respond quickly to any divergence between expected and actual returns. Depending on the exact content of the capital and labour compromise, the related flexibility may affect wages, working hours, or even job security. However, on the other hand, some workers may have access to financial gains through equity holdings, or more likely by the intermediation pension funds. As a result, the prospect of gains in the financial market has a direct impact on household decisions to save or spend. Boyer referred to the equity base as *patrimonial*[17] because wealth, as measured by the financial market, tends to influence household consumption of both durable and non-durable goods, and indebtedness to banks (Boyer 2000; Aglietta and Rebérioux 2004).

The structuralist influences are apparent in regulation theory as it stresses the significance of specific institutions over and above production function. Boyer (2000) identifies five distinct, but interrelated socio-economic institutions, and how they are organised to examine the different forms capitalism has taken. These include i) how competition is organised between firms; ii) the monetary institution – the functions of money and circulation; iii) the relation between the state and the economy; iv) the international economy insertion; and v) the wage-labour nexus – wage determination, flexible labour market.

Moreover, Becker et al. (2010) distinguished between productive and financialised accumulation based on the sectoral direction of investment. These are extensive and intensive accumulation based on whether workers consume goods that are bought primarily in the market, and whether the increase in surplus-value is due to increase work intensity; and lastly, introverted and extroverted accumulation, determined by the direction of output towards domestic or international markets.

Drawing on case studies from South America and Eastern Europe, Becker et al. (2010) postulated further types of financialisation. These include financialisation based on fictitious capital in the core, which meant inflation of financial prices; financialisation based on interest-bearing capital, which meant the expansion of banks, and high-interest rates in the periphery. They further distinguish between 'elite' financialisation in the semi-periphery countries – the involvement of a new bourgeoisie and the upper-middle-class; and

---

17   Aglietta and Roberioux (2004) introduced the concept of 'patrimonial capitalism' where income accrues via shareholding and could reimburse stagnant wages.

'popular' financialisation – which meant that workers and other middle class have also been drawn into the realms of financial operations. Regardless of the validity of these categorisations, drawing a distinction among varieties of financialisation is significant in examining the phenomenon in its entirety. For instance, the World Bank and the IMF financial inclusion policy has drawn the underserved, the unbanked and the rural poor in Ghana into the realms of the financial sector.

Although the regulations accumulation regimes concept acknowledges the systemic importance of the rise of finance in recent decades, the specification of the financialised regime is not precise than that of the *Fordist regime* of accumulation. However, even the *Fordism* regime of accumulation, Brenner and Glick (1991) argue whether it ever accurately captured the character of accumulation in the core countries, including the US in the period outlined. It is therefore essential to note that doubts surrounding the notion of the *Fordist regime* since the US economy is the standard reference for the regulation school when it comes to *Fordism*. Lapavitsas (2013) questions whether the regulation school analysis of financialisation goes beyond a reworking of the theories of shareholder value and the dominance of the stock market. While the above discussions have been rooted in the Marxist tradition, Post-Keynesians also provide yet another current that explains the emergence of financialisation.

6   Post-Keynesianism and Financialisation

Post-Keynesian theory of the providence of financialisation shares some similarities with Marxist analysis, but also has some decisive differences. The post-Keynesian theory focuses on how the growth of financial markets has paved the way for financial fragility and instability. The scholarly work of Minsky (1986; 1996) has been the cornerstone of Post-Keynesian financial analysis. Many post-Keynesian writers use Minsky's Financial Instability Hypothesis (FIH) to explain the rise of finance in the economy.

The hypothesis offers both empirical and theoretical aspects. The empirical aspect is that from time to time, capitalist economies show inflation and debt deflations[18] which could be possible to spin out of control. The theoretical argument begins with the description of the economy as a capitalist economy with high-priced capital assets and intricate, sophisticated financial systems. Thus, in the capitalist system, there exist private property and private

---

18   See Fisher (1933) for the classical description of debt deflation.

ownership of the means of production. For Minsky, the capitalist financial system is a complex of inflows and outflows of money transactions.

Minsky (1996) identifies three distinct income-debt relations, which are labelled as hedge finance, speculation finance, and ponzi finance. Hedge finance units are those finances that can meet all their contractual payment requirements. That is, borrowers' expected stream of income cash flows would be sufficient to repay principal plus interest. Speculative finance units are where revenues only repay interest without the principal. Such units need to roll over their liabilities by taking on new debt to meet commitments on maturating debt. For ponzi finances, the revenues are insufficient to fulfil their contractual payment obligations of either repayment of the principal and/or interests due. Here a new loan should be taken in order to service existing debt. Thus, the FIH is a theory that exhibits the impact of debt on system behaviour and also how debts are validated. Thus, income-debt relations will eventually be dominated by ponzi finance.

Firms' willingness to fund investments is conditioned by both the cost of borrowing and future profit from the investment. Any rise in interest rates could lead a firm whose income-to-debt nexus was initially branded as a hedge, to become speculative and eventually ponzi. To avoid mass insolvency and bankruptcies will require the injection of liquidity by the government and the central bank.[19] The particular mix of these three income-debt relations reflects the historical development of the economy and shapes long-term expectations.

When the ratio of speculative and ponzi finances increases as a share of total liabilities, firms and the economy become sensitive to interest rate variations and changes in asset prices. The economy then becomes unstable. If access to credit dries out (credit crunch) for whatever reason, inability to meet debt obligations will trigger a process of deleveraging, which, in turn, will cause asset prices to fall (Minsky and Kaufman 2008).

Minsky (1996) further outlines five stages of American capitalism, which are commercial capitalism; industrial capitalism and wild-cat financing; financial capitalism and state financing; paternalistic, managerial and welfare state capitalism; and money manager capitalism. It is the fifth stage – money manager capitalism that Minsky posits a large amount of financing occurring without financial intermediaries. This, he argues, was due to a consequence of neoliberal privatisation and pension system, resulting in the ascendancy of institutional funds and shareholder value orientation in the financial system. Wray

---

19   See Ivanova (2013) for a summarised criticism of the Financial Instability Hypothesis.

(2011) believes that money manager capitalism spells out a structural shift in the core countries, including the rise of financial engineering and shadow banking, pressure for deregulation and less supervision, and most importantly, increasing household debt. Palley (2011) argues that Minsky's money manager capitalism proposes a 'super-cycle', which allows more and more financial risks into the system. The cycle, according to Palley, involves twin developments of 'regulatory relaxation' and 'increased risk-taking.' These developments increase both sides of the balance sheet – increasing both the supply of and demand for risk.

Minsky's FIH and the money manager capitalism offer a scholarly analysis of policy changes in the US, but very little if any direct insight into the dynamics of financialisation in the peripheral economies. As pointed out by Lapavitsas (2013), there is a minimal discussion on Minsky's work on the long-term balance between finance and the real economy, and the broader implications of money manager capitalism were not critically analysed. Ivanova (2013) adds that Minsky's theory is vague as to the factors that trigger substantial changes in the behaviour/conduct of the financial actors and the working of the financial systems over the economic cycle.

The post-Keynesian literature on financialisation is generally based on the rise of the rentier layer, and in particular, money lender as a rentier. Keynes referred to the rentier as a parasitical economic entity that extorts profit due to the scarcity of capital and might, therefore depresses investment and profitability for active capitalists. The objective of the rentier lies in the perpetuation of financial profits at the expense of productive investment and broader welfare. For Keynes, successful capitalism requires the *euthanasia of the rentier* that could be attained through a low-interest rate (Keynes 2018, 24).

The rise of the rentier in recent decades has been linked with a series of policy initiatives undertaken by the core countries (see, for instance, Lazonick and O'Sullivan 2000; Epstein 2005; Epstein and Jayadev 2005; Crotty and Lee 2005; Lazonick 2014). Although this literature deliberately deals with the issue of global in its view, the links between the growth of the rentier layer in such a varied range of institutional contexts are not critically analysed primarily in sub-Saharan Africa and other peripheries.

The ramification of the rising power and dominance of the rentier is the transformations in corporate governance, in the name of *Shareholder Value Orientation*. Managerial capitalism assumes that managers' preference is growth, while shareholders are dividend out of profit. This principal-agent conflict was resolved through some fundamental institutional changes. These changes include the use of performance-related pay and stock options as managerial compensation, and the growth in mergers and takeovers (Lazonick and

O'Sullivan 2000). Lazonick (2010; 2014) argues that firms move from an outlook of retaining and invest to one of downsizing and distribute as a consequence of executive stock options, share buybacks and the increased mergers and takeover activities.

Sharing evidence from France, the US and the UK, Stockhammer (2004) posits that there is an inverse relationship between the part of income given out in dividends and interests and real economic sector investment. Orhangazi (2008) and Crotty (2005) find evidence from the US that rising financial profit since 1980 has reduced real economic sector investment and increased dividend payouts, and share buybacks have led to firms substituting their own capital with borrowed capital and thus shortening planning horizon and increased uncertainty. This has increased firms' debt-capital ratio, forcing firms to reduce costs by cutting wages and reducing labour and real sector investment.

Within post-Keynesians, financialisation characterises the ascendency of the rentier because of the neoliberal economic policies espoused by the state in the last four decades. The dominance and power of the rentier have supported financial profit at the expense of industrial profit, and therefore financialisation has induced poor performance of real investment and output in the core countries. Like Marxists, post-Keynesians recognise the connection between stagnating production on one hand and financial expansion on the other in the era of financialisation.

However, the critical distinction between post-Keynesians and the Marxists is the fact that post-Keynesians consider the rapid expansion of the financial sector at the expense of the production sector is due to inappropriate economic policy in the core countries. That is, policies such as shareholder value orientation have directed investment into finance rather than the production sector of the economy. Thus, the ascendency of the rentier has a dismal impact on the real economic sector. Marxists, on the other hand, argue that the expansion of finance is due to the malfunctioning production sector. Thus, both post-Keynesians and Marxists agree on the falling rate of profit in the real economic sector but differ on the causation.

For post-Keynesians, the ascendency of the rentier layer symbolises financialisation, and this is because of the inappropriate economic policy. However, these inappropriate policies are inadequately specified and critically addressed. Toporowski (2010) suggests that economic boom and shared prosperity in the golden age of capitalism enlarged the middle-class, particularly in the US. These middle-class demanded higher-yielding assets for savings. He argues that the privatisation of pension funds endorsed these funds to be channelled into corporate securities. As more inflows flooded the stock market, the share prices rose. The capital gain is therefore paid by the next buyer or the institutional investor, who is more interested in the capital gain than investment in long-term sustainable profits from real production. This process, therefore, increases firms borrowing, and further results in higher interest and dividend obligations than their cash-generating capacity in expanding.

For such firms that are over-capitalised, holding financial assets against liabilities is safer than investment in plants and machinery that tie up funds and slow returns. In view of this, corporations invest in financial assets and engage in mergers and acquisitions rather than investing in production. Toporowski (2008) further adds that households also manage their liquidity with excess capital. Households hold increasing bank debt against real estate and financial assets, with house owners relying on housing inflation rather than income for consumption.

Toporowski provides a significant/scholarly examination for the understanding of financialisation in the US without the covert rentier layer. However, he believes that financialisation is cyclical and argues that *financialised capitalism is over* (Toporowski 2009, 146). It is worth acknowledging that the impact of capital market inflation in the core countries or the peripheral countries was not sufficiently clarified in detail, although presumably capital market spillovers and the changing investment trends of the multinational corporations would figure prominently. Thus, the successes of financial markets inflation retard the performance of the under-invested industrial sector. This is because financial innovation continues to mobilise financial resources in order to sustain the rising asset price. Toporowski (2009, 153) argues that in an era of *finance* (financialisation), *finance mostly finances finance*. The absorption of financial resources in the financial market to buy financial assets will eventually result in financial inflation.

Another thread in the literature is the rising inequality in the era of financialisation. Post-Keynesians link rising inequality to a neoliberal policy agenda, which has strengthened a small minority whose wealth comes from financial profit.[20] Stockhammer (2012b) has extended this argument globally, where he hypothesises two growth models – debt-led and export-led. In debt-led growth economies, households maintain consumption levels through borrowing due to falling or stagnating wages. In the export-led growth countries, suppressing wages supports international competitiveness, with profit recycled. The two groups are complementary because the current account deficit of debt-led countries and capital inflows of the former match the current account

---

20 Palma's (2009) seminal work describes the class and race implications of inequality.

surpluses and the capital outflow of the latter. That is, financial deregulation has permitted one group of countries to run a protracted current account deficit.

However, it is difficult to position sub-Saharan Africa specifically in any of these models proposed by Stockhammer. Stagnant wages characterise the region, yet it is less internationally competitive due to the export of primary commodities whose demand is price inelastic, and the high importation of manufactured goods from the core countries. This has resulted in current account deficits for most countries in the region. On the debt-led model, lack of collateral security in the region impedes household ability to borrow, finance, or smooth out consumption. The confluence of these factors is the rising of chronic poverty in the region. Another tenet of financialisation is the trans-nationalisation and the liberalisation of finance.

7 Trans-nationalisation and Liberalisation of Finance

Financialisation has also had significant impacts on the international dimension. The liberalisation of global capital flows has led to increasing fragility of exchange rates, often resulting in a violent exchange rates crisis. Central to neoliberal reforms are deregulation and liberalisation of the financial systems. This public policy is based on the standard neoclassical economic theory that financial globalisation would allow capital to be re-allocated to its most efficient use. Accordingly, Stockhammer (2012a) questions the implication for core-periphery capital flows and the impact on growth and development indicators, especially in the periphery.

The earlier proponents of financial globalisation and liberalisation, Mckinnon (2010) and Shaw (1973), and later Mishkin (2006) argue that alleviating financial restrictions will allow market forces to determine real interest rates and can have a positive impact on economic growth as interest rates rise toward their equilibrium in a competitive market. This tradition argues that artificial interest rates ceiling such as what was being used in Ghana pre-structural adjustment period in 1983 reduces savings, capital accumulation and results in inefficient allocation of resources. They contend that financial liberalisation encourages higher interest rates, which will stimulate more savings that could provide a source of funds for investments in the real economy and bring about economic growth and development. This has informed global economic policies, especially through IMF's Structural Adjustment Programmes imposed on periphery countries, in particular, sub-Saharan Africa.

The classical economist assumption of higher interest rates leading to more investment has been challenged. Keynes (2018[1936]) argues that a rise in a rate of interest intended to encourage higher savings which could be directed to real production will instead have the effect of reducing real investment. He remarks that withholding consumption (i.e., savings) would depress the business of producing for current consumption without necessarily stimulating the business of making ready for some future act of consumption automatically. That is, the insufficiency in effective demand, culminating from too much household savings, will constrain rather than promote the process of production. He asserts that capitalist agents must usually save from their existing profit – 'real savings' before investing in the future.

It can then be argued that real savings by the capitalist agents are primarily determined by the increased demand for the products, which will influence the amount of capital that is invested in the productive process. Therefore, if individuals deferred consumption, it will depress today's investment and will subsequently reduce the rate of real savings and invariably reduce the scale of future investment. Keynes' (2018[1936]) argument is that it is the rate of profit that induces investors to accumulate capital wealth and even to require any loanable funds at any interest rate. That is, the scale of investment depends on the relation between the rate of interest and the rate of profit, with the rate of profit dependent on the individual's ability to spend on the capitalist products. Arrighi (1994) sums it up as the reason why capitalist agents invest money in a given input-output combination is to make a profit.

The globalisation of finance disrupted sub-Saharan Africa's domestic approach to financial systems. Global financial markets enable governments and large corporations in the periphery to benefit from offshore borrowing and capital markets. Thus, borrowers searching for funds are no longer limited purely to domestic markets as they can raise funds from the global financial market. Likewise, investors with surplus funds can reach out to borrowers in both domestic and international markets. Valdez and Molyneux (2015) argue that the purpose of international financial markets is matching those who want capital with those who have capital. This reduces borrowing costs and ensures efficient global financial markets.

However, as Mandell (2002) points out, capital account liberalisation has reduced the independence of policymaking in the periphery countries. Capital movements disrupt any changes in monetary policy, particularly in the periphery. Hanson et al. (2003) suggest that countries could adopt a floating exchange rate system to offset the impact of capital flows. However, adopting a floating exchange rate in Sub-Saharan Africa has encouraged financial contracts to be denominated in foreign currency, notably the US dollar onshore as well as offshore.

In contrast to the neoliberal account, Stockhammer (2012a) argues that financial globalisation and liberalisation have led to frequent exchange rate crises caused by unpredictable capital flows, and long-lasting global imbalances. Fluctuations in exchange rates are increasingly determined by global capital movements rather than domestic macroeconomic fundamentals such as growth, inflation, and current account positions. It is normally profitable to take part in interest arbitrage[21] in a liberalised international market than investing in the real economic sector. This interest arbitrage means that higher interest rates in the periphery countries induce capital inflows from the core. Any changes in interest rates will lead to a sudden and sharp capital outflow with a devastating effect on the exchange rates. Incidents of exchange rate crises as a result of capital inflows followed by sudden and sharp outflows have been a common feature in semi-periphery countries (Epstein 2005; Harvey 2005; Reinhart and Reinhart 2009). The effects of exchange rates volatility as a result of rapid capital movements on macroeconomic have been felt severely in Mexico 1994, Turkey 1994 and 2001, South Asia crisis 1997–1998, Argentina 2001, and have all led to a severe recession with some long-lasting with double-digit fall in real GDP (Stockhammer 2004; 2012b).

Despite these risks and potential disadvantages, periphery countries were forced to liberalise the capital accounts as part of the conditionalities for structural adjustment loans. The World Bank and the IMF policy of privatisation and deregulation through the Structural Adjustment Programme created a climate where domestic (periphery) bourgeoisie are freer than ever to transfer their nation's wealth into financial markets and financial institutions of the core countries. As we shall see later, on the net basis, capital has been flowing from the periphery to the core and the majority of studies are unable to give sufficient evidence in support of financial globalisation and growth benefits (Stiglitz 2000; Kose et al. 2009; Stockhammer 2010; Powell 2013). However, some advocates of financial globalisation argue that the benefits materialise indirectly, and direct impact will show up if more sophisticated methods were used (Mishkin 2006).

Furthermore, in contrast to the orthodox economics vision, financialisation has resulted in the growth of financial investment and financial profit with

---

21   That is, to borrow in one country or currency and invest in another country or currency (sometimes called carry trade).

adverse repercussions for the real economic sector. This has occurred in both core and semi-periphery countries (Orhangazi 2011).

The literature on trans-nationalisation and liberalisation of finance, unlike stagnation of production, incorporates analysis of changes in the peripheral countries. It offers specific empirical insight into the commonality and divergence between how these developments are witnessed in the core and the periphery. For most periphery countries, deregulation and liberalisation of their economies were through the Structural Adjustment Programme (SAP).

8 Financialisation and Poverty Alleviation: Banking the Unbanked

The essential vehicles used to transplant financialisation of households in the developing countries have been microfinance and financial inclusion policy under the auspices of the World Bank and the IMF. It is therefore crucial to consider the transformation of global economic alignment to appreciate the macroeconomic context in which microfinance and financial inclusion imposed themselves as a new frontier of capitalist development. The weakening of industrial capitalism and the growth of the finance-led regime of accumulation have resulted in new channels through which credit has been flowing to the private sector. Consequently, the predicament of social reproduction caused by neoliberal economic austerity measures and the spread of new market-based alternatives to the classical social safety nets has made it possible for new credit creation. In this context, Harvey (2011) and Marazzi (2010) argue that expanding access to microcredit and loans has been the solution associated with falling effective demand as a result of neoliberal economic policies.

In the era of neoliberal capitalism, financial inclusion is commonly portrayed as a useful poverty alleviation tool, which is also facilitating the democratisation of the financial market. The growth of microfinance[22] and the recent emergence of financial inclusion, a new frontier of global development in the periphery countries have given rise to the debate about whether the neoliberal restructuring of banking the unbanked[23] are actually benefiting the poor. Mader (2015) argues that financial inclusion has expanded the financial sector by transferring the social and creative skills of the unbanked, underserved and

---

22 Microfinance is a type of financial service providing small credit/loans to the most vulnerable customers who lack access to traditional banking services.
23 Those individuals and businesses that have no or minimal access to any financial services are known as the unbanked and underserved, respectively.

the poor into financial products. That is, the unbanked have been fully integrated into the global financial market, and neoliberal's omniscient market-based projects have replaced the government programmes aimed at the poor. The new market-oriented poverty alleviation strategies place on individuals and households to be more responsible and develop an investor mentality by either accepting market conditionalities or by contracting debt.

Consequently, this neoliberal ideology acts as a moral force aimed at changing the behaviour and conduct of the poor and those at the margins. (Demirguc-Kunt and Klapper 2012) argue that financial inclusion systems equalise opportunities by reducing inequality and famished off poverty while at the same time stimulating economic growth. Thus, finance is seen as the only way of improving the welfare of every citizen, and not just the poorest households. Therefore, the prudent way of alleviating poverty is to encourage and incentivise the impoverished households to access financial products to induce borrower behaviour (Rojas-Suarez 2016).

The free-market argument is that regular repayments promote self-discipline on the part of the poor borrowers. This idea of self-control, good behaviour makes borrowers liable for controlling irregular income streams, something which has been possible through receiving microcredit/loans. On this evidence, Lavinas (2017) contends that poverty is still viewed as a consequence of laziness and passivity, moulding it as a choice. Thus, the over-indebtedness, power relations and concerns of well-being, status and dignity are all ignored.

The general concept of financial inclusion is that the poor lack access to microcredit due to the substantial collateral required by the formal financial system. This idea views poverty as due to the condition of financial exclusion encountered by poor people (Yunus 2007). Therefore, by using social bonds as the preferred form of collateral, as in the case of group loans and solidarity lending, microfinance aims to provide the right to an economic initiative to the poor, in order to empower them to self-improve their life condition (Nowak 2005). It has been argued by Reed et al. (2015) that there has been a substantial growth of the Microfinance Industry (MFI) and its clients in the era of neoliberal capitalism. The vast majority of these are in the periphery regions – Africa, Asia and Latin America.

It is essential to recognise that the pioneering microfinance institutions have gone through an extensive transformation. The initial MFI were either small or medium-sized organisations managed by Non-Governmental Organisations (NGOs), savings and credit co-operative, which depended on public subsidies and contributions to cover operating costs (Robinson 2001). Members can draw loans from it in times of need and pay them back later. The interest charge for these services is very low as these microfinance institutions operate a non-profit making trade.

The essential aspect of the earlier MFI is that the credit money they issue has directly come from savings deposits within them. That is, their resources are derived from the past production of value in the economy through workers' wages earned in production. Contemporary MFIs are managed and operated by large financial institutions governed by the neoliberal market-based notion of financial self-sufficiency. These institutions demand exorbitant interests from poor borrowers in order to cover their high operating costs and also to reward investors for the capital collected from the market. The transition from the public subsidised/state-driven model to a market-oriented one has been enthusiastically supported by neoliberal global institutions such as the World Bank and the IMF through the Consultative Group to Assist the Poorest (CGAP), an organisation aimed to promote the best practices in the financial inclusion industry.

Aitken (2013) remarks that microfinance, microcredit and financial inclusion are vehicles of extracting further financial profit from the poor and the unbanked. He postulates three ways in which microfinance and financial inclusion paradigm of poverty alleviation have been financialised:

> Practices of valuation, in which microcredit is made legible in the metric associated with financial markets; techniques of intermediation which facilitate flows of global capital into micro-credit networks; and processes of securitisation which have provided a vehicle through which global investors can access micro-credit receivables as investable objects.
> AITKEN 2013, 474

Aitken is of the view that delivering Microfinance (MF) through commercialised ways has attracted investor interest in the sector. This interest has resulted in the growth of rating agencies in the MFI with the main aim of providing investors with financial information relating to the financial performance, quality of loan portfolio, risk exposure and return on investment. The overall purpose they claimed, has been to offer relevant information to promote transparency of MFI to facilitate investors' continuous interest to ensure regular capital flows into the sector.

However, Bateman (2010) argues that financial analysts, investors, fund managers and consultants have profited from this incentive-driven arrangement with rising incomes. Since microfinance and financial inclusion advocate individual self-reliance – a feature of neoliberalism, it endorses the slashing of state social security for individual security and effect facilitates the withdrawal of state public services. Bateman concludes that commercialised microcredit/loans are an anti-poverty variant of capitalism.

The emergence of microfinance investment vehicle dominated by global capital oligopolies – an intermediary operating between private investors and MFIs have increased the total assets of microfinance investment vehicle from $2.3 billion in 2005 to $13.5 billion in 2016 (Symbiotics 2017). The growth of microfinance investment vehicles demonstrates that there is sufficient reward to keep private investors in MFI.

Central to financialisation is the securitisation of consumer credit – a new technique adopted by financial markets. This model involves the pooling of credit receivable into financial engineering/securities which can be traded in the financial market. The price of this securitised credit is derived from the income streams generated from the interest payments. This financial engineering/securitisation distinct the risk of credit from its owners onto investors. It converts the consumer credit market into the sphere of generating/yielding tradeable financial products based on the cycle of regular monthly payments.

MFI has also embraced securitisation similar to the subprime mortgage market. Consequently, consumers' microcredits and loans are converted with all the risks attached to special purpose vehicles and selling their related cash flows to an investor. It is therefore not difficult to conclude that the purpose of MFI is to generate a tradeable financial product that will earn regular monthly repayment to the capitalist. This activity generates further income to fund additional microloans. This facilitates investors to borrow short-term from the money market to fund microcredits and loans. In short, this fictitious money (as discussed in chapter 3) does not come from previous production activity rather from expectations that it will be validated by future production processes.

Securitisation has been a critical feature in the contemporary financial market but is usually applied to middle-class financial products in the form of mortgages and loans of high value to middle and upper classes of society (Lazonick 2012). Nevertheless, in a finance-led accumulation regime, financial institutions have exploited other markets to extract financial products. This has been possible due to the enormous database constructed by specialised credit-ratings agencies with new forms of credit-scoring algorithms that invent new forms of risks and new geographies apparent.

Although the retail financial market has always been about generating new financial products, the shift in the last four decades has been significant. Previously bank assets, in the form of loans and mortgages were matched by their liabilities such as deposits and savings. However, in a financialised capitalism, financial products have been drawn on not for the proceeds that can be earned from the interest rates spread on savings and credit/loans, but rather the raw materials for bonds and other securities that can be invented from the regular income payments that such assets can provide (Leyshon and Thrift 2007).

The Initial Public Offering (IPO) of Compartamos, a leading MFI in Mexico accused of charging high-interest rates raised $467 million in the Mexico stock market in 2007, providing healthy returns on investment for investors. An Indian MFI, SKS also raised $1.5 billion in the Bombay Stock Exchange in 2010, an amount which is over forty times its entire year earnings (Reille 2010; Feasley 2011). These examples illustrate that the interest of the poor borrower is irrelevant, and the real mission of financialised MFI is to serve the interest of profit-maximising private investors.

It has been argued that microfinance and the financial inclusion of the poor will offer a win-win solution for all. Thus, the poor who are financially excluded would be assisted to emerge from a condition of social exclusion, while at the same time microfinance companies make profits for their investors. However, the profit motive of the industry has resulted in high interest in microcredit to the most vulnerable people in society. This has drawn attention to the level of interest rates considered appropriate to satisfy the social mission that microcredit and financial inclusion companies claim to offer and what has been recognised as a profit maximising objective of these industries.

Bateman (2010) argues that the high-interest rates charged have been justified on the grounds of financial self-sufficiency and continuous expansion to offer more microloans to increase the number of beneficiaries. This proposition shows that the financial inclusion industries are using poor individuals at a point in time to kindly accept to help other poor households some other time in the future. That is, in order to get out of poverty, poor households should accept high market interest rates to help themselves and others in similar conditions. This is not the equitable vision of banking the unbanked. Bateman concludes that financial inclusion firms have failed to deal with their moral and ethical missions.

The exorbitant interest rates, however, are just one of the contradictions that have accompanied the neoliberal financial inclusion paradigm of poverty alleviation. Cutthroat competition amongst firms in the industry has resulted in predatory lending in a rising saturated market. This has pushed many poor borrowers into a condition of over-indebtedness and suicide as reported in India and Nicaragua (Priyadarshee and Ghalib 2011; Mader 2015). The authors argue that microcredit is being used for consumption purposes in most cases and explain why multiple borrowing has become a feature in the industry – credit from one financing firm could be the only way to meet the repayment obligation from the previous loans – ponzi financing discussed above. Consequently, micro borrowers are at risk to face a situation in which loan repayments have to be made at the expense of food, education and health expenditures. Failure to repay microloans is likely to result in exposing insolvent borrowers, harassment and further social exclusion (Guérin et al. 2014).

The World Bank argues that individualising the process of poverty alleviation means freeing the poor people of reliance/habituation on an estranging system of social protection and therefore empowering the poor for their destiny. This neoliberal idea manifests itself to be generous; however, it is severely disputed by the social relationships of the market, where it is the survival of the fittest. The privatised state enterprises make access to social amenities unavailable for the poor, and by transferring social policies, provision of which is a challenge in the periphery countries to the realms of the market in the form of contracts contradict any effort to alleviate poverty. Financial inclusion has been generally supported as an effective poverty alleviation tool, which is also fostering to democratise the financial sector. However, rising over-indebtedness has increased the level of suicides and non-performing loans in poor communities, undermining the trust in the whole microfinance and financial inclusion system as a way of alleviating the misery of poverty.

9 Conclusion

The post-war capitalism was in contrast to the pre-war era. The rise of neoliberal capitalism is not an accident but a well-planned and orchestrated approach. The collapse of the Bretton Woods system and the cross-border integration and production processes facilitated this. The global integration of production and financial systems was facilitated by technological changes in transport, communication and data processing. The dominant neoliberal idea of individual freedom and liberty assumes that responsibilities for successes and failures rest on the individual but not the state. It also limits state intervention and advocates the importance of the rule of law.

Political economists and other disciplines have captured the exponential rise of finance in the concept of financialisation. The literature on financialisation offers both contradictory and complementary accounts drawn from diverse disciplines. Four strands that stand out in the literature are the stagnation in production; French regulation theory of financialisation, post-Keynesianism and financialisation, and the trans-nationalisation and liberalisation of finance. All these strands deliberately addressed issues on the global as opposed to national accumulation. However, they failed to critically examine the changing behaviour/conduct of the agents of capitalism – banks, industrial enterprises and households, both within countries and across borders. Like post-Keynesians, Marxists recognise the connection between stagnating production on the one hand and the ascendency of finance on the other in the era of financialisation. However, they differ on the root cause of this financial expansion. Post-Keynesians argue that the rise of finance is due to inappropriate economic policy, while Marxists believe the rise of finance is due to the declining productive sector.

The brief literature on financialisation provides very little theoretical insight into the emergence of the phenomenon across the world market; however, it offers essential case studies on the transformation of various institutional settings.

Increasing financial flows remain the main feature of financialisation. However, it should not be assumed that financialisation in SSA will be homogeneous. The study of financial systems and the dominance of finance must acknowledge the global hierarchical foundations of this process. The restrictions imposed by international imperialism is mediated by domestic economic restructuring with rooted class implication and interactive transformations between economic agents. The relationship between the global financial systems and its international accumulation processes and the specific country's trajectories of integration should be incorporated into the research of financialisation in the periphery. For instance, SSA capitalists' access to the global pool of liquidity has resulted in mixed outcomes because of the floating exchange rate systems. SSA governments have also adopted contractionary monetary policies aimed to attract capital inflows, with sterilisation efforts driving the growth of domestic bond markets. Thus, a distinctive aspect of financialisation as it unfolds in the periphery.

The next chapter examines the long-standing debate on financial development and economic growth. It brings together the rise of finance and the financialisation of everyday life and unpacks the financial profit conundrum. The chapter distinguishes between fictitious accumulation and real commodity accumulation.

CHAPTER 3

Finance-Growth-Nexus

Theoretical and Empirical Literature

1 Introduction

Heterodox currents of economic thought have mostly addressed financialisation as a particular configuration of the core. The previous chapter presented the rise of neoliberalism and the emergence of financialisation. The chapter discussed the shift from the *Keynesian-Fordist* mass-production mass consumption economic principles and management to the late 1970s neoliberal era and the contradictions of neoliberal capitalism.

This chapter examines the long-standing debate of finance-growth nexus. It starts with the rise of finance and the financialisation of everything by examining the collateralisation of everything that could be collateralised. The financial profit conundrum is explained by examining Marx's profit upon alienation, in particular financial profit extracted from individuals and profit derived from trading financial assets. The chapter further provides a clear distinction between real commodity accumulation and fictitious accumulation, and the balance of power between them. The contemporary heterodox perspective on the finance-growth debate is also examined in this chapter by providing the supply-leading hypothesis relative to demand following theory.

2 The Rise of Finance and the Financialisation of Everything

Contemporary financialisation epitomises the second bout of financial dominance in the history of the core countries, the first covering the latter part of the nineteenth century and the early twentieth century lasting until the interwar years. During that period, the growth of large monopolist corporations as the dominant units of production emerged, most of the time organised as cartels operating in exclusive trading zones. Likewise, capital export and international financial markets grew strongly, typically associated with giant monopolist banks that dominate international finance (Orhangazi 2008b; Lapavitsas 2013).

Contemporary financialisation has clear resemblances or comparisons but also distinctive features with the previous bout of financial dominance. The growth of Multinational Corporations (MNCs) dominates the international economic activity – (a feature of globalisation); international banks play a prominent role in global finance; capital exports have grown significantly. However, there are also noteworthy differences between these periods.

The ascendance of finance – financialisation has not resulted in exclusive trading zones associated with territorial empires as it did in the first stint. Besides, banks are not dominant over large industrial enterprises, at least in the core. However, there has been significant interpenetration and interconnectedness between the realm of finance and the sphere of production, while financial relations have flourished in the economic life of workers and households in general. Panitch and Gindin (2004) assert that globalisation and the ascendency of global finance have been driven by the US state, capital, and imperialism in the modern era, and has necessitated the restructuring of other states according to the dictates of globalisation and ascendant finance (a debatable exception could be China and Russia).

The first bout of financial dominance in the international economy led to a passionate debate among Marxist theorists. An essential contribution to this debate is the work of Hilferding (1981), which attempted to incorporate the growing significance of banks in monopoly capital (as discussed in chapter 2) and the consequences of growing monopolisation, which he argued will result in the formation of a general cartel. Thus, the entire capitalist reproduction will be dominated by a single entity, which would control the volume of production in all divisions of industry. The conclusions drawn from his work do not apply directly to the contemporary conditions of financialised capitalism. Nevertheless, the theoretical concepts he sets out, the issues he raised, and the links he drew between economic, social and political phenomena are vital for the examination of contemporary financialisation. Hilferding argues that as production becomes monopolised, large firms will increasingly depend on bank credit for real productive investment.

Consequently, the relationship between financial institutions and industrial capitalists will lead to finance capital. Finance capital is therefore hypothetically resting on close links between the banking and industrial sectors through interconnecting appointments, information sharing, and making mutually beneficial decisions. It is essential to recognise that Hilferding's analysis ignores the supposed opposition between what Lapavitsas (2013) calls the 'active' industrialist and 'idle' financier. Consequently, the power of rentiers imposing their interests in industrial capital and reducing investment rate and growth was largely ignored. Somewhat, finance capital was perceived as an amalgam of banking and industrial capital, and therefore real economic sector took an interest in the operations and profitability of the financial sector and vice-versa. Also, Hilferding's argument of the formation of a cartel is hampered by powerful counter-tendencies such as the breaking up of monopolies and the founding of new firms to compete with existing monopolies. His notion of a general cartel also limited his ability to develop any meaningful theory to examine the modifications in capitalist accumulation connected to monopolistically/oligopolistically competitive market, regulated by a few large firms.

A new form of profit emerged as finance capital developed. Hilferding discerned profits from the stock market discounted at the rate of interest; however, industrial capital earns the profit. Given that, the rate of profit should normally be higher than the rate of interest, the purchase price of shares exceeds the capital invested, if future returns are translated into net present value, this conforms to Marx's analysis of finance. The difference between the two (profit and interest) is 'founder's profit,' which is extracted and given as a lumpsum to those money manager capitalists who manage the shares on the stock market. Part of this founder's profit also accrues to banks for their investment banking activities.

The concept of the founder's profit remains important in examining contemporary financial profit, including capital gains (Krippner 2011; Lazonick 2014; Orhangazi 2011). Hilferding saw shareholders in the same way as moneylenders and that the expected return on shares should be the same as the rate of interest (in addition to a risk premium). Hilferding's work outlined the expansion of capital export and transnational rivalry between large multinational corporations.

The concept of *Finance Capital* was used by Lenin (1999) to build the theoretical core of his analysis of imperialism, which could be defined from the view of Lenin as the highest stage of capitalism or the concentration and centralisation stage of capitalism – monopoly stage of capitalism. He stresses the importance of the tendency towards monopoly for both industrial and banking capital, although Hilferding was aware of monopolisation. Lenin posits rentier[1] as a vital social group within the capitalist class in the era of imperialism. He stresses the significance of the re-division of the world by countries dominated by finance capital, therefore leading to imperialist rivalries and wars. However, Lenin, like many other Marxists in the 1920s and 1930s, did not examine the consequences of monopolisation for the underlying theory of accumulation.

It is worth noting that neither Hilferding nor Lenin tried to explain the ascendancy of finance as a result of capital escaping to the sphere of circulation looking for speculative financial profit. Lapavitsas (2013) argues that

---

1 Lenin borrowed the notion of *'rentier'* from Hobson.

these authors and other leading Marxists at the time treated crises as a complex and multidimensional phenomenon that could not be associated with a simple theory of the rate of profit to fall. He argues that classical Marxists are alien to the concept that the normal state of capitalist production is to malfunction due to a continuously excessive organic composition of capital, or even due to falling 'surplus' absorption. Again, these authors would have been surprised at the notion that the rise of finance epitomises the '*autumn*' of capitalist hegemonic power, as suggested by Arrighi (2007) in his analysis of systemic cycles of accumulation. Lenin, however, saw imperialism as parasitic and decaying, but he referred to the capitalist mode of production as a whole, rather than to the sphere of production in countries where finance capital was robust.

The theoretical analysis of Hilferding's *Finance Capital* demonstrates an epochal transformation of capitalism that transpired in the nineteenth century until the interwar years of the twentieth century, related to the significant rise of finance during the same period. However, if this epochal transformation of capitalism has taken place, then its roots are likely to be found in the forces of production/industrial enterprises and labour process/households. However, Hilferding did not discuss this thoroughly and there is no relevant empirical evidence provided in *Finance Capital*. This weakens the overall analysis of finance capital. Hilferding's analysis does not critically capture the complexity and range of the contemporary relations between industrial enterprises and bank capital. In the era of contemporary financialisation, banks do not hold the dominant position in bank-industry relations.

As argued by Harvey (2005), Orhangazi (2011), Lapavitsas (2013) and Storm (2018), banks compete with pension funds, insurance firms, and other financial institutions in providing external funds to industrial enterprises. Similarly, large industrial enterprises engage in financial activities in the open markets on their own account by issuing shares and bonds. Furthermore, they can engage in trade and consumer credit, as well as transacting forward, futures and derivatives markets on their account without the need for banking services. For instance, Mobile Money Operators in Ghana can issue shares to the public/customers to raise capital for their operations[2] without the need of investment banks.

The ascendancy of finance in the mid-1970s was empowered by the nexus of supportive neoliberal thought, the global stagflation during the period, and the improvement in information technology tools. The improvement in financial

---

2   See chapter seven for detailed analysis of Mobile Money.

technology eased the cost of financial engineering with the help of complex mathematical tools for pricing financial assets and supported by the 24/7 global financial trading with speed (Epstein 2005; Van der Zwan 2014; Davis and Kim 2015). What makes the current ascendency of finance different is how financial intermediation has shifted from banks and other financial institutions to financial markets. Storm (2018) calls this process a move from the *visible hand* of relationship banking to the axiomatic *invisible hand* of apparently self-correcting, self-regulating efficient financial markets.

For example, households' mortgage debts have been financially engineered into securities and traded in international financial markets, while pension and savings are invested in mutual funds and stock markets (Epstein 2005; Krippner 2011). Besides, the unbanked and underserved on the other hand have been entangled into the realms of the global financial market through their daily dependence on microloans, credit and mobile money, like banking (see chapter seven for detailed analysis of mobile money services) in the name of financial inclusion. The development of *enforced indebtedness* proposed by Steindl (1989) is worrying for a financial crisis. Thus, the life of households everywhere revolves around finance. Steindl remarks that households organise their daily lives around *investor logic*, active individual risk management, and involvement in international financial markets.

Storm (2018) argues that conglomerate corporate bodies, which previously provided secure employment and stable retirement benefits, have been broken up into disaggregated international commodity chain structures to comply with global financial markets principles *of shareholder value maximisation* (SVO). Lazonick (2014) contends that contemporary decision-making powers have shifted away from corporate boardrooms to global financial markets. Consequently, falling real capital formation as investors transfer their funds to more lucrative global financial markets. The excess funds in the financial markets are used mainly to invest in short-term financial instruments, which yield high returns that precipitated the systemic meltdown of the recent global financial system in 2007/08 (2018). That is, in pursuit of high return investments using the liquidity to generate more money from money – $M \rightarrow M^1$ (*in the money circuit of capital*).

Financial markets are deeply penetrating social space by financialising everything and opening new enclosures/fields; for instance, insurance firms issuing healthcare bonds where the payoff comes from the savings made from the healthcare intervention for the insurer. A similar case is the International Red Cross collaboration with a German insurance firm to issue bonds to fund rehabilitation services in conflict zones (Van der Zwan 2014; Storm 2018).

The roles of financial actors[3] have occupied bigger geographical scales in markets of items significant to human survival and development. The global markets for food, primary commodities, healthcare, education, and energy have all been financialised. These financial actors and financial institutions have converted nature into an object of accumulation strategy and have created various financial products aimed at the environmental crisis in the form of carbon trading markets, climate-sensitive derivatives, biodiversity asset bonds and disaster bonds. Keucheyan (2017) calls it the *'assurantialisation'*[4] of climate risk. He explains the deliberate privatisation of risk, which has removed government responsibility and protection that was previously given to farmers against any personal misfortune to market-based individualised insurance for farmers, workers and households. Thus, in a contemporary financialised economy, *trading* in commodities and food markets has nothing to do with the current and future consumption needs of households/consumers but the directives of the financial market's alternative collateral, store of value, and assets role in the international economy (Clapp and Isakson 2018).

Consequently, the value gained/derived from the futures contract of these commodities neither supports its capacity to meet consumers' demand for food nor smoothens output prices for farmers, but rather uses it as collateralised securities to endorse speculative shadow banking transactions. The consequences are higher food and commodity prices and an increase in price of farmlands. With big financial investors into agricultural commodities trading, farmers, agri-food firms and food retailers now seek gains in the financial markets; they have prioritised the interests of their shareholders as they branch into more financial activities. As a result, wages have been reduced, and external costs have been ignored by shifting risks to workers/consumers.

With reduced or no government support, farmers must now manage their risks (price and weather) by taking out insurance – commodity exchange as hedging (Clapp and Isakson 2018). These developments underpin rising inequalities in power and wealth within the food industry and produce further unpredictable food markets. As a result, they weaken the resilience and sustainability of the industry, and have impeded collective actions to tackle these challenges. Storm (2015) remarks that in the era of financialisation, anything that can be collateralised will be collateralised. Access to affordable financial products is being reconceptualised as the rights and responsibility of every citizen. Thus, the displacement of financial institutions by financial markets has

---

[3] Financial actors here refer to financial intermediaries such as banks, bond investors, pension fund, insurers and speculative hedge funds.
[4] The insurance of nature.

had an inescapable impact on the way households; industrial enterprises, as well as governments, make decisions and choices.

Governments around the world have adopted finance-friendly policies at the expense of social welfare to welcome cross-border capital flows. Some of the policies include reducing capital controls, promoting liquid domestic stock markets, given independence of the central banks, decreasing and in some cases abolishing the taxation of wealth and capital gain (Chandrasekhar and Ghosh 2002; Storm 2015; 2018; Bortz and Kaltenbrunner 2018). To compound the problems of the poor, the international institutions, notably the World Bank and the IMF narrowed the definition of poverty to mean lack of access to quality and affordable finance.[5] Consequently, the neoliberal economic policy comes to produce more financial relations – a new institution to manage the poor, the unbanked and the underserved in the society (Mader 2015).

The hegemony of finance has shifted the focus of governments, industrial enterprises and households away from the real economic sector production towards returns/income earned through financial instruments, a process Davis (2009), Kiely (2018), and Storm (2018) describe as the transformation from an industrial to a post-industrial society and the financialisation of everyday life. This has an important implication on the direction of government policy towards poverty alleviation in a country such as Ghana. Rising financial profits at the expense of industrial profits have been the cornerstone of contemporary financialisation. The imbalance of power relation between holders of capital and households resulting in exploitation of the latter is examined below.

3   The Financial Profit Conundrum – Profit in Marxist Economics

One of the critical features of financialisation is the rising financial profit, empirical evidence for which is provided in chapter 4. Many theoretical approaches to contemporary financialisation have classified increasing financial profit as a sign of limited profitability in the sphere of production and a resultant escape of capital in the sphere of finance (Arrighi 2007; Krippner 2011; Lazonick 2014; Orhangazi 2011). Arrighi's historical systemic cycle of accumulation suggests that financial expansion is the '*autumn*' in the cyclical trajectory of hegemonic prowess in production and trade. That is, as finance grows, capital migrates

---

[5] See chapter six for the theoretical and empirical analyses of the Issue of poverty- definition, measurement and debates.

from production and trade to financial speculation, financial intermediation, and profit gradually and progressively come from financial deals.

The concept of profit can be contended to be one of the main innovations in the field of political economy by Marx (2019[1867]), although his notion has not been generally accepted. In his view, profit is the money-form of surplus value created in production. Wage workers earn the equivalent of the value of labour-power as money wages but usually indulged in working for longer than the time-equivalent of the value received, thus creating extra, or surplus value. This labour-process is exploitation in production and constitutes the defining feature of capitalism – the difference between 'necessary labour time and surplus labour-time'.[6] Thus, the surplus-value is determined by the extra portion of the working day that the labour works. The rate of surplus-value is therefore an expression of exploitation of labour by the capitalist in the production process.

For Marxist Political Economy, profit is basically treated as a flow of surplus-value and of net output – newly created in the sphere of production. Surplus value realises a monetary form in the sphere of circulation through the sale of the finished product and ensues as the exclusive property of the capitalist who owns the means of production. Different forms of return emerge as the total flow of surplus-value is unevenly distributed among sectors under various headings in the sphere of circulation – rent for property owners, profits for entrepreneurs actively engaged in the production and trade, and interest for owners of money capital available for lending.

Although Marx's theory of surplus-value diverged significantly from Ricardo's *Principles of Political Economy of Taxation*, there are some similarities in their investigation of profit. Ricardo (1891) theorises that profit is a newly created flow of value (embodied labour) that accumulates per period. However, profit is not a self-standing part of production/output emerging due to a normal profit-generating process. Instead, profit is the left-over net output that accrues to capitalists once labourers have claimed their share corresponding to wages. Thus, profit or the residual tends to fall as wages, and other costs rise.

Similarly, Marx treated profit as part of net output accruing to capitalists. However, Ricardo's notion of profit as residual contrasts with Marx's theory of exploitation to explain the emergence of profit as a result of a typical capitalist process. Although Marx treated profit as part of the flow of net output accruing

---

6 'Necessary labour-time' is the portion of the labour-process which produces the value of the labour means of subsistence. Surplus-labour time is the labour-process that is no longer necessary labour because it creates no value for himself but creates a surplus for the capitalist (Marx 2019[1867]).

to capitalists, he rejected Ricardo's view that profit is a residual and proposed his theory of exploitation to explain the emergence of profit as a consequence of a feature of the capitalist process.

Essential for this book is Marx's theory of profit, which has influenced other strains of classical political economy, which identified types of profits independent from the flow of production. This strain of Marx's theory is vital to examining financial profit. The central notion in this regard is 'profit upon alienation,' initiated by Steuart (1767). He posits that 'real value' and 'profit upon alienation' are inherent in the price of a commodity. The necessary labour needed for production, the cost of materials and the subsistence of workers form the real value, while the profit upon alienation is derived from the residual/surplus of price above the cost of real value.

The profit upon alienation is what forms the profit accrued to the industrial capitalist. Steuart further distinguishes between 'positive profit' and 'relative profit'. Positive profit is determined by the overall increase in value and output, which expands the 'public good'. This is qualitatively different from relative profit, which is extracted from trade and unrelated to the expansion of output. The distinction is significant because, on the one hand, profit could come from the expansion of productive capacity – an addition to earlier output. On the other, profit could come from purely a zero-sum trading game relative to output – a gain by one party will lead to a loss by another party in the sphere of circulation (Lapavitsas and Levina 2010; Lapavitsas 2013). The latter is what Steuart refers to as 'profit upon alienation', which constitutes 'relative profit'.

The analysis of 'profit upon alienation' has many strengths relevant to this study. However, since it classifies the overall capitalist profit with 'profit upon alienation', it considers capitalist profit as it emerges from a zero-sum game in exchange. In contrast, Marx (2019[1867]) argues that capitalist profit is already enclosed in 'real value', not least as part of normal labour required for production. Nevertheless, Marx points out that one party's gain in circulation could come as a loss of another party. There is a distinctive feature of this form of profit from the flow of surplus value created in production through the exploitation of labours.

Marx adopted the concept of 'profit upon alienation' in his examination of financial transactions relating to the personal income of households. He contends that financial dealings extracting profit from household income are exploitative and not related to surplus-value. That is, there is qualitatively a distinction between exploitation occurring in financial transactions and exploitation occurring in the sphere of production. The financial exploitation is derived from a direct extraction of rent from households' income to the rentier. This exemplifies the World Bank and IMF financial inclusion policy in Ghana and other periphery countries. Lapavitsas (2013) remarks that the social factors that account for exploitation are related in the sphere of circulation, reflecting in particular the imbalance position of power between households/workers and capitalists in the financial transaction, as discussed in chapter seven.

The exploitation in production as outlined by Marx amounts to creating a new flow of value out of unpaid labour, which accrues as the exclusive property of the capitalist who owns the factors of production and the finished products. The social factors underpinning this exploitation as outlined by Lapavitsas and Levina (2010) and Lapavitsas (2013) are the absence of property rights by households/workers over the means of production, as well as the lack of power of households/workers over the production process. In short, capitalist profits originate from a new flow of value created in production through the exploitation of labours.

However, profit upon alienation emerged from zero-sum relations relating to the current stock of money originating through financial dealings. This concept is adopted in this book to analyse financial profit, and in particular financial profit for rentiers advancing money to households, governments and profit extracted from financial assets. Financial profit contains elements of surplus value but broader in construction to include other forms of monetary increments. For Lapavitsas and Levina (2010), Orhangazi (2011), Lapavitsas (2013) and Storm (2018) financial profit is similar to the primordial type of profit capturing purely the excess of money returned over money advanced- $M \rightarrow M^1$ *in the money circuit of capital.*

The notion of 'profit upon alienation' is significant to the analysis of financial profit earned from a mortgage, consumption loans (through mobile money services in Ghana) to households, and from handling pension and other funds. It is important to note that these forms of financial profit could be accrued to the lenders of financial assets, or financial institutions as fees, commission and proprietary profits. Lapavitsas (2013) argues that the social underpinnings of financial expropriation are partly with the non-capitalist character of personal income. Workers and other households go into a financial transaction in order to obtain use-values, whether directly in the form of wage goods or in the future through a pension. In contrast, financial institutions enter financial transactions to make profits. There are systematic differences in information, organisation and social power between the two parties, which permit financial institutions to exploit the holders of personal income. Indeed, it is also possible for individual households/workers to enter a financial transaction from the perspective of making a profit, but this does not eliminate the systematic difference between individuals and financial institutions as counterparties to transactions. The two-way relationship between real commodity accumulation and financial accumulation and the change in the balance between them is examined below.

4   Real Commodity Accumulation and Fictitious Accumulation

A contemporary financial system (financial services and monetary services) provides a variety of purposes in capitalist accumulation. Monetary services offered by the financial systems include credit creation, savings, transfer of money across the economy, enabling foreign exchange transactions, and other monetary services. Financial services, however, include mainly the mobilisation of loanable funds in the economy and its subsequent advance through loans/credits. Besides, financial services include collecting spare money funds across society as well as trading loanable capital in the open markets (Lapavitsas 2013, 201). The monetary services of the financial system are often ignored or overlooked in the debate on financialisation despite its vital importance to financialised capitalism. The monetary and financial services are closely intertwined through the creation of credit by financial institutions.

The importance of distinguishing between real and financial/fictitious accumulation originates with Marx[7] who argued that '*money*' capital available for lending takes a separate form of accumulation compared to capital employed in production. From this viewpoint, financialisation could be seen as a change in the balance of power between real and financial/fictitious accumulation, thus, financialisation represents the asymmetric expansion of fictitious compared to real commodity accumulation since the neoliberal era.

Real commodity accumulation comprises industrial, agricultural and merchant's capital, and this occurs in both production and circulation. The actual form it takes includes the addition and improvement to the means of production, the expansion of real value, the growth of the labour force, and the development of the means of communication, amongst others. Moreover, it further relates to the sphere of distribution since it leads to the division of output between wages and profit. The key aspect of real commodity accumulation is the production and expansion of surplus-value, which yields positive profit from the sale of the product, which later facilitates real investment. The pointers of real commodity accumulation, thus, include expansion of output-value and use-value, an increase of the workforce and enlargement of real capital investment.

---

7   See Marx's *Capital* Vol.3, pp. 599–607.

Fictitious accumulation, on the other hand, originates in the sphere of circulation and remote from the real production, but could also be seen in the scope of distribution primarily through the creation of financial profit as discussed above. Financial/fictitious accumulation mainly takes the form usually undertaken by financial markets/institutions in the form of mobilising, trading, and advancing loanable capital. One key feature that sets real accumulation apart from financial accumulation is that the latter does not offer a quantifiable final product-value and use-value (Orhangazi 2011; Harvey 2005; Lapavitsas 2013). Just like the real commodity accumulation, financial/fictitious accumulation provides jobs needed to undertake the various sophisticated financial products and transactions.

However, the relationship between the expenditure of the workforce and the degree of fictitious accumulation is somewhat incongruent (Krippner 2011; Orhangazi 2011; Storm 2018). Likewise, the huge capital investment in establishing financial intermediaries does not match the degree of fictitious accumulation. This is because it mainly deals with mobilising, trading and advancing loanable capital. The critical aspect of financial accumulation is heaping up claims on others – mobilising financial assets which have their own (fictitious) prices.

Another distinctive feature is that whereas real accumulation relates to stocks, financial accumulation is mainly a flow concept. That is, financial accumulation involves the flow of mobilising and advancing of loanable capital, and in contrast, real commodity accumulation relates to the expansion of industrial, agricultural and merchant's capital – the stock concept.

The balance between these two is shaped by the characteristic difference between the forms of accumulation. The operation of the financial systems varies across countries, regions, and even cultural frameworks within which industrial, agricultural and merchant's capital interact with loanable capital. Therefore, the connection between real and financial accumulation has historical and geographical dependent characters (Orhangazi 2011). Real accumulation requires a complex financial system, and therefore necessarily requires the development of financial accumulation; however, the outlook and the conduct of financial systems vary according to specific and historical factors. A given state of real accumulation in terms of growth rates, employment, and profitability could correspond to significantly varying states of financial accumulation.

Since historical, institutional, political, and cultural factors play a pivotal role in the relationship between real and fictitious accumulation, there can be no perfectly optimal balance between them. Orhangazi (2011) outlines two main channels in which financial/fictitious accumulation could impede real accumulation. Firstly, he argues that diverting capital into financial assets crowds-out real sector accumulation. Thus, if firms put more money into financial assets, there will be less available for real investment. Given the incentive to earn higher returns in financial assets, more capital flows into financial assets at the expense of the real economic sector. This, however, assumes external funds are limited, and any extra capital comes at a higher cost. Secondly, he remarks that the pressure on management to generate short-term profit shifts investment to the financial sector due to the lucrative quick returns as opposed to real investments. However, it could be argued that earnings from financial investment, albeit rapid returns in the short run, could be used to fund real investments in the medium to long run.

Another way to assess how financialisation hampers real investment is through pressure on industrial enterprises to increase payments to financial markets in the form of dividends and stock buybacks by firms. Tobin (1965) argues that there is an inverse relationship between real accumulation and fictitious accumulation. He argues that real and financial investments are substitutes. Thus, if financial assets provide better returns, it will attract more capital to the detriment of real sector investment. He concludes that investment in financial assets could not compensate for the detriment in the real sector at the macroeconomic level by merely reallocating funds.

Equally, Crotty (2005) presents that in the era of neoliberal capitalism, industrial enterprises have expanded their financial investments by acquiring financial subsidiaries or expanding existing ones to accrue financial profits. He argues that industrial enterprises diversifying into financial markets was a response to the falling rate of profit in the real economic sector in the last four decades.

Stockhammer (2004) remarks that contemporary transformation in corporate governance as a result of rising financial profit has resulted in different priorities and incentives of firms' management. Management adopts the preferences of financial markets due to rising financial profit. The consequences of managerial preferences for short-term financial profit, as opposed to long-term growth, are the declining real sector investment and falling productivity. He concludes that the transformation since the 1980s can be conceptualised as a displacement of the earlier regulated capitalist objectives of long–term growth through real capital accumulation for a short-term investment in financial assets. This process of managerial objectives of long-term growth prevailed until the late 1970s when the neoliberal ideology of institutional investors interested in short-term growth in share/stock prices emerged.

Lazonick and O'Sullivan (2000) describe the approach as a shift from a 'retain and invest' strategy to a 'downsize and distribute' approach. They contend that management prioritise allocating firms' revenue in a way that will increase the firms' share prices as well as the valuation of stock options. These institutional changes have given priority to 'shareholders value' together with the increase of institutional investors, the alignment of the interests of managers with those of shareholders through the use of stock options, and the threat of takeover in the active markets for corporate control. Duménil and Lévy (2004) note that real capital accumulation processes follow the rate of retained profits in the economy. Thus, increased financial pay-outs in the form of interest and dividend payments reduce retained profits and so should reduce the rate of accumulation.[8]

Although it could be argued that in efficient financial markets firms could raise capital to fund profitable investment opportunities, it is clear from the above that industrial enterprises are in a position in which, managers first transfer a considerable part of their earnings to the financial markets and then compete with all other borrowers to re-acquire their funds back. Froud et al. (2000) describe this process as *'coupon pool capitalism.'* This process of discharging the earnings to the financial markets and then competing with everyone else to re-acquire these funds increases the degree of uncertainty and reduces the planning horizon for investment funding. Thereby, unlike the earlier period of 'retain and invest', managers now could not be sure of the amount of the funds they will get back and at what cost. Thus, the pressure to offer rising short-term returns to shareholders impedes investments that have more extended periods of gestation by creating uncertainty about the ability of the firm to finance future projects.

In summing the above, Gowan (1999) remarks that global financial markets assert mitigation charges upon the real economic sector, and that the contemporary financial system is not a source of finance for productive projects. In his view, it is erroneous to assume that international financial markets are financing the development of the real economic sector. Thus, the international financial market and the productive sector are not integrated and the trillion of dollars traded on the financial market do contribute to the development of the productive sector.

The confusion about the key function of the global financial market comes from mergers and takeovers under neoliberal capitalism. Whenever acquisitions occur, it is erroneously assumed that some form of capital investment has taken place. However, such takeovers and mergers may not have anything

---

8 Duménil and Lévy (2004) observed huge data from France and the US, which were consistent with a slower pace of capital accumulation on the one hand and rising interest and dividend payments on the other.

connected to real investment; indeed, the opposite may be happening. Asset stripping and running down the activity of the acquired assets so that the buyer can outcompete rivals and gain greater market share could be the motive. In the era of neoliberal capitalism, much has been argued about the benefits of Foreign Direct Investment. However, in most cases, especially in the periphery countries (as we shall see in chapter 4), it could simply mean a change of ownership or companies, with little or no new real investment to expand production activity.

Gowan is of the view that when neoliberals and advocates of financial liberalisation argue that a growing capital market will have a positive impact on capitalist production, it is as erroneous as imagining that a huge expansion of the insurance industry heralds safety economy/community. Insurance can operate in both ways, as the more anticipated crime the larger the premium and insurance market. He concludes that when huge bonanzas are made overnight on capital markets, it signals that something has gone wrong from a social point of view.

5 Contemporary Heterodox Perspectives on Finance-led Growth Debate

The 2007/08 financial crisis reignited the debate of the relevance of deepening the financial system.[9] There is a sharp disagreement among economists concerning the impact of the financial sector on economic growth and development. The dominant hypotheses are the demand-leading hypothesis and supply-leading hypothesis. According to heterodox economics, financial crises and the more recently 2007/2008 global financial crisis is a result of deregulation and liberalisation policies in the 1980s, which contributed widely to the instability in the global financial and economic systems.

Heterodox economists generally argued that unregulated financial markets are inherently unstable, vulnerable to fraud and manipulation by insiders and capable of causing long and deep economic crises accompanied by political and social tension and unrest in countries across the world. The consequences of this financial fragility are compatible with endogenous financial instability

---

9 Financial deepening is a term used by economists to refer to the increasing provision of financial products. It can refer to both a wider choice of services and better access for different socioeconomic groups. Financial deepening can affect both individuals' and societies' economic situations. It is used in this book to represent the development of the financial sector.

theories pioneered by Keynes and later extended by Minsky. The internationalisation/globalisation of the financial systems allows the crisis to spread across borders. Crotty (2011) asserts that it would have been difficult, if not impossible, to enact radical liberalisation and deregulation policies in the financial market if financial economists had opposed efficient market theory. This is a theory which favours minimal regulation in the financial market with the assumption that individuals and institutional investors will maximise returns for a given level of risk. Thus, by choosing the amount of risk that is optimum for them will enable scarce resource allocation to their most productive uses, hence making the real sector more efficient.

The disastrous consequences of recurring financial crises facilitated heterodox assessments to gain extensive attention in academic discourse and several policy institutions. The growth of global capital flows as a result of the neoliberal policies – liberalisation and deregulation, have been described as the new phase of contemporary capitalism – financialisation, a phenomenon whose effects are described by many scholars as damaging to real capital accumulation and sustainable economic development (Orhangazi 2011; Stockhammer 2012b; Lapavitsas 2013). That is, there is a gravitational shift of the economy from real production to financial/fictitious engineering.

5.1 Banks, Financial Markets and Economic Growth: The Dilemma

Among the notable contributions to finance-growth nexus studies are Bagehot (1873), Schumpeter (1911), Goldsmith (1969), McKinnon (1973), and Shaw 1973) who offer prudent arguments in favour of deregulation and liberalisation of the financial sector to induce economic growth. However, the studies of Robbinson (1952), Lucas (1988), Miller (1998) Miotti and Plihon (2001), (Loizos (2006) and Wolfson and Epstein (2013) reject finance as an 'over-stressed' deciding factor of economic growth and postulate that where *enterprise leads, finance follows*. Thus, finance in their view is not a critical determining factor of economic growth, but instead, economic growth drives financial development; hence, finance merely responds to growth needs.

On the one hand, Bagehot (1873), Schumpeter (1911), Goldsmith (1969), McKinnon (1973), Shaw (1973) and Gurley and Shaw (2002) dismiss the view that the relationship between financial sector development and economic growth can be ignored without significantly restricting the understanding of economic growth. This is important for policymaking, because if finance merely acts to changes in demand of the real economic sector, then it will lessen the intensity of studies on the causes and development of financial sectors. In contrast, if there were convincing evidence of a long-run positive impact of financial development on sustainable economic development, then this will call for an urgent need for intensifying research on the political, legal, regulatory, and policy determinants of financial systems.

As noted by Bagehot (1873) in his reference to British industrialisation,[10] finance promotes capital accumulation and reduces risks that are inherent in particular investment projects. Bagehot suggested that British investors and managers had sufficient knowledge concerning businesses together with market and economic environments in the country. As a result, by improving the information on firms, managers, and market conditions, financial intermediaries can drive economic growth. Financial intermediaries produce better information, improve resource allocation, and foster growth. Thus, besides identifying a market niche, an entrepreneur requires finance provided by financial systems.

Financial intermediaries as King and Levine (1993) and Morales (2003) remark that it may also boost the rate of technological innovation by identifying those entrepreneurs with the most excellent chances of successfully initiating new goods and production process. This supports the central view of Schumpeter's (1911, 74) argument about finance in the process of economic development: *'the banker, therefore, is not so much a middle man. ... he authorises people in the name of society. ... to innovate'*. Thus, in the view of Schumpeter, the supply of credit by banks was a crucial determinant for growth in the industrialisation eras by providing capital for technological innovation and productive ventures. Therefore, financial systems re-allocate resources to the best productive projects by advancing credit to entrepreneurs to produce goods and services.[11] In contemporary capitalism, Schumpeter's view could be achieved by public financial systems as opposed to private financial systems seeking the short-term return from the financial market.

However, the assumption that capital somehow will be inexplicably flowing towards productive ventures is less convincing because banks require the multifaceted task of mitigating information as well as transaction costs. Besides, what Schumpeter failed to mention in the bank-firm relationship is the absolute power of the bank managers, which could severely weaken the corporate governance of firms. This is because it will be relatively easy for the bank insiders to exploit their creditors and may not be immune to corruptible influences.

---

10   The industrial revolution in England characterises the transformation from labour intensive (manual production) to capital intensive (machine production) that changed the social structure of the British economy.
11   See Lapavitsas (2013), and Marx *Capital* vol. 3 for a critique of borrower, lender and *monied* capitalism.

Keynes (2018 [1936]) however, attached partial importance to the role of finance on the principle of an efficient and perfect money market. That is, equalling the money market equilibrium to the macroeconomic equilibrium. He remarks on the importance of financial intermediaries in mobilising savings that could be channelled to investment projects to facilitate capital accumulation, employment and economic growth. Consequently, disequilibrium in the financial sector could impact the real economic sector in multiple ways.

The deepening of financial systems can accelerate economic growth (Demirgüç-Kunt and Levine 2004). Thus, a well-developed financial sector with varying financial services ahead of time of their demand will accelerate economic growth by reallocating scarce resources to the competing needs. Hence, the financial sector deepening as a crucial determinant of economic growth cannot be overlooked (Goldsmith 1969; Hicks 1969). When a significant portion of domestic income is reinjected into the economy, it creates domestic capital accumulation, which enhances economic growth. Financial intermediations that connect savers with borrowers and other financial services stimulate growth rates as well as improving the performance of the economy. The establishment of financial institutions facilitates new financial instruments and a variety of financial assets that are critical in the production process.

The core argument here is that the financial sector deepening impacts positively on economic growth and development through efficient use of capital stock. As Goldsmith (1969) argues, there is no doubt that the impact of financial sector development on economic growth results in an alternative circulation of capital expenditure within the economy, whether the outcome is positive or otherwise.

The hypotheses of McKinnon (2010[1973]) and Shaw (1973) extended Goldsmith's (1969) finance-led theory by adding that financial sector development does not suggest singularly higher productivity of capital, but higher savings rates that promote savings mobilisation which could reallocate for investment in the real economic sector. Contrasting Goldsmith's (1969) view that financial sector development and growth are mutually thought of as endogenous, McKinnon and Shaw's central point which is an extension of Hayek's (2014) thesis (of omniscient markets), is the effect of economic policies that impede the development of the financial sector. They assert that financial repression damages economic growth and develop a theoretical model with debt intermediation. Goldsmith (1969), McKinnon (1973), and Shaw (1973) argue that development in the financial sector impacts positively on economic growth. They suggest that inefficient financial systems and weak capital markets deter global investors because underdeveloped financial markets lack liquidity and suffer from high transaction costs. Thereby, the local economy becomes unattractive, and investment activities remain underdeveloped.

These authors advocate financial liberalisation programmes and the adoption of structural reforms in the banking and financial sector to attract foreign investors to boost the domestic economy. They argue that financial market financing is effective than financing through debt because it is less expensive and more flexible and secure for lenders; and above all, it allows optimal allocation of scarce resources which leads to the acceleration of growth rate. They conclude that financial intermediaries could increase the real returns to savers and likewise decrease the real cost to investors by way of accommodating liquidity preferences, reducing risks as a result of diversification, enhancing operational efficiency and cutting information costs.

The works of Goldsmith (1969), McKinnon (1973), and Shaw (1973) contend that liberalisation of interest rates promotes banking competition that will stimulate capital investment and economic growth. The development of the banking sector through liberalisation of interest rates will spur the accumulation of savings. Higher interest rates will encourage savers; this saving accumulation will serve as a source of investment financing. The investment adds to the capital stock and creates employment and increases productivity that leads to economic growth. According to this tradition, there is a strong positive relationship between developments in the financial and banking systems and economic growth.

The supporters of the McKinnon-Shaw (1973) hypotheses argue that state restrictions on banking system policies over time slow down financial developments and damage economic growth. The imposition of governmental restrictions obstructs the dynamics, efficiency and competitiveness of the financial system. Consequently, households' incentive to save will decrease as the real interest rate falls, which in turn will reduce savings mobilisation and therefore decrease the amount available for investment. This process will limit capital investment, which will reduce productivity and economic growth. Accordingly, it is expected that financial liberalisation will include interest rate reforms that will promote savings which will facilitate the rate of real capital formation, increase productivity and economic growth in the periphery countries.

The *Neo-Structuralist School*,[12] on the other hand, has argued that there is an inverse relationship between financial market deepening and long-term

---

12 Neo-structuralism is a contemporary version of a structuralist current of thinking, which argue that underdevelopment is not a cause of exogenous factors or bad policy, but an intrinsic feature ingrained in social and economic structures. Advocates oppose neoliberal mantra of stabilisation, privatisation and liberalisation.

economic growth rates. Advocates of this tradition focus on the consequences of the implementation of the liberalisation programmes on real economic activities and recommend financial repression. Loizos (2006) asserts that liberalisation of financial markets may impede growth if *curb* markets (trading shares outside the official stock market) become dominant over the official channel of financing investments.

The work of Jeanneney and Kpodar (2004) on the impact of financial sector deepening on financial instability, found that the expansion of the banking industry and financial sector deepening through financial liberalisation and deregulation, led in the vast majority of cases to financial instability and financial crises followed by slowdown and recession in domestic economies.[13] Miotti and Plihon (2001) assert that the financial liberalisation policies adopted by (or in many cases forced on) many periphery countries to develop their banking sectors and strengthen the financial market structures, were closely followed by an accentuation of the banking crisis and the precipitation of new risky behaviours. Thereby, trade and financial liberalisation of the capital account could be viewed as a catalyst for the recent financial instability. Therefore, development in the financial sector has adverse effects on long-run economic growth.

The proponents of this tradition argue that finance is *demand-following* and suggest that a growing economy culminates in demand for credit and financial products, which will facilitate financial institutions to respond spontaneously to the rising demand for these financial products/services. Robbinson (1952, 86) argues that *'where enterprise leads, finance follows.'* Thus, financial sector development is not a critical determinant for long-run economic growth. In his view, the financial sector deepening is *'demand following'* and not a cause of economic growth. Ang (2008) asserts that when an economy is growing, the demand for financial products stimulates the development of the financial system by establishing new financial providers, financial actors and financial services in the domestic economy. Thus, the financial sector deepening per se does not cause economic growth, but instead follows the growing demand emerging from the real economic sector. Others such as Lucas (1988) and Singh (1997) contend that financial sector deepening may obstruct economic growth and sustainable development.

In support of demand-following tradition, Lucas (1988) and Epstein (2005) question the role of the financial sector deepening in sustainable development.

---

13 See David Harvey (2005) for an account of Chile's economy before and after the liberalisation of the financial market.

He dismisses financial deepening as an *'overstated'* determining factor in the growth debate. He argues that total factor productivity is determined exogenously, suggesting a somewhat weak relationship between financial development and economic growth. This, in his view, is the consequence of diminishing returns to capital, suggesting that financial variables may influence the level of income but not the growth of income in an economy.

The effects of financial instability on economic crises have been presented by Wolf (2014), a former World Bank Economist, and the Financial Times editor, in his book *The Shifts and the Shocks: What We've Learned – and Still Have to Learn – From the Financial Crisis.* Wolf argues that the World Bank and the IMF liberalisation processes in developing countries have created financial instability with evidence from Latin America in 1982, the Asian financial crisis in 1997/98, and the more recent financial crisis of 2007/08. All these financial crises affected the real economy with stagnant growth, mass unemployment and underemployment, falling real wages and rising inequality and poverty headcount. Thus, the period of neoliberal market liberalisation has also been associated with a period of financial crises, which reverberate to the rest of the economy with dire consequences.

The neoliberal restructuring of the 1980s brought into the world a mammoth: a financial sector able to demolish economies from within. Confidence in unrestrained financial markets that promote ever-rising private debt is a risky form of economic hubris – arrogance or self-assurance, which leads neoliberals to believe that financial development may do no wrong. In summer 2005, Raghuram Rajan, an IMF Chief Economist, asked whether financial development has made the world riskier.[14] His work was much criticised and ignored at the time when the US Federal Reserve chairman and other prominent economists and financial regulators argued that unfettered financial market is too big to fail. Nevertheless, Rajan argued that financial development had made the global economy riskier due to technological change, market liberalisation and institutional change. The opportunities associated with financial development also provide added risks, especially in the presence of perverse incentives. Financial market development in the era of neoliberalism is inherently unstable, swinging from extreme optimism to excessive pessimism. Historical evidence has shown that financial crises have a habit of bringing with them economic stagnation and severe and long-lasting real sector recession.

---

14   Raghuram Rajan, an IMF Chief Economist, available at www.ted.com/speakers/raghuram_rajan. Accessed 10/01/2021.

6   Economic Functions of Financial Intermediaries

Financial systems have influenced the allocation of resources throughout the history of capitalism. The emergence of banks that enhance the acquisition of information about firms and managers undoubtedly alters the allocation of credit. Besides, financial contracts that make investors more confident about returns on their investment affect how people allocate their savings. Likewise, money and capital markets development promote liquidity of the financial system that encourages the mobilisation of savings and facilitates resources to flow towards its most efficient use (Merton and Bodie 1995).

A practical approach in understanding how financial systems impact savings and investment decisions and hence, economic growth, has been the work of Levine (1997; 2005). She presents ways through which financial systems promote economic growth. These include the mobilisation of savings, efficient allocation of capital, supervision of managers, simplifying risks trading and enforcing contracts in the trading of goods and services. Although there are alternative ways of classifying these functions,[15] Levine suggests that financial development provides quality financial services and therefore reduces the impacts of asymmetric information and transaction costs. As a result, financial development involves improvements to i) production of ex-ante information about investments, ii) monitoring of investments and implementation of corporate governance, iii) trading, diversification, and management of risks, iv) mobilisation and pooling of savings, and v) exchange of goods and services (Levine 2005, 870). Each of these financial functions may stimulate savings and investment decisions and hence, economic growth. Thus, decreasing the cost of financial intermediation facilitates investment due to the lower cost of borrowing; as a result, stimulating economic growth. Likewise, mobilising savings comprises of the ability to overcome the transaction costs of accumulating from individuals as well as information asymmetries. This suggests that banks play an essential role in channelling resources from surplus unit-lenders to deficit unit-borrowers for investment projects. Ben123civenga and Smith (1991) remark that the process climaxes in capital accumulation, productivity gains and therefore, economic growth. Thus, by mobilising savings from households, financial intermediaries provide reasonable returns to savers and advance credit to a largely diversified range of ventures facilitating the capital accumulation process and economic growth.

---

15   See for instance, Merton and Bodie (1995; 2004) for alternative ways of categorising the functions provided by the financial system.

However, the adverse effect of the illiquid stock market on growth rates in periphery countries is more significant than banks (Singh 1991; Levine 2002; Demirgüç-Kunt and Levine 2004; Masoud and Hardaker 2012). For instance, Singh (1991) argues that the instability of the stock market, deterrence of risk-averse savers, the growth of short-term speculative investors looking for quick returns relative to long-term growth are the major drawbacks in the periphery and have considerable influence on the performance of the economy. Moreover, the critical drawback of the Harrod-Domar Growth model[16] in the periphery is its limited application. There is a high marginal propensity to consume in many periphery countries, and therefore, any extra income earned would be spent rather than saved, which would result in a domestic savings gap. Besides, the lack of sound financial systems and the high cost of capital (see chapter 5) also limits the viability of such a model. Increased household savings may not necessarily mean the availability of capital for real sector investment. Weaknesses and deficiencies in human capital in many periphery countries limit the capital-output ratio of the model.

6.1   *Empirical Evidence on Finance and Growth*

Studies on the interaction of finance and growth assess the impact of the operations of the financial systems on economic growth. That is, whether the impact is economically significant and whether specific components of the financial system (such as banks, and stock markets) play any significant role in fostering growth at different phases of economic development. The discussion starts with cross-country studies of finance-growth nexus. The second part examines econometric approaches to finance and growth based on cross-country case studies and recent econometric studies in the context of Ghana.[17]

6.2   *Cross-country Studies of the Finance-Growth Nexus*

The pioneering cross-country work on finance-growth nexus was led by Goldsmith (1969, 390) who posits that 'one of the most critical problems in the field of finance, if not the single most important one. ... is the effect that financial structure and development have on economic growth.' Thus, he sought to examine whether finance exerts a causal effect on growth and whether the combination of markets and intermediaries operating in an economy

---

16   Harrod-Domar Growth Model argues that the level of national savings and the productivity of capital investment (input-output ratio) are the significant determinants of economic growth. The model stresses the cyclical relationship between domestic savings, investment, capital stock and economic growth.

17   See chapter nine for econometric analysis of finance-growth-poverty nexus in Ghana.

influences economic growth. Goldsmith based his work on data compiled from 35 countries between 1860 and 1963 on the value of financial intermediation assets as a share of economic growth. He presumed, albeit with ample qualifications, that the depth of the financial sector is positively related to the quality of financial activities offered by the financial systems. His cross-country studies pointed to the fact that over time, the size of the financial sector relative to the economic output increases as economies develop and peak at about three times of a country's GDP. His result shows a positive relationship between the development in the financial system and the level of economic activity, but he failed to deliberate on the direction of the causality. As Levine (2005) pointed out, Goldsmith did not take a stand on whether financial development causes growth. Besides, he was unable to provide much cross-country evidence of the connection between economic growth and the structure of the financial system due to lack of data on securities market development for a wide range of countries.

Thus, Goldsmith's work raises several key issues, all of which he presciently stresses, that subsequent studies have tried to resolve. These include the fact that the investigation involves only 35 countries. Also, the investigation does not systematically control other factors that could influence economic growth. Furthermore, the study did not investigate whether financial development is connected with productivity growth and capital accumulation, which they stress. Last but not least, the examination did not shed light on whether financial markets, non-bank financial intermediaries, or the combination of markets and intermediaries matter for economic growth.

Building on the pioneering work of Goldsmith (1969) and addressing some of the limitations of his work, King and Levine (1993) examined 77 countries over 29 years. To rectify the problems identified in Goldsmith's work, they systematically control other factors influencing long-run growth. The findings show that financial development measured by private credit relative to GDP (PRIVY), the size of the financial system (DEPT) and how central and commercial banks allocate credit to the household (BANK) has a positive and significant effect on growth indicators. These growth indicators are real GDP per capita, capital stock and productivity growth. They concluded that the initial level of financial development and growth is significantly large. However, this example does not explain the causes of financial development. They only hypothesise the possibility of a significant long-term impact of financial development on growth. Although they addressed some of the limitations of previous studies, cross-country regression cannot eliminate them all. Thus, though King and Levine (1993) demonstrated that finance has a positive impact on economic growth, they failed to address the issue of causality. The authors also centred their investigations simply on banks and did not consider other aspects of the financial market.

The work of Levine and Zervos (1998) and Demirgüç-Kunt and Levine (2004) examined the performance of stock markets on economic growth. They considered about 50 economies and found a positive relationship between stock market development and long-term growth rates. However, due to the speculative and illiquid nature of stock markets in SSA and other periphery countries, such fundamental conjecture from cross-section techniques could be precarious(Arestis and Demetriades 1997).

A study by the McKinsey Global Institute (1999) on the effect of financial sector performance on growth rates, reported that the performance of the financial sector positively influences capital productivity. The report studied the productivity of capital in three core countries from 1974 to 1993. The findings indicate a higher per capita wealth in the US ($26,500) than in Germany ($21,900) and Japan ($20,900) using 1993 US Prices. They argued that there is a positive relationship between the productivity of capital and wealth accumulation (www.mckinsey.com). Accordingly, the financial market in the US performs better in facilitating profitable projects, and in return, rewards savers better than those in Germany and Japan.

6.3 *Contemporary Literature on Econometric Models for Ghana*

Empirical research on finance-growth nexus is limited in Ghana, except for the inconsistent/conflicting studies by Quartey and Prah (2008) and Adu et al. (2013) found some evidence of finance-led growth when examining the ratio of broad money to GDP. However, the evidence presented using private credit (as a proxy for financial deepening) relative to GDP demonstrates no relationship between financial sector development and economic growth. That is neither *supply-leading response* nor growth-led finance (*demand-following*). Esso (2010) also examined the relationship of financial system deepening and growth rates in six West African countries (Burkina Faso, Cape Verde, Cote d'Ivoire, Ghana, Liberia and Sierra Leone) and found that economic growth leads to financial development in only Burkina Faso, Cote d'Ivoire and Sierra Leone. Adusei (2013) conducted annual time-series (from 1971 to 2010) using private credit and broad money as financial development proxies. His findings show that development in the financial system in Ghana impedes economic growth.

Frimpong (2020) provides a robust insight into the conflicting findings in the literature. He argues that the choice of financial sector proxy on growth effect is significant to the outcomes. His findings show that private credit provided by financial institutions stimulates capital accumulation, economic growth as well as poverty alleviation. Therefore, policy recommendation is to encourage financial institutions to provide long-term affordable capital/credit to SMEs and other industrial enterprises to facilitate real capital investment. This he maintains will promote employment, productivity, and enhance household income, which is crucial for sustainable development. The high cost of capital as a result of neoliberal financialisation in Ghana is inimical to sustainable development. Therefore, financialisation, as defined in this book, has contributed to the chronic poverty levels in Ghana.

Similarly, Adu et al. (2013) examined the long-run impact of the financial sector deepening on economic growth in Ghana. The model findings show an adverse effect of broad money growth on economic growth. However, they found a positive impact of private sector credit on economic growth. Their findings, therefore, suggest the choice of financial sector proxy is a critical factor in the finance-growth nexus.

The World Bank, IMF and other orthodox economists have contended that development in the financial systems drives economic growth. However, the evidence is mixed, and the argument on whether financial development is the cause or the effect of the growth process is still not settled. Another debate is the issue of a correct measure or appropriate indicator of financial development.

7 Dynamics of Financial Development, Income Distribution, Economic Growth and Poverty Reduction in Ghana

The interplay between the ascendency of finance, economic growth, and poverty alleviation has captured the attention of both policymakers and researchers since the divergences between theory, and the result of practical policy application concerning the relationship of these factors have been rather conspicuous. Theoretically, the financial sector has a strong relationship with the real economy through the provision of financial resources to the factors of production, stimulating the production of real output, increasing employment opportunities and reducing poverty levels. Paradoxically, in many cases, countries experiencing fast financial development have demonstrated greater income inequality, implying that the effort to reduce poverty levels may not have been realised despite rapid development in the financial sector. Using data from Indonesia Central Statistics Agency, Dewi et al. (2018) argue that a 1-percentage increase in economic growth as a result of financial development was tagged to reduce the poverty level by 0.116% over the period 2010–2015; however, in reality, it only reduced the poverty levels by just 0.059%.

Understanding the relationship between financial development and poverty reduction is of particular significance for Ghana. Over the last few decades, the financial sector, albeit liberalisation and deregulation policies, has become the engine of growth for the economy through the accumulation of capital and technological advancement. The contribution of the financial sector to economic development, as measured by the ratio of broad money to GDP increased from 20.5% in 2004 to 33.3% in 2018. Private credit relative to GDP also increased from just under 7% in 2004 to 17.7% in 2016. Ghana achieved a nationwide poverty reduction target set by the Millennium Development Goals (MDGs) in 2000. Poverty rates in Ghana halved to 24.2% in 2013, two years before the target date of 2015. Since then, poverty alleviation has stalled; between 2013 and 2017, poverty rates reduced by just 0.8% to the new rate of 23.4% (Ghana Statistical Service 2018).

Furthermore, there are wide regional variations with the rural-urban divide. With its substantial growth in the population currently estimated at 29 million (Ghana Statistical Service 2018), it is estimated that nearly seven million Ghanaians are living below the poverty line. This absolute figure is not different from the 1990 levels. That is, poverty rate (measured in percentage) has been reduced but there is little improvement in poverty headcounts (the number of poor individuals).

As Ghana aspires to achieve a higher middle-income status sooner than later, it is evident that a concerted effort to reduce poverty in Ghana is urgently needed. Since the various economic development programmes undertaken to eradicate poverty will likely be effective with the assistance of resource mobilisation, substantial developments in the financial sector are expected to attract these resources. Many multi-lateral agencies, including the World Bank, International Monetary Fund (IMF), and Africa Development Bank (AfDB) have long been accelerating the development agenda of the financial sector in Ghana to attract external resources as part of broader efforts to eradicate poverty. On the domestic level, the Bank of Ghana has consistently made concerted efforts to provide a stable and enabling environment for financial sector growth. However, without close regulation by the state, neoliberal financial development will only promote financial speculation and will plant the seed of financial and economic crises.

Previous research on the impact of financial development on poverty reduction documented conflicting and debatable findings across countries, data and methodologies. For instance, Jalilian and Kirkpatrick (2005), Inoue and Hamori (2012) and Chemli (2014) reported causality running from financial sector development to poverty reduction. However, the work of Ho and Odhiambo (2011) and Uddin et al. (2014) presented a bidirectional causality between development in the financial system and poverty. Although the majority of studies reported a positive relationship from the development in financial systems on poverty reduction, Beck, Demirgüç-Kunt, and Levine (2007), Dhrifi (2014) and Shahbaz et al. (2015) suggest that financial sector development is apparently causing poverty levels to increase.

In the context of SSA countries, minimal empirical research has been made to investigate the interaction between financial systems development and poverty reduction. The few empirical research includes Odhiambo (2009) for South Africa, Odhiambo (2010b) for Kenya, and Odhiambo (2010a) for Zambia, which presented a positive impact of financial sector development on poverty reduction. However, Aye (2013) provided evidence from Nigeria, showing causality from poverty to financial development. Dauda and Makinde (2014) maintain that there are no significant effects of the financial system deepening on poverty levels in Nigeria.

Keho (2017) investigated six SSA countries and found that development in the financial system causes poverty alleviation but not directly. He found that in Cameroon and Gabon, financial development causes economic growth, which creates job opportunities and higher wages, hence poverty reduction. However, his findings from Nigeria and South Africa show that poverty alleviation causes financial sector deepening. Therefore, it is difficult to conclude from Keho's findings that there is a direct causal link running from the financial sector deepening to poverty reduction. The author concludes that there is no empirical evidence to suggest that the development in the financial system causes poverty reduction in many periphery countries. That is, an expansion of private credit relative to GDP does not necessarily lead to improved well-being for the poorest households.

While most of these studies were conducted in Asia, Latin America and SSA, none has focused on the Ghanaian case. This book examines the relative strengths of the financial sector in reducing poverty and the degree to which changes in financial development cause poverty levels. Given that poverty reduction has been a critical issue in Ghana, I provide empirical evidence on the financial sector-poverty reduction nexus in Ghana using the more recent national poverty data published in 2018. I investigate the relationship between the financial sector development and poverty reduction, assessing the relative strengths of the dominance of financial institutions, financial actors and financial motives in the war against eradicating poverty.

8 Poverty and the Pandemic: The Case of Ghana

I argue that globalisation did not alleviate poverty in Ghana and current deglobalisation trends amidst the global pandemic would increase poverty levels as Ghana's rural society is not conducive to digitisation and social distancing.

As the number of COVID-19 cases continues to rise around the world, and the global economy enters a recession that is predicted to be deeper than the great recession of 2008–09, low and middle-income countries and the poor brace for yet another shock that threatens to deepen global inequalities and exacerbate an already challenging situation. Already one year since the pandemic started, the working class has been confronted with a massive frontal attack on its living and working conditions, job security and even itself. This is on top of what they have endured over four decades under neoliberal restructuring.

In one sense the pandemic affects the rich and poor in the same way. But the preventive measures taken to reduce the spread of the virus seem to strike a disproportionate cost on the working class and the poor who can least afford the burden. Mwainyekule and Frimpong (2020) cite Ghana, a country whose nature of the working-class jobs in the informal sector that account for about 80% of the labour force is improbable to permit them to work from home. This means that a shutdown of most parts of the economy will choke their livelihoods. They are doubtful to have savings or substantial wealth to fall back on to sustain them throughout the public health measures. Their meagre incomes were affected, and their mediocre savings and assets reduced in value. Across every industry, nonessential firms have closed sending workers home with no idea when they might return to work.

Poverty in Ghana is a rural phenomenon (see chapter 6) and those urban dwellers live in overcrowded settlements lacking basic social amenities. This segment of the population can hardly cope with strict public health measures such as social distancing and lockdowns, and are prone to any economic shocks that directly impact on their income. Even before the emergence of the global epidemic, growth rates (GDP) were only weakly translating into inclusive social outcomes. Thus, the argument that globalisation alleviated poverty in Ghana is a complete myth.

The relationship between the global pandemic outbreak, the contraction in demand and the falling commodity prices will inevitably slow or even reverse the limited progress that has been made in the fight against poverty alleviation. This is likely to undermine the United Nations Sustainable Development Goals (UNSDGs) of no poverty and zero hunger by 2030.

Until now, Ghanaian authorities have had big plans for the future. However, the pandemic has left the president wondering how best to salvage the economy from a deep recession that has not been seen for decades. He talks about the unthinkable (Mwainyekule and Frimpong 2020). The World Health Organisation (WHO) in its report on 8th May 2020 widely commended Ghana for using effective COVID-19 measures. However, with infection cases on the rise, governments all over are scrambling to save not only lives but also livelihoods. The President of Ghana, Nana Akuffo-Addo stated: "We know how to bring the economy back to life. What we do not know is how to bring people back to life" (Akufo-Addo 2020).[18] The dilemma facing governments across the globe is that the more they try to improve public health measures such as 'social distancing and stay at home,' the more the economy sinks into recession with dire consequences for inequality and poverty.

The pandemic is said to have a devastating effect on global poverty. Even though it has not had the dreadful effect in sub-Saharan Africa (SSA) as feared, the region is predicted to be the hardest hit with a further 23 million people pushed into poverty. The latest projections by PovcalNet (an online tool provided by the World Bank for estimating global poverty) show the share of the global population living on less than $1.90 per person per day to increase to 8.6% in 2020 from the 2019 rate of 8.2%. This is compared with the projected decline of 7.8% over the same period before the pandemic. With more people in low and middle-income countries living close to the International Poverty Line (IPL), the World Bank projects that these countries are likely to bear the most consequences in terms of rising numbers of extreme poverty.

8.1 The Economics of It All

Ghana recorded its first 2 cases of COVID-19 on 12th March 2020, and since then the number of confirmed cases continues to rise. The pandemic comes on the backdrop of years of strong and sustained economic growth in Ghana, casting doubt on favourable projection outlooks for the economy. Sub-Saharan Africa (SSA) region as a whole is estimated to witness its first economic contraction at 1.6% for almost three decades largely due to the global pandemic. Although the Ghanaian economy is not projected to contract in 2020, the economy's real GDP growth in 2020 has been revised down significantly from the initial forecast of 7.5% to 1.5% in the recent IMF World Economic Outlook (International Monetary Fund 2020b). In light of this development, the incidence of poverty

---

18   President Akufo-Addo addresses nation on measures taken by government to combat the coronavirus pandemic. *Speeches* (15 March 2020).

is likely to increase as a result of the possible decrease in GDP per capita resulting from a falling growth rate. Bearing in mind the high concentration of workers in the informal sector, with ongoing public health directives of social distancing as well as declining economic activities, the impact on the vulnerable communities would be severe. This could in turn erode the economic gains achieved in recent years and slow down Ghana's economic development considerably.

However, the IMF growth forecast for 2021 has been revised upwards to 5.9% from the initial 4%, though much of this will depend on how long the global pandemic is contained. This also reflects the fact that the growth rate would be based on the lower base from which it will emerge. The projected impact on tax revenues is a shortfall of $764 million through a decrease in conventional tax revenues, a decline in import duties, and other planned tax relief as part of fiscal measures to mitigate the adverse effect of the pandemic. This shortfall will impact on the country's ability to develop, given that the additional spending needed to mitigate the adverse impact of the pandemic is likely to increase the country's fiscal deficit as well as the debt stock. The government estimates a fiscal deficit of 6.6% of GDP, which is above the de facto fiscal rule of 5% of GDP set by the Fiscal Responsibility Law.

Mwainyekule and Frimpong (2020) explain how the Government of Ghana was one of the first in the sub-region to implement the COVID-19 economic response package. The monetary measures included the Central Bank reducing monetary policy rate and the primary reserve requirement to provide liquidity to accelerate domestic investment. The fiscal stimulus consisted of tax forbearance and three months absorption of water bills for all households, full electricity bill rebate for 'lifeline customers' – poorest households, and 50% for non-poor households based on March 2020 electricity consumption, and distribution of food supplies to the poorest communities. To further lessen the economic impact of the pandemic on Ghanaians, parliament approved COVID-19 Alleviation Programme Fund to support businesses and households. This included $ 170 million to support households and Micro, Small and Medium Scale Enterprises (MSME

s). Ghana's effort to combat the virus caught the attention of the international community and donor agencies. This prompted the IMF to approve a $1 billion package as direct budget support to the government. The World Bank also approved a financing package worth $100 million, which consisted of $35 million in emergency medical support and $65 million in long-term health capacity building (International Monetary Fund 2020a). This indicated confidence in the government's effort in fighting the pandemic.

The irony is that those petty traders and street hawkers toiling in the blazing sun to make ends meet may not benefit from this generous economic package. Even though petty traders account for a large number of traders in Ghana, their activities have been seen as undermining the healthy function of the formal economy. Consequently, they are always in conflicts with the authorities over licensing, taxation, site of operation, sanitation, working conditions as well as accessing credit from the formal financial sector. Thus, the lack of documentation and recognition will prevent these traders from accessing the credit on offer. Likewise, the poor in rural areas and those urban dwellers who live in overcrowded settlements without pipe-borne water and electricity are likely to miss out on the rebate approved by the government. This segment of the population can hardly cope with strict public health measures such as social distancing and lockdowns and are prone to any economic shocks that directly impact on their income. As Mwainyekule and Frimpong (2020) put it succinctly, they are adversely affected by public health measures but may least benefit from the economic package.

The recent gains from the country's strong economic growth, fiscal consolidation and macroeconomic stabilisation have created a bit of headroom for the government; nevertheless, COVID-19 is poised to impact significant disruption in the coming years.

The immediate effects of the pandemic come from its disruption to the global demand for and supply of goods and services. As a primary commodity exporter, falling global commodity prices will affect the balance of payment and the nation's finances. Given that the performance of Ghana's external sector will have a considerable multiplier effect on its domestic affairs, export revenue is of paramount importance to the country's economic development. The economy has become increasingly export-driven, with the share of exports increasing from 25% of GDP in 2013 to 35% of GDP in 2018.

However, it is important to note that the country's export is highly concentrated with few primary commodities such as oil, cocoa and gold accounting for over 80% of all export earnings. Thus, the fortune and performance of these commodities on the global market will have a significant impact on Ghana's export earnings and its ability to cope with the pandemic and economic development. However, the projections of these commodities vary considerably in the international market. The effect of the pandemic and the measures taken by governments have had substantial impacts on commodity markets and supply chains. Prices of most commodities have declined since the beginning of 2020. The combined factors have been weaker demand and unexpected rising supply for some of these commodities. The World Bank's Commodity Market Outlook (April 2020) provides a bleak picture of the market (World Bank 2020).

The prospects for crude oil were already subdued when COVID-19 hit the globe. Crude oil has been adversely affected by the pandemic due to the unprecedented combination of negative demand and positive supply shocks, simultaneously. Oil accounted for over 30% of Ghana's export earnings in 2018, indicating the collapse in global demand, and falling oil prices will likely cause significant disruption in the economy. China alone accounts for more than half of Ghana's oil exports, and though the Chinese economy is not projected to contract in 2020, the COVID-19 pandemic and the ongoing trade disruption with the US caused a decrease in demand from China in the first quarter of the year. Economic development in China is of paramount importance to the Ghanaian economy. Ghana's 2020 fiscal budget was drawn on the assumption that global oil prices will be at the World Bank's average of $62 per barrel for the fiscal year; therefore, any deviation will disrupt the nation's budgetary position.

A sudden drop in demand coupled with a price war between Russia and Saudi Arabia caused Brent Crude prices to fall to $21.44 per barrel at the end of April 2020 (Figure 1). Although OPEC agreed to cut supply to mitigate the falling prices, it is uncertain the extent to which this action will impact on the price, given the anticipated fall in demand due to transport disruption and a slowdown in economic activity. The government of Ghana expects oil revenue to fall by as much as $9.7 million, should oil price average $30 per barrel projected for the rest of the fiscal year. One way out of this is for the country to diversify its exports and economic dependence on crude oil.

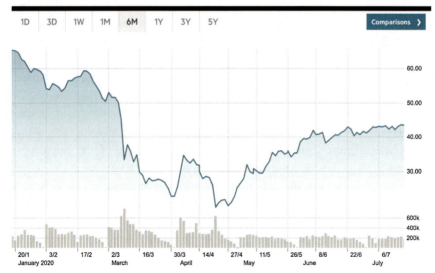

FIGURE 1   Brent Crude oil six months price to July 2020
SOURCE: MARKETS.FT.COM/DATA/COMMODITIES/TEARSHEET/SUMMARY?C=BRENT+CRUDE+OIL

Another important export commodity is cocoa, which contributed nearly one-fifth of Ghana's export revenues in 2018 and has seen plunging prices of about 20% since the outbreak of COVID-19 pandemic. With the uncertainty and falling disposable incomes in chocolate-consuming countries such as Europe and North America, demand for the commodity continues to fall. Most indices forecast a further weakening demand as the travel and tourism industry that accounts for a large portion of the chocolate market is also in decline. However, the impact on Ghanaian cocoa producers is likely to be minimal in the short-term, at least in 2020, because most of the year's harvest has been completed and pre-sold to COCOBOD – the state-run monopoly. Despite this, the rural farmers engaged in cocoa farming are vulnerable in the community with a high percentage living just above the poverty line. A sustained decline in export revenues from cocoa due to depressing global cocoa demand will inevitably affect the incidence of poverty in rural areas.

Gold on the other hand may be the lifeline for the Ghanaian economy during the pandemic due to its attractiveness as a safe-haven asset in crisis, and also as a hedge against economic shocks. Gold contributed to over a third of Ghana's export earnings in 2018.

The precious metal reached a quarterly high price in August 2020 at almost $2,070 per troy ounce (Figure 2). It is projected for further increases in 2021 and 2022. This may provide some mitigation impact on the country's export earnings. Although price and demand for gold are on the rise, Ghana may not be able to take advantage of the rising demand to increase supply in the short term. The closure of gold mines, borders and air routes has left stockpiles idle, thus, delaying any benefit associated with the surge in demand and rising gold prices.

Global industrial commodity markets, hence globalisation, have been more adversely affected than agricultural staple food markets. The food security market remains relatively stable. However, panic buying and border closures may have a widespread impact on this in the coming months. Particularly, in SSA where most vulnerable people live with one-fifth of the population suffering from malnutrition, food makes up a large proportion of their consumption; therefore, any disruption to the food supply chain will likely have a devastating impact. The export sector has already been disrupted, particularly for perishable products such as fruits, vegetables and fresh flowers. Continuous disruption to global trade is likely to have an impact on essential inputs such as fertilisers and pesticides, which will adversely impact on crop protection and likely reduce yield in the coming years. A shortage of pesticides is already impeding the efforts to control locust outbreaks in the Upper East region of Ghana. Thus, while most agricultural markets for staple foods are well supplied at least in

FIGURE 2   Gold prices 12 months to July 2020
SOURCE: HTTPS://GOLDPRICE.ORG/GOLD-PRICE-HISTORY.HTML

the short-term, concerns about food security have increased as governments impose trade restrictions and panic buying.

Investment in physical and human capital is a key driver towards poverty alleviation. Certainly, the inflows of Foreign Direct Investment (FDI) and remittances to Ghana will fall over the next few years; what is not certain is the extent to which it might fall. As COVID-19 impacts on the negotiation of international investment agreements, UNCTAD's (2020) most recent estimate forecasts a drop of up to 40% in global FDI in 2020–2021, similar to the 41.6% decline during the most recent financial and economic crisis of 2007–09. However, during the great recession, inflows of FDI to Ghana only fell by around 13%, though this was on the back of the country's first oilfield discovery in 2007, making it hard to assess the real impact the crisis would have had otherwise. The situation makes a comparison with the extent to which the latest UNCTAD projections will impact on the country difficult. But without a doubt, the 13% drop will certainly be on the low side for the effect of COIVD-19 on FDI inflows in the coming years. This will adversely affect job creation, wages and likely increase the incidence of poverty.

One way to mitigate the decline in FDI and de-globalisation trends is to increase domestic investment. The government fixed capital formation is expected to increase from the current 1.8% of GDP to 2.2% of GDP as a result of the increasing expenditure in the health sector to improve the sector's infrastructure. Also, the Central Bank has reduced both the monetary policy rate and the primary reserve requirements to improve liquidity to boost domestic investment. However, aggregate domestic investment is projected to fall, with gross capital formation expected to fall from 16% in 2019 to 12% of GDP this year, though 2021 gross capital formation is expected to bounce back to 15.5% of GDP.

The recent depreciation of the domestic currency has eroded all the gains at the start of the year. With the projected decline in export revenues, FDI, remittances, tourism and investors' capital flight, further deterioration is inevitable. This depreciation should make exports more attractive, but the impact on oil and cocoa exports is uncertain, given that these commodity markets tend to be price inelastic at least in the short run and therefore currency depreciation will not have much impact on export earnings. Gold export, on the other hand, could benefit from the depreciation due to its being price elastic in the short run, in places like India, Ghana's largest gold market. Given that the Ghanaian economy is an import-driven one, the pandemic is likely to have a considerable negative impact on the economy's international trade and reserves. If this situation persists longer than anticipated, the country could suffer from a significant decline in government revenue and expenditure, leading to potential job losses and rising poverty. This could erase the economic gains achieved recently and slow the country's economic development making Sustainable Development Goals (SDGs) of no poverty and zero hunger by 2030 under considerable threat.

The pandemic arrived in Ghana at a time when a severe banking crisis was coming to an end, causing a further blow to the economy. The banking crisis started in 2017 when the central bank realised that most of the local banks were at risk of defaulting on their loans. The Bank of Ghana approved a takeover bid of UT Bank and Capital Bank Ltd by Ghana Commercial Bank (GCB) Ltd. The central bank in its press release cited insolvency as the main reason for revoking the operational licenses of these indigenous financial institutions (Bank of Ghana 2018). They asserted that the banks have failed several times to meet the minimum capital requirements of a universal bank. As result, to safeguard customers' deposits, the operation licenses were revoked under a Purchase and Assumption Transaction with Ghana Commercial Bank (GCB) Ltd. These twin events – banking crisis and COVID-19 pandemic have had and continue to have a devastating effect in the fight against poverty in Ghana.

9 Conclusion

The rise of finance and the financialisation of everything examined the consequences of the shift in financial intermediation from banks and other financial institutions to financial markets. The consequences of this shift are the rising profit of financial assets and the collateralisation of everything that can be collateralised. As financial profit grows, capital then migrates from the real economic sector to financial speculation. The concept of profit upon alienation provides the reasons why so much financial profit is accrued from mortgage, consumer loans, and from handling pension and other funds to the rentier money lender.

The distinction between fictitious accumulation and real commodity accumulation provided a balance of power between them. While real accumulation is a stock concept, financial accumulation is a flow concept. There is no perfect optimal balance between financial and real accumulation due to historical, political, institutional as well as cultural relationships in each geographical setting. However, increasing financial investment crowds out real accumulation. Thus, as firms increased investment into financial assets, there will be less for real accumulation. Consequently, rising financial profit will attract financial/fictitious accumulation at the expense of real accumulation. The pressure on firm managers to increase profit in the short run can shift investment into financial assets that yield quick returns.

The contemporary heterodox perspective on finance-growth debate provides supply-leading hypothesis relative to demand leading theory arguments. Supply-leading hypothesis, on the one hand, provides prudent arguments in favour of deregulations and liberalisation of the financial system to stimulate economic growth and argues that the development of the financial systems cannot be overlooked in addressing the economic growth debate. Consequently, a well-developed financial system together with financial products ahead of their demand will induce the real economic sector by connecting lenders with borrowers. Thus, financial sector development impacts positively on economic growth rates. However, the demand following hypothesis presents inverse relationships between development in the financial systems and economic growth. Advocates of this tradition argue that financial systems respond spontaneously to the increase in demand for financial products, and hence, finance is demand following.

Cross-section studies of finance-growth nexus pioneered by Goldsmith (1969) argued that financial development fosters economic growth. However, the evidence presented in the context of Ghana provided mixed outcomes. The reported growth effects of financial system development depend on the choice of financial proxies employed. The interplay between the ascendency of finance, economic growth and poverty alleviation has attracted the attention of policymakers and researchers. Theoretically, development in the financial system induces economic growth, job creation, and reduces poverty levels. However, rising economic growth in Ghana has resulted in income inequality with a marginal reduction in extreme poverty.

CHAPTER 4

The Case of Ghana

1   Introduction

The previous chapter examined the shift in financial intermediation from banks and other financial institutions to the financial markets, and presented the lack of consensus on the long-standing debate of finance-growth-poverty nexus. Chapter four is a case study of Ghana and presents the country's profile from independence in 1957 to 2020. The chapter also discusses the evolution of the financial sector and investigates the effects of banking reforms on the economy. Section 2 presents recent economic performance, including some key economic indicators since 2000. Section 3 is divided into two parts and examines the political economy of Ghana from 1957 to 1982, the trajectory of state-led accumulation to neoliberalism. Sub-section 3.2 covers the political and economic developments from 1983–2019. This sub-section explains the reason why Ghana adopted the Structural Adjustment Programme (SAP) and the transition into multi-party democracy in 1992. The consequences of neoliberalism are investigated in section 4. The various waves of financial sector reforms pre- and post-adjustments periods are presented in section 5. Section 6 presents the distinctive features and the commonality of financialisation in the core and the periphery. This section analyses why the Ghanaian economy is under-financed yet financialising. Section 7 concludes with the empirical study of net capital flow from Ghana to the core countries, notably the US.

2   Country Profile and Overview of Recent Economic Performance

Ghana is one of the most relatively stable and peaceful countries within the sub-Saharan African sub-region (SSA) and was the first country within the sub-region to gain independence in 1957 and to experience neoliberal's Economic Recovery Programme (ERP) together with Structural Adjustment Programme (SAP) in 1983. Recently, the country has made significant progress in its political and economic developments compared to the challenging years of political instability and economic policy inconsistencies that branded its initial years after independence. With a Gross Domestic Product (PPP) of $132.5 billion in 2015, Ghana's economy ranks second largest after Nigeria in the West Africa sub-region and twelfth largest economy in Africa – African Economic Outlook

2017[1] (Africa Development Bank 2017). Ghana has consistently achieved year-on-year economic growth, with an average yearly GDP growth rate of 8% during 2009–2014; compared with the SSA average growth rate of 5% over the same period. Consistent economic growth coupled with the recent discovery of oil in 2007 and subsequent production in large quantities raised Ghana's GDP per capita (current prices) to $ 1,648 in 2017. In 2015, Ghana's GDP per capita reached $ 1,480 and was therefore classified as a low-middle income country as per the World Bank's country classifications (World Bank Group 2016; Bank of Ghana 2018).

The economy of Ghana has historically depended on two major sectors – the agricultural sector (mainly cocoa production),[2] and the mining sector (mainly gold). However, other minerals such as diamond, bauxite and manganese are also produced in commercial quantities. The service sector has in recent years surpassed the primary industry, thanks to the rise of financial services, information and communication sub-sectors. The country is therefore in an enviable position of few commodity-dependent economies that are blessed with all the three significant commodities of interest to Africa trade – agriculture, minerals, and oil. Therefore, there is a high expectation for accelerated growth and development and structural transformation of the country. Table 1 highlights selected key economic indicators from 2000–2017.

Table 1 shows positive real GDP growth rates ranging from a low of 3.7% in 2000 to a high of 8.5% in 2017. This was achieved thanks to substantial growth in financial services and information and communication as well as mining production, which was helped by the relatively stable prices of its key export commodities (gold and cocoa) during the period. The decline in economic growth in 2009 is due to the global financial and economic crisis, and subsequent fall in cocoa price, fall in remittances, tourism, and other capital flows, together with the increase in global oil prices. Other internal problems such as severe energy challenges and deterioration of fiscal deficits also compounded its external balance of payment deficits to limit economic growth in 2009. The strong economic growth in 2011 was supported by the oil sector when Ghana started full oil production in commercial quantities (Figure 3).

Historically, the agricultural sector has been the main contributor to Ghana's GDP. However, in recent times, the service sector has overtaken the agricultural

---

1   Based on GDP at PPP as at 2015, the 12 largest economies are Nigeria, Egypt, South Africa, Algeria. Morocco, Angola, Sudan, Ethiopia, Kenya, Tanzania, Tunisia, and Ghana.
2   Ghana is currently the world's second-largest producer of cocoa. It held the first position for many decades before the 1980s bushfires that destroyed the crop.

TABLE 1   Selected key economic indicators, 2000–2017

Economic indicators	2000	2002	2004	2006	2008	2009	2010	2012	2014	2016	2017
Real GDP growth (%)	3.7	4.5	5.6	6.2	7.3	4	8	9.3	4	3.7	8.5
Inflation (year-end)	40.5	15.2	11.8	10.5	18.1	15.9	8.6	8.8	17	17	11.8
Monetary policy rate (%)	n/a	24.5	18.5	12.5	17	18	13.5	15	21	25	20
91-day Treasury bill (%)	42	26.6	17.1	10.2	24.7	23.7	12.3	22.9	25.8	16.8	13
Fiscal balance (% of GDP)	-9.7	-6.7	-3.7	-7.55	-11.48	-5.6	-6.8	-11.5	-10.2	-7.9	-6
Balance of payments (US$m)	-117	40	-11	415	-941	1159	1463	-669	-85	247	1091

SOURCE: AUTHOR'S ESTIMATES, FIGURES FROM GHANA STATISTICAL SERVICE (GSS) AND THE US FEDERAL RESERVE

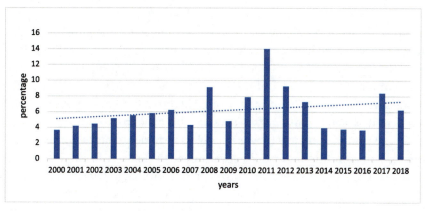

FIGURE 3   Real GDP growth rate (%) 2000–2018
SOURCE: AUTHOR'S ESTIMATES USING FIGURES FROM GHANA STATISTICAL SERVICE (2018).

sector's dominant contributions to the GDP. Between 2010–2016, the service sector accounted for over 50% of the total GDP, while the contributions of the agricultural sector declined every year from almost 40% in 2002 to just 19.5% in 2016. The growth of the industrial sector declined between 2006 and 2011 before rising in 2012 due to the production of oil in commercial quantities. The recent growth in the service sector has been engineered by the strong growth in the financial services, and information and communication sub-sectors, as shown in figure 4.

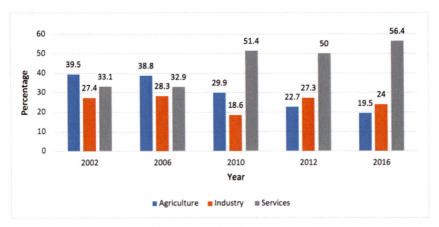

FIGURE 4   GDP composition by sector 2002–2016
SOURCE: AUTHOR'S ESTIMATES, DATA FROM GHANA STATISTICAL SERVICE (2018)

The macroeconomic policy objectives for the country are set to achieve a stable macroeconomic performance together with the fiscal discipline to facilitate private sector development to accelerate the economic growth agenda. However, there have been some challenges in achieving these stability objectives. The intermittent high inflation accompanied by high-interest rates and the continuous depreciation of the domestic currency (Ghana cedi) usually troubles the economy. The instability often happens during the political election period, which occurs every four years. This could be seen in 2000, 2004, 2008, 2012, and 2016, mainly because of excessive budget deficits from expenditure overruns by the incumbent government to hold on to power. Table 1 illustrates fiscal deficits throughout the period with large deficits notably in 2000 (9.7%), 2008 (11.48%), 2012 (11.5%) and 2016 (7.9%) election years. Fiscal deficit financing has crowded out private sector investment. Besides, the occasional deterioration in the country's terms of trade and capital movements have created a large balance of payment deficits as seen in particular in 2000,

2008 and 2014. These twin deficits (budget and balance of payment deficits) adversely affect the macroeconomic stability coupled with high inflation and high-interest rates, and weaken the domestic currency, as well as affect the economic development of the country.

The historical high inflation rate was brought under control from 2000–2007, except for a brief rise in 2003 due to fuel price hikes, and remained relatively stable after that between 10–15%. A combination of policies accounted for this relatively stable inflation. The automatic fuel price adjustment mechanism, as well as prudent fiscal and monetary policies coupled with a relatively stable exchange rate of the Ghana cedi, were due to savings made because of the external debt cancellation under the HIPC initiative.[3]

Monetary policy rates have moved in tandem with inflation rates and therefore witnessed a fall during 2000–2007, after which it was raised to reduce inflationary pressures that occurred during 2008–2009. The two election years – 2008 and 2012 resulted in high fiscal deficits; consequently, interest rates on government securities increased as the government borrowed to finance the deficits.

The review signifies that Ghana's recent macroeconomic performance has been relatively stable compared to the historical years. However, the occasional deterioration in the twin deficits coupled with high inflation and rising interest rates obstruct private sector development. Nevertheless, continuous political stability, increasing economic growth and sound economic policies have played a significant role in stabilising the current economic performance.

3 The Political Economy of Ghana: From State-led Accumulation to Neoliberalism

The political and economic arrangements of Ghana are classified under two distinct periods: the period after independence from British rule, to the end of 1982 – where the state-led accumulation provided social welfare to the citizens; and, the neoliberal accumulation ushered in April 1983 and dismantled government intervention by glorifying and justifying individual freedom and market-led economic arrangements.

---

3   Highly Indebted Poor Countries (HIPC), an initiative signed by the government of Ghana under the auspices of the IMF/World Bank, which resulted in debt cancellation.

3.1 Political and Economic Developments from Independence (1957) to 1982

Before proceeding to examine the process of Ghana's stabilisation and Structural Adjustment Programme (SAP), it is essential to assess in detail the structure of the country's economic and political decay. That is, the confluence of factors that precipitated the catastrophic state of affairs within which the recovery effort was launched. I argue in this section that the state apparatus is to be blamed for most of the crisis that prompted the excruciating process of SAP in Ghana.

The economic crisis that swamped Ghana since independence can be argued to involve the intensification of three interrelated problems that had their roots in the policies pursued after independence – in an attempt at building an integrated and self-reliant national economy.

Firstly, there was a structural crisis within the economy epitomised by an asymmetry between high domestic demands on the one hand, and sharply declining industrial and agricultural production on the other. Secondly, there was a fiscal crisis, exemplified by swelling external and domestic debt, massive budget deficit, and apparently uncontrollable expansion in government spending. Furthermore, there were deep-seated patterns of state instability, debilitation and increasing *delegitimation*, proven by frequent regime changes accompanied by frequent policy changes and revisions, increasing loss of policy control and effectiveness, and of popular confidence and support (Hutchful 1989; Killick, Malik, and Manuel 1992).

I argue in this book that these three components, which reciprocally reinforced each other to deepen the crisis, also functioned to create a context in which a decrease of state control over the country's political economy steadily originated – as demonstrated in a rapid expansion economic activity outside the reaches of state control during the 1970s.

Ghana's prospects for development were bright when it gained independence from the British in March 1957. The abundant natural resources aided the first president, Dr Kwame Nkrumah, to embark on a state-led strategy, focusing on import substitutions. Other Latin American countries had successfully started state-led development strategies during the period (Hutchful 1989; 2002). It is important to also acknowledge that, Keynesianism was the main orthodoxy during the period – the state grew larger relative to the economy and took a more active and interventionist role. The state established more or less comprehensive social welfare programmes and used fiscal and monetary tools to manage the economy. Government intervention was paramount in the private sector in several ways through regulation, taxation and subsidies, as well as dominant control over the financial sector.

Politicians are characterised by their distinct ideologies, and President Kwame Nkrumah was no exception. Atta-Boakye (2006) argues that he used his political ideology as a weapon and transformed the political landscape of Ghana into ideological concepts. Nkrumah established an institute to teach his doctrines of socialism, communism, and *'Nkrumaism'* – his ideologies became the blueprint in all public places – educational institutions, market places, and workplaces. He argued that capitalism was too complicated for a newly independent country like Ghana, hence the need for a socialist society.[4]

President Nkrumah established several State-Owned-Enterprises (SOEs) ranging from food, timber, Sanyo manufacturing to Cocoa Marketing Board. The government's 7-year development plans emphasised industrialisation through domestic production of import substitutes. The state provided the necessary welfare services from healthcare to public housing. Socialism became the engine of Ghana's economic development. As Killick, Malik, and Manuel (1992) and Hutchful (2002) observe, this socialist-oriented policy was based on the hope of a continuous increase in the price of cocoa and other minerals that Ghana was blessed with. The state-led approach encountered some problems, which precipitated the overthrow of President Nkrumah's party in 1966. Hutchful noted that since the focus of the state-led strategy was on redistributing the national prosperity, the state then became the father and mother, which resulted in colossal state expenditure. The rising deficit or national debt is not a bad thing if the proceeds were used to expand material economic production with full employment and rising wages, as these would lead to positive economic outcomes for the nation. However, with the sharp decline in export revenues following the fall in commodity prices, it became extremely difficult to fund these socialist-oriented policies.

The new military government of the National Liberation Council (NLC) led by General J.A. Ankrah and Kotoka abandoned Nkrumah's socialist-oriented economic development projects and sort to empower the private sector. They started the country's first negotiation with the Washington Consensus. The standby deal included a reverse of most of Nkrumah's state-led policies. The IMF prescribed trade liberalisation, contractionary fiscal and monetary policies, removal of subsidies, and the devaluation of the cedi (Boafo-Arthur 1999, 147). This free-market approach to economic growth and development was not received well by many recognised professional bodies such as the teacher's union, lawyers and industrial workers' union in 1969. This compelled the

---

[4] Kwame Nkrumah, *Ghana: An Autobiography* (London: Heinemann 1957), pp.xv-xvi.

military government to hand power to Dr K. A. Busia's constitutional government to form the second republic.

Interestingly, the second republic[5] was also pro-neoliberal and started to address the inefficiencies with market-based policies. This free-market ideology was evident in the 1971 contractionary budget, where new taxes were imposed, development levy was introduced, withdrawal of state subsidies, abolishing of free education, devaluation of the currency (cedi) by 44%, and liberalisation of trade. These reforms were not received well by most of the population and resulted in a military coup by a former student of the Kwame Nkrumah Ideological Institute, Colonel Kutu Acheampong, and the National Redemption Council (NRC). The NRC reversed almost all the neoliberal policies of Busia's government. The local currency was revalued by 42%, state welfare services were reinstated, and some external debts were crucially rejected. Despite how damaging some of these policies were, they received widespread support, but in the end, worsened the country's developmental position. Shillington (1992) asserts that the economic mismanagement, corruption, and incompetence of the Acheampong regime drained off Ghana's scarce resources. He contends that the hard-foreign exchange realised from the increased cocoa prices were primarily diverted from the state coffers. It was this high-level corruption that precipitated the first coming of the Armed Forces Revolutionary Council (AFRC) led by Flight Lieutenant Jerry John Rawlings in June 1979, intending to stabilise the economy. Gyimah-Boadi (1993, 6) reckons the AFRC fought corruption, mismanagement, and profiteering before handing power to Dr Hilla Limann's constitutional government to form the third republic.

The government considered seeking external assistance to address the empty national coffers. However, domestic pressure did not permit Limann's government to seek and implement the World Bank and the IMF neoliberal packages. The continued hardship of Ghanaians prompted the military-led by Rawlings, again, to stage another coup to overthrow Limann's government in December 1981 – and formed PNDC government – what most Ghanaians refer to as 'the second coming of Rawlings'.

The efforts by successive governments in Ghana to provide national self-sufficiency and to disassociate the economy from neoliberal institutions have been futile. Like many periphery countries, the lack of the necessary material base makes it challenging to reject neo-colonialism. This weakness means that Ghana is forced to depend heavily on external economic forces, particularly

---

5 The constitution of the Republic of Ghana provides the basic charter for the country's second attempt at republican democratic government since independence in 1957.

the western countries and neoliberal institutions. The integration of the economy into the capitalist world, therefore, reduces the opportunity for policy manoeuvre. This dependency culture makes the country vulnerable to capitalist interests. Smith (1979) argues that periphery countries cannot exist without their dependency on the core, but they also cannot exist within it. This is the challenge faced by many periphery countries within the capitalist world economy.

It could be argued that the reason why some leaders in Ghana would accept neoliberal measures is because of the country's subordinate/inferior bargaining status to that of the neoliberal institutions. Ghana had limited ways, if any, of dealing with its economic woes. In his analysis of modernisation, Frank (1971) argues that underdevelopment is a consequence of the unequal distribution of resources and the exploitation of the periphery countries by the core. He argues that resources/raw materials flow from the periphery to the core countries while manufactured goods flow in the opposite direction to enrich the core countries. Thus, countries in the periphery are underdeveloped because the core requires cheap raw material and labour. The appropriation of economic surplus to the core is the cause of underdevelopment in the periphery. Emmanuel (1972) adds that international trade leads to the core countries becoming richer at the expense of the countries in the periphery. He argues that high wages in the core countries are the critical factor in their development. This is because rising consumer incomes stimulate aggregate demand which leads to economic growth and development. Thus, any attempt to de-link a periphery country from such a structural-dependent arrangement will be difficult, if not impossible. The inability of Ghana to process and add value to some of its raw materials places the economy at the periphery of the world market. The country, therefore, exports raw materials and a dumping ground for western manufactured products. The economy depends on external sources for most of its needs, thus, making it challenging to de-link itself from global economic institutions. Thereby, successive governments have been compelled to seek international assistance to embark on national development.

The problems in Ghana were worsened by various domestic and international shocks. A severe drought hit the SSA sub-region accompanied by a series of bush fires, which destroyed cocoa and other cash crops. The global oil crises in 1973–74 and 1979–80 followed by global recession outstretched and magnified the domestic deterioration. Furthermore, the Nigerian government deported over one million Ghanaians who went there to seek greener pastures during the hard times in Ghana. The continuous economic deterioration and its political consequences for the PNDC government forced them to accept the neoliberal orthodoxy (Boafo-Arthur 1999). In her book, *The Shock Doctrine: The*

Rise of Disaster Capitalism, Klein (2007) argues that neoliberal orthodoxy is so unpopular that the only time it wins an argument is through deception and coercion. Thus, neoliberal restructuring depends on crises, a time when citizens and nations are disoriented, confused and preoccupied with their own immediate survival. This desperate situation allows neoliberals to embark on trade liberalisation, privatisation of state own enterprises and austerity measures without any serious opposition from the people. Thus, neoliberalism embraces crises as opportunities to initiate its radical free-market ideologies.

3.2 *Political and Economic Developments 1983–2019*

This period witnessed a stable political and economic environment, albeit under the PNDC military rule until December 1992 when the nation restored its multi-party democracy to begin the fourth republic. The stable political environment, albeit some failed coup attempts, empowered the PNDC government to embark on economic reforms. The reforms covered both the real and the financial sectors (see sub-sections 5.1 and 5.2).

A general election was held in December 1992 and won by Rawlings and the (p)NDC[6] party and was re-elected in December 1996. It is worth acknowledging that the re-election of Rawlings and the NDC government was the first time that an elected government had completed its term of office in the history of Ghana's multi-party democracy. The market-based policies adopted from the IMF and the World Bank continued. However, significant budget deficits accompanied the return to constitutional regimes. Huge government spending in election years resulted in excessive government borrowing, accompanied by rising inflation.

The year 2000 election witnessed the first transfer of political power from one political party to another and from one civilian government to another. This momentous event was historical in the politically turbulent SSA subregion. The new administration – New Patriotic Party (NPP) government continued with the neoliberal economic agenda and empowered the private sector through various government policies. The Centre For Policy Analysis (2003) contends that the dividend from a stable democracy was the massive external financing support to the private sector. The NPP government opted for the HIPC initiative offered by the IMF and World Bank. This initiative saved the country a substantial amount of external debt obligation. The NPP was voted out of power in 2008 after serving two terms and power was smoothly

---

6 The PNDC military government formed the National Democratic Congress (NDC) political party to contest the 1992 general election. The 'p' was usually used by the opposition parties to claim that the NDC party is still under a military rule.

and peacefully transferred back to the NDC. The NDC handed power back to the NPP after losing the 2016 general election. These political processes have enhanced Ghana's democratic credentials. It is important to note that successive governments and political parties have embraced the political stability and the free-market ideology started in 1983/1992.

4 Neoliberalism in Ghana

Since the mid-1970s, SSA countries have suffered from slow economic growth, food shortages and famine, mass unemployment with widespread poverty, declining export earning, mounting national debt, and increasing marginalisation and isolation from the global economy. Although many periphery countries shared these experiences, the problem was more severe in Africa for many reasons, which included African democracy and its peasant transformation. These issues made social, political and economic reforms imperative. Table 2 presents some of Ghana's macroeconomic indicators from 1960–1995.

TABLE 2   Basic indicators of economic performance (percentage annual average growth) 1960–1995

	1960–70	1970–83	1983–89	1990–95
Real GDP	2.2	-0.8	5	4.3
Gross domestic investment	-3.1	-5.9	16.6	21.9
Exports	0.1	-4.4	11.7	10.1
Imports	-1.5	-7.2	13.5	8.6
Total agriculture	2.6	-0.5	3.6	2
Population	2.3	2.3	3.5	3

SOURCE: AUTHOR'S ESTIMATES FIGURES FROM THE WORLD BANK (1960–1990) AND GHANA STATISTICAL SERVICE (1990–1995)

Table 2 illustrates the deterioration of the Ghanaian economy between independence and the early 1980s. The output of the economy declined while the population grew at an average rate of 2.7% per annum. Cocoa, the main cash crop and the primary foreign exchange earner for the country declined, which worsened the trade balance. As the foreign exchange problem became more severe, imports contracted from -1.5% in 1960–70 to -7.2% in 1970–83. The massive jump in gross domestic investment (1990–1995) was due to a substantial investment in gold mining in 1993 because of the privatisation of the sector. The dual oil crises in the 1970s (1973 and 1979) coupled with the depreciation of the local currency added to the deterioration of the economy. Table 2 also demonstrates a relatively stable economy from 1983 onwards with 5% annual average real GDP growth and 3.6% yearly growth in agriculture output between 1983 and 1989. The high imports after SAP reduced to 8.6% with exports average of 10% in the early 1990s.

Other economic indicators showed deterioration in the Ghanaian economy as inflation was running over 100% and imbalances in both domestic and external accounts became a permanent occurrence. These factors worsened economic development, as food and basic medical supplies became unaffordable for ordinary citizens. Inflation stayed above 100% in 1977, 1981 and 1983, where it peaked at 123% (figure 5).

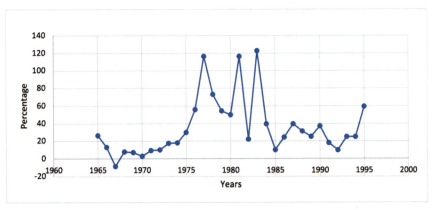

FIGURE 5   Inflation rates in Ghana 1965–1995
SOURCE: AUTHOR'S ESTIMATES, FIGURES FROM THE FEDERAL RESERVE HTTPS://FRED.STLOUISFED.ORG/ AND GHANA STATISTICAL SERVICE (1999).

Many interpretations have been given to explain the origin of the crisis, which has emaciated the Ghana economy and the wider society. The main schools of thought are the *'internalists'* whose view reflected neo-classical liberal, and the *'externalists'* whose view mirrored neo-Marxist dependency approaches.

The neo-classical liberal argument points to internal variables such as economically damaging developmental policies pursued by successive regimes, implementational problems due to inadequate state administrative capacity, excessive and debilitating state intervention, and corruption as the central causes of the crises in Ghana. The critical message that unites neo-classical liberals is their tendency to search for internal, predominantly political, often normative accounts as opposed to international, economic or structural explanations (Chazan 1982).

By contrast, *neo-Marxist cum externalists* have tended to argue that Ghana's economic deterioration can be attributed to the country's structural position at the peripheries of the global capitalist economy, a situation which inflicts severe restraints on independent attempts to create an integrated and self-reliant national economy. The advocates of this view contend that Ghana's underdevelopment is an unavoidable consequence of a colonial legacy, which bestowed an economy dependent on the primary export sector to acquire resources necessary for its further development in the absence of any sustainable mode of internal accumulation. This dependency, they argue, has left the economy at the mercy of exogenous shocks and fluctuations in a manner that wrought (in the medium and long-term) against any significant development, an argument shared by Frank (1971) and (Emmanuel 1972). They also highlight the hurtful operations of MNCs, whose activities have served to 'decapitalise' the economy through profit repatriation and the use of numerous under-the-counter strategies for surplus transferring like transfer pricing. This has been done in collaboration with their local comprador bourgeoisie[7] ruling elite, which has served parasitically off the resources of the *'swollen state'* and has freely 'mortgaged' the economy to foreign concerns in return for the benefits which accrue to them through their control of the state.

Although *externalists'* argument is tenable in the context of Ghana, there is no doubt that no coherent explanation of the country's economic woes can omit concerns raised by the *internalists* – such as state ineffectiveness, incompetence, and corruption. Gyimah-Boadi and Jeffries (2000) argue that the liberals' explanation offers a clear perspective of the root cause of Ghana's economic decline. However, they acknowledges that the approach alone is insufficient in accounting for the catastrophic decline of the economy. Chazan (1982, 14) remarks that:

---

[7] This is a section of the domestic middle class who act as agents for foreign investors and multinational corporations for their private gains (at times) at the expense of the whole country.

If the government alone were responsible for the decline, (as the pragmatic-liberal school suggests) or if outside forces in consort with the state-linked classes must bear the blame (as the dependency school argues), then the unit of analysis remains the state or the state as it relates to the external variables.

What is lacking in this approach is any careful scrutiny of the central position of the state vis-à-vis the society it purports to reflect. Therefore, there is a belief that government may represent the society or outside interests, but not much attention has been given to the impact of governmental policies on society as a reason for Ghana's underdevelopment. However, Fouskas and Gökay (2018) argue that a key feature of neoliberal capitalism is its uneven combined development across time and regions/territoriality; and as long as the political and economic policies in the periphery are designed and dictated by the core, there will always be winners and losers. They argue that the core countries are imperial in nature and impose their own political and economic systems as well as principles and cultures through the recruitment of local elites. Consequently, the domestic government may be forced to represent outside interests at the expense of society.

While subscribing to the argument that the state has contributed greatly to the country's economic woes, it is vital to qualify this position, for the centrality of the state should be understood as a reflection of the country's underperformance as well as a factor aiding to create further underdevelopment.

The trajectory of Ghana's economic and political decline since independence to the early 1980s made it indispensable to pursue the painful process of SAP under the second Rawlings regime.

The economic factors leading to poor performance, according to Sowa (2002) could be summarised as follows:

1) The overvalued exchange rate that discourages exports and encourages imports;
2) The printing of money to finance government deficit and its resultant inflation;
3) The imposition of price controls at the manufacturing stage; and
4) Misallocation of and misuse of imports licence which created inefficiencies and denied inputs and equipment to high priority areas.

Other structural weaknesses included:

1) The over-reliance of agriculture as the leading sector with little investment in the industry to address the declining productivity;

2) Non-diversification of exports from cocoa, subjecting the economy to the volatile world commodity prices;
3) Large public and service sector; and
4) Insufficient mobilisation of internal resources for domestic capital formation.

The consequences of economic decline after independence resulted in the deterioration of the standard of living and the general impoverishment of the citizens as a whole. Most indicators point to a worsening standard of living. Real GDP per capita declined from 634 cedis in 1971 to 394.8 cedis in 1983. Most Ghanaians could not afford basic necessities of life such as food, water and shelter. Index of food production per capita fell to 72 in 1982 with 1971 as the base of 100 (Ghana Statistical Service 1999; Sowa 2002).

After more than two decades of abysmal economic performance, Ghana and at least 33 other African countries adopted, or were forced to take the Economic Recovery Programme (ERP) together with SAP (Britwum, Jonah, and Tay 2001). The initial years of SAP involving stabilisation appeared successful. The economy grew at about 5% between 1984 and 1989. Killick and Malik (1992) observe that the reforms attracted unprecedented capital inflows and led to an overall balance of payment surpluses, despite a large continuous deficit on the current account due to imports. They also argue that the more realistic exchange rate, together with good weather, the decline in smuggling due to better producer prices and an increase in cocoa export revenue supported the GDP growth of 5% per year. Sowa (2002) observed budget surpluses from 1986, although he argued that it was due to an increase in foreign aid, which was included in the calculation. Although domestic credit did not expand as much, the increase in external inflows kept the growth of aggregate money supply high; inflation reduced from three-digit to about 25% per annum. The initial improvements in the macroeconomy had a positive impact on society and enabled the rising incidence of poverty to be stabled. However, some of the conditions attached to the stabilisation, such as the retrenchment of public sector workers and the privatisation of state-owned enterprises forced many people back into poverty.

The proponents of SAP attribute a significant part of Africa's malaise to the magnitude of state intervention, and thus, the relatively large size of the public sector in SSA is to blame for the woes of the region (Logan 1995). Africa is likely more interventionist than other regions; however, the interventionist explanation of the African problem is rather reductionist. Stiglitz (2002) argues that intervention in the periphery countries can be useful at times to the development and expansion of the private sector. Thus, Stiglitz advocates the East Asian model of economic development, where governments, though relying on the free market, actively intervene in creating, shaping and guiding markets. This has invigorated new technologies, promoting an environment in which firms take considerable responsibility for the social welfare of workers.

The drawback of neoliberal reforms is that it does not differentiate between types of state intervention in Africa, what Stiglitz (2002) calls *'one size fits all'*; a policy based on the out-of-date belief that markets are omniscient and by themselves, lead to efficient outcomes. Adewumi (1997) refers to the IMF policy as a *'bogus'* doctor who prescribes the same medicine for different ailments – market forces for the exchange rate, interest rates, and economic ailment. It is also doubtful whether SSA countries can be fully integrated into the global economy when there are internally disintegrated, and SAP does not address issues of international trade. Although SAP seems to address structural reforms in the domestic economy, it fails to appreciate the dynamics of the peasant sector. Due to these and many other issues, SAP continues to face opposition among many scholars and policymakers despite the general acknowledgment of the crisis of statist socio-economic systems in Africa.

The dominant position of the subsistence sector within SSA economies is one of the most striking differences between Africa economies' structure and those of other peripheral countries. In no other periphery region does the subsistence sector account for as much as 70–80% of the working population. Since the subsistence sector has significant implications for the performance of African economies as well as for their ability to absorb international market shocks, any developmental policy that ignores this vital sector may struggle to have a positive impact.

The key elements of SAP are the neoliberal doctrine of market-based policies, limited government intervention, export-led growth, financial discipline, absolute and comparative advantage, and prosperity and economic growth. The World Bank and the IMF have widely cited the economies of Pacific Asia as good examples of the success of such neoliberal policies of market-oriented, outward-looking development strategies (World Bank 1993), despite generally accepted evidence that the newly industrialised Pacific Asia countries developed with a maximum rather than a minimal state intervention. As Chang (2010) asserts, the economic success stories of the East Asian miracle, where the region's GDP per capita increased significantly accompanied by a drastic decrease in poverty, demonstrates the significance of strategic, rather than unrestricted integration with the global economy. For instance, Singapore embraced free trade more extensively than other Asian countries, and also relied on FDI for its economic development; however, it doesn't conform to many aspects of neoliberal doctrines. Singapore provides extensive support in the form of subsidies to attract MNCs into sectors that are considered strategic for national development. State infrastructure development and targeted academic and vocational courses at particular sectors and industries have been used widely. Singapore is a global leader in State Owned-Enterprises. The State Housing Development Board, for instance, provides about 85% of all housing units, and the government owns and controls almost all land in the country.

China and India's integration into the global economy was based on nationalistic inward-looking vision rather than global outward-looking dreams. China adopted high tariffs to protect its strategic industries, in particular the manufacturing base of the economy. The average Chinese tariff was about 30% in the 1990s. Nevertheless, the country attracts more FDI but still imposes foreign ownership ceiling and local content requirements, which mandate foreign firms to acquire a certain proportion of their inputs from domestic businesses and suppliers. Therefore, there is no evidence to suggest that these countries would have been better off had they adopted a neoliberal open-door policy as prescribed in SAP.

There was a general belief that the long-run benefits of SAP outweigh the short-run social costs. It was not known that the long-run was what Keynes refers to as *'when all may be dead!'* (Keynes 2018[1936]). Ghana implemented two phases of SAP. The first phase – SAP 1 or ERP1 covered the period 1983–1986 and was focused on resuscitating the ailing economy. The aim was to stabilise the economy from further declining. It was centred on fiscal, monetary, and trade policy reforms. The second phase of SAP covered 1987–1992, intending to consolidate the gains made from SAP 1. In the second phase, medium to long-term goals were set to try to incorporate stabilisation and economic growth. These goals include a 5% economic growth rate through increasing investment to over 25% from 10% of national income; increase savings to 15% by 1990 from SAP 1 level of 7%; implement Public Enterprise Reform Programme (PERP); reduce government spending, denationalisation of non-performing SOEs; and establishing Programme of Actions to Mitigate the Social Cost of Adjustment (PAMSCAD) (Donkor 2019, 124). The state-centric method to development pursued since independence made these measures very risky for the government. Nevertheless, SAP made SSA more integrated into the global economy because the conditions meted out were measured to open up the adjusting nations' economies to FDI, imports, and possible export-led growth that can be used to reduce debt and poverty.

However, some authors have argued that the negative aspects of SAP aimed at poverty alleviation, lightening debt burden and saving sinking economies of the SSA is enormous. According to Ismi (2004) and McGregor (2005), SAP was forced on SSA by the IMF and the World Bank to create conditions that benefit MNCs from the core. The liberalisation enabled these monopolies facing falling profits and stagnation of capital accumulation to move out from their home countries to protect falling profits and engage in financialisation cum globalisation of production. Strengthening this assessment, Osabu-Kle (2000) asserts that during the period of SAP, the income of the poorest fifth of the world's population fell from 2.3% to 1.4% while the wealthiest fifth of the world's population saw their income increased to 85% from 75%. Those who make the rules on trade and liberalisation benefited at the expense of the poor. This demonstrates that at least in the short-run, SAP made conditions worse and eroded some of the social gains such as employment, education and export earnings.

There are several areas where the SAP initiative impoverished Ghanaians. The privatisation of state enterprise resulted in mass unemployment, forcing families into extreme poverty; trade reforms also led to a reduction of income for rural peasant farmers, and spending cuts on education, health and other social services deepened poverty in communities. Even if there were some benefits of SAP, these were not evenly distributed as cuts to government social services affected the poor the most. Even the (World Bank 1997) acknowledged that conditions in 11 out of the 33 countries that adopted SAP deteriorated and further 9 countries only showed a slight improvement. For many years of SAP, the cries of the poor were largely ignored by the neoliberals. The poor who laboured in rural areas knew something was wrong when they realised cuts to government spending and subsidies they receive. But they were powerless to change the rules or influence the neoliberal institutions that made the rules.

On trade liberalisation, Adewumi (1997) challenges the World Bank and the IMF to show a country in the world that does not protect its agriculture and the industrial sector(s) in one way or the other. He questions why international financial institutions and donor countries compel poor African countries to liberalise their trade. He argues that these liberalisation measures are the cause of the destruction of African industries, with millions of job losses and conversion of SSA economies into a mere export of cheap primary products and the dumping grounds for finished goods of the core countries. This unjust and unequal liberalised trade could be argued to be one of the leading causes of chronic poverty in Africa. Trade liberalisation policy often involves the removal of subsidies on food, fertilisers, education, and other agricultural inputs; these have resulted in high food prices, malnutrition and hunger, and falling education enrolment. These inhumane policies affect the poor and the vulnerable in the community.

In his analysis of unequal exchange, Emmanuel (1972) contends that peripheral countries consistently have unfavourable terms of trade; whatever they undertake and produce will always exchange a more substantial proportion of the nation's labour for a smaller proportion of foreign labour. He argues that capital and labour expended do not determine the value of exchange, but rather the reciprocal demands of the exchanging parties that determine prices. The prices received will determine the reward given to labour and capital. Emmanuel rejects Ricardo's comparative costs advantage and the international division of labour and posits that in peripheral countries the produce of labour will never match the value of a product of a comparable amount of labour in a core economy on the international market. This unequal exchange results in low wages and unfavourable terms of trade in the periphery for the benefit of the consumers in core countries. He concludes that any form of imperialism is mercantile in nature.

The World Bank and the IMF justified the massive retrenchment on the grounds that the public sector was unproductive and over-bloated. However, as too many professionals were forcibly retrenched in Ghana as part of the SAP agreement, it is difficult to understand who is going to tap and develop both human and natural resources for the development of Ghana.

On privatisation of State Corporations, evidence from Chile[8] suggests that this is to the benefit of the foreign investors and very few super-rich Ghanaians. The neoliberal ideologies of privatisation have been centred on efficiency and profitability, with little attention on the social costs and cultural dynamics of Ghana. The state has been the mother and father since independence, no wonder privatisation in Ghana was partly successful under a military regime. In its concluding seminar in Accra, the Organisation of African Trade Union Unity (OATUU) argued that the existence of every government should be the satisfaction of the basic needs of the people. The public sector is, therefore, the backbone of any government and the vehicle for development.

Although many critics of SAP agree to some forms of reforms to resuscitate the economies, they disagree with the diagnosis. They argue that the volatility in the international economy was to be blamed for the crisis, in particular, the harsh commodity price changes in the 1970s. Kahler (1990) argues that low-income African countries were destabilised by various market imperfections, bottlenecks and rigidities, and as a result, the neoliberal prescriptions were improper. Others question the economic wisdom of devaluation and trade liberalisation given the elasticities of supply of exports and demand for imports[9] in SSA. Africa exports mainly primary commodities and imports manufactured

---

8 See for instance, Harvey (2005) *A Brief History of Neoliberalism*.
9 The Marshall Lerner condition advocates that for devaluation to be effective, the sum of elasticities of imports and exports should be more than one- elastic.

finished goods. The low exports and imports elasticities increase domestic costs of servicing debt and the cost of imported inputs; as a result, the prescriptions were inappropriate (Cornia et al. 1992).

According to Shah (2013), poor countries were forced to cut spending on education, health and other development projects, but debt servicing and other economic policies have been made the priority. That is, the World Bank and IMF are asking the poor countries to lower the standard of living of their citizens in order to meet their debt obligations. Shuh further argues that periphery countries have been encouraged to export more to raise sufficient funds to pay off debts promptly. This has resulted in a price war, making their commodities even cheaper on the international market, which favours the western consumer at the expense of the poor as imports become expensive. This unequal exchange could be argued to be exploitation to the exporting country.

Interestingly, Ayittey (2000) remarks that many Africans oppose economic liberalisation purely on ideological grounds. This, he argues, is because of the deep-seated resentment to capitalism or free markets, an attitude that dates back to the colonial era. Because the colonialists were capitalists, thus, capitalism is as evil and exploitative as colonialism. Some intellectuals viewed the World Bank involvement as a neo-colonial institution amplifying this bias against capitalism. Ayittey concludes that the government opted for what he calls *safe budget cuts* on education, health and road maintenance. Real per capita spending on health and education was reduced drastically as a way of reducing government spending while protecting spending on militaries and bureaucracies. The cut in social expenditures undermined economic growth and shrank revenue collection.

4.1 *Neoliberalism and Housing Provision in Ghana*

Ghana, like many low-middle income countries, is plagued with an acute housing deficit. This remains one of the central development challenges. The rising demand for housing, coupled with supply constraints has resulted in a huge gap, especially in the urban areas of the country. It is estimated that the country requires a minimum of 100,000 housing units yearly, but the estimated supply is just 35% of the requirement (ISSER 2013). Although there is a lack of comprehensive housing policy in Ghana, it is essential to distil a distinct policy focus between pre-SAP and post-SAP periods.

The pre-SAP (post-independence) era involves active and direct state provision of public housing. State institutions such as Bank for Housing and Construction, First Ghana Building Society, State Housing Corporation and the Tema Development Corporation were established with the view of facilitating sustainable and affordable housing provision and finance. This Keynesian intervention in housing delivery provided low-cost houses in the district and regional capitals which ended in early 1983 when Ghana adopted SAP. Government policy on housing took a different turn after SAP, with much emphasis on private sector involvement in housing delivery from production, financing to the production of building materials. Thus, the role of the state in neoliberal housing policy is to provide a regulatory and economic framework for the market to thrive. However, as pointed out by ISSER (2013), the private sector has never provided any significant role in building low-cost houses for poor and low-income segments in the country.

Most of the housing units in Ghana are provided by the private informal sector, where individuals finance house building through informal sources such as self-financing and remittance. With an unstable macroeconomic environment coupled with high inflation and persistent depreciation of the domestic currency, Obeng-Odoom (2012) reckons it could take up to 15 years for an average person to acquire a two-bedroom housing unit. This incremental building tied funds into uncompleted buildings which could otherwise have been used for other productive projects. Nonetheless, these self-financing remain the most popular viable option for many individuals wishing to own a house.

Housing finance is a significant part of the World Bank's financial sector strategy and the overall aim of poverty alleviation and improving lives. Housing finance plays a major role in the strengthening of the housing market, the development of the financial sector and the overall health of the economy. Vibrant housing finance supports labour mobility, job creation in both high and low-skilled sectors, investment and the overall improvement in the quality of life.

Across the world and especially in Ghana, housing financing is one of the major development challenges due to a variety of factors, including demand as well as supply-side constraints. Despite the various financial sector reforms in Ghana, financing arrangements in the housing market remain underdeveloped and unattractive to a large segment of the population. Teye, Teye, and Asiedu (2015) argue that the prevailing housing financing system in Ghana is minimal and only designed for high-income earners in the urban areas and those in the diaspora. Consequently, for many people, informal sources – self-financing remain the only option available. Warnock and Warnock (2008) examined housing finance systems as a proportion of GDP in 62 countries, including Ghana. Their findings reveal that housing financing (formal) in Ghana accounts for just 0.5% of GDP, the least among the countries investigated compared with 15.7% average in the sub-region. The UN Habitat (2011, 98) presents that:

> The pattern through history has been to establish institutions to provide housing finance ostensibly targeted at ordinary urban Ghanaians. Governments have then watched them decline and fail and then established new institutions which have also failed. In the cycle of decline, each has turned to the high-income market for a safe environment for its lending. In reality, none of the institutions has targeted the majority of urban households who have remained without any recourse to housing finance.

Indeed, while most of the above focused on inadequate housing financing in urban areas, the problem is even worse in rural areas. The rural housing market is unattractive due to low-income and high levels of poverty. This has contributed to the poor housing conditions in rural communities of the country, and the rural occupants lack the necessary resource to make any improvement to their housing conditions.

In most of the core countries, especially the UK and the US, the mortgage market is a capable and vibrant financier of the housing needs of the citizens. However, an efficient housing finance system is crucial for the supply and demand for houses and its accompanying services. The supply obstacles in Ghana involve high costs of land (especially in the urban areas), lack of adequate capital of universal banks to finance long-term projects, partly due to liquidity problems and the benefit gained from short-term government securities. Besides, the inability of mortgage providers to assess the credit-worthiness of potential borrowers as well as other unstable macroeconomic conditions (for instance, currency depreciation) in the country amplify the problem. These supply-side constraints limit the number of providers in the mortgage industry. Even in situations where supply is available, demand constraints, such as high house prices often quoted in foreign currencies (notably in US$) as a hedge against domestic currency depreciation, priced out many low and middle-income segments to enter the market. Persistent high inflation and interest rates accompanied by unfavourable terms of loan repayment, and the cultural belief in many communities that it is forbidden to be in long-term debt amongst others have constrained demand for external financing for housing. These demand and supply constraints reinforce each other to limit the formal channels for housing financing system in Ghana. Thus, the reluctance of mortgage providers to lend to prospective homeowners is matched by prospective borrowers (homeowners) averse to enter the mortgage market due to demand-side constraints. It is within this context that self-financing and informal means of housing in Ghana flourished.

These challenges are evident in the number of loans disbursed for housing financing in 2011. According to the (Bank of Ghana 2015), less than 3% ($ 26.1 million) of bank loans went into housing finance. This is very small even when compared with other low-middle income countries such as Sri Lanka and Kenya, where housing finance portfolios were over $1billion and $668 million, respectively, over the same period (Teye, Teye, and Asiedu 2015).

The 'real estate bubble' is a major part of the mechanisms of financialisation, which happened in the world economy during the last four decades. Economic expansion in the neoliberal era is heavily dependent on debt-financed household spending/consumption. Asset bubbles/inflation encouraged households to borrow against inflated assets. To augment the process, neoliberal institutions offer a transformed financial system ready to provide risky loans to homeowners. In simple terms, the main source of purchasing power in the housing market is bank credits/loans, in the form of mortgages, rather than households' income. The more banks are willing to lend, the more money floods into the housing market. This is one of the key reasons that housing prices have been able to race ahead of most household's income. Even the deregulation policies in the 2000s made second loans to low and no-income households possible. This was accepted because it was believed that housing prices would rise in perpetuity. The credit that banks lend for mortgages is not money in someone else's savings account, but new money created specifically and artificially to fund the loan. As banks become more and more willing to grant risky mortgages, the supply of money to the economy increases, and with that, the purchasing power of the individuals increases even if the actual income of the most household does not.

It was the deregulation and liberalisation of the credit market in the 1970s and 1980s that kick-started the shift towards this preference for mortgage lending over other activities, as banks and building societies were for the first time allowed to grant credit to households against the value of their homes. The incentive for the banks for this preference is clear: If a bank or mortgage company lends against a property and the borrower does not keep up their repayments, the bank ends up repossessing the house, and the land it sits on, and sells it at a higher price since the prices continuously grow, or at least expect to grow. As land and house prices rise, households are compelled to take out larger mortgage loans to get on the housing ladder, boosting banks' profits and capital. The boost in profits and capital enables banks to issue more loans, which further pushes up prices. This process can continue even when house prices are more than the households' incomes, sustaining the expectation that prices will continue to rise.

The practice can continue until there is an economic shock and a very large number of people's incomes can no longer keep up with debt repayments. Nevertheless, this practice has triggered a secular rise in consumer debt in the neoliberal era. As presented by Kotz (2008; 2013) the ratio of consumer debt to disposable income before the 1980s was relatively stable, and moves in line with the business cycle – rising during peaks and falling during economic slowdowns. The ratio of debt-income, however, more than doubled between 1982 and 2007, from 59% to 128.8%, respectively. Likewise, financial sector debt to GDP skyrocketed from 20% in 1980 to 120% in 2008. Consequently, the housing bubble that burst in 2007 rendered many financial institutions insolvent, notable among them are Northern Rock in the UK and Lehman Brother in the US.[10]

Indeed, as the ratio of house prices and mortgage debt to income increases, the economy becomes more susceptible to any change that would spark a larger portion of households' income to be taken up in debt repayments on their mortgages: such as a fall in salaries or rise in interest rates. Such a change, if significant enough, would render the whole process go into reverse, consequently, mortgage defaults, falls in house prices and therefore falls in households' net wealth. This would trigger a contraction of bank lending, a recession in spending and, potentially, a financial crisis. As argued by Minsky, a sudden shock to the economy or if job and wage growth slowed, households' capability to sustain heavy debt load would be compromised. This could shift hedge financing to Ponzi financing – where borrowers cannot afford the repayment of capital plus interest and therefore require new credit to service previous loans. This would impact consumer spending, aggregate demand and slow down economic growth.

There is almost a uniform agreement amongst experts that the 2007/08 global financial crisis started in the US sub-prime housing market[11] as a result of such practices and failures (Storm 2018; Fouskas and Gökay 2018). It seems in Ghana too, neoliberal financialisation has relied on the housing market to some extent, in particular in the major cities. The economic liberalisation and

---

10 The collapse of Lehman Brothers' founded in 1847 was attributed to its involvement in the subprime mortgage crisis and its exposure to less liquid assets. Its filed for bankruptcy proceedings in September 2008. Lehman's collapsed played a leading role in the unfolding of the financial and economics crisis of 2007/08. Northern Rock (founded in 1965) on the other hand was nationalised during the financial crisis caused by the subprime mortgage problem.
11 Subprime mortgage crisis was the considerable increase in high-risk loans to overvalued assets, with limited or no collateral to borrowers who often lacked the income for repayment, went into default in 2007.

a corresponding increase in domestic and foreign private investments, especially in the housing industry, affected the situation in the urban areas where one can observe an overproduction of housing for high-income earners, and this led to a dramatic rise of gated communities. On the other hand, however, there has been virtually no provision of housing for low-income earners, thus exacerbating their continued dependence on the informal sector for housing provision in these areas.

In Ghana, the private sector involvement in the housing market is dominated by a few large firms such as Regimanuel Gray Ltd, which controls almost 50% (market share) of houses built by real estate developers. This is followed by NTHC properties with 12%, State Housing Takoradi and Trasacco Estate Development with 8% and 7%, respectively. Although these oligopolies offer mortgages for prospective homeowners, the target segments have been the high-income group due to the high cost of buying, large deposit requirement and the high interest rate on mortgaging. Houses in the open market are too expensive for the low-income segments. Certainly, the high cost of housing is due to the high cost of land, which is a consequence of the liberalisation of the land market and its accompanied speculative activities escalating land prices. Thus, the adoption of neoliberal housing policy in Ghana has resulted in the overproduction of housing for the high-income segment with little to none for low-income earners. Consequently, worsening the marginalisation of low-income groups, especially, the urban poor to depend on the informal sector for housing provision. Indeed, lack of direct government involvement in the housing market has resulted in the development of slums and inadequate housing in the country, especially in urban areas where domestic and foreign private developers focus on expensive houses for high-income earners.

5 Financial Sector Reforms in Ghana – A Historical Perspective

This section presents events in the pre- as well as post-structural adjustment financial sector reforms that cover the privatisation of state financial institutions together with the various changes in the financial sector.

5.1 Pre-structural Adjustment Financial Reforms 1957–1982

The financial sector in Ghana was dominated by state ownership between 1957 and 1982. Successive governments, since independence, established state banks to widen access to credit facilities to SMEs. The reason that prompted this was the fact that Barclays Bank Ghana Ltd., and Standard Chartered Bank (the only two existing (foreign) banks at the time) were reluctant to lend to domestic households, farmers, and SMEs due to high default rates. In response, eight state banks were established between 1953 and 1977 to provide credit to priority areas. Furthermore, the state acquired a 40% stake in Barclays and Standard Chartered Banks (Bank of Ghana 2000). Thus, the state banks dominate the banking industry pre-financial liberalisation era.

The pre-liberalised era also featured a fixed exchange rate and state control of the money supply. Different economic policies by the successive governments resulted in a series of devaluations notably in 1967, 1971 and 1978 (discussed above). There were some re-valuations in the period as well. The lack of a competitive environment in the banking sector coupled with political patronage led to inefficiencies in the industry. However, the priority sectors in the economy were not starved of the needed credit.

The high inflation rate accompanied by the negative real interest rates discouraged savings in the banking sectors, which led to excess liquidity stored outside the formal financial system. This undermined the mobilisation of savings to facilitate the private sector's investment. The inefficiencies also impeded financial deepening and solvencies in the banking sector. Consequently, policy recommendations concluded that the Ghanaian economy could attain faster growth with financial sector reforms. Husain and Faruqee (1994) assert that mobilising the 16% savings stored outside the banking industry could stimulate growth rates and reduce poverty levels by a percentage point. In response to these financial sector inefficiencies, the government accepted, as part of SAP, the Financial Institution Sector Adjustment Programme (FINSAP 1 in 1983) and (FINSAP 2 in 1990).

5.2   *Post-liberalised Reforms*

The contemporary financial liberalisation has its roots in SAP. FINSAP 1 was aimed at restructuring the banking sector by mobilising savings and facilitating credit allocation. It also featured the establishment of Non-Performing Asset Recovery Trust (NPART) with interest-bearing bonds, which were redeemable in yearly instalments within 6 years. The Banking Act of 1970 was not explicit on the minimum capital requirements and risk exposure. This was amended under the 1989 Banking Act, which mandates banks to hold 6% as the minimum capital requirement and operational rights to set interest rates.

FINSAP 2 was implemented in 1990 with the aim of establishing money and capital markets, speed up loan recovery by NPART and privatisation of state-owned banks. These were embarked on to promote competition and efficiency in the financial sector. The argument was that it would facilitate the private sector as the engine of growth. The Ghana Stock Exchange was established in 1990 with 12 listed companies and one government bond.

The government of Ghana initiated the Financial Sector Strategic Plan (FINSSP) in 2001 to further liberalise and deregulate the financial sector. The major development under FINSSP included central bank independence to promote price stability. Accordingly, the Monetary Policy Committee was established to set the policy rate to act as a benchmark rate for setting interest rates by other financial institutions. One notable development under FINSSP central to the argument in this book is the concept of Universal Banking ACT 2003.[12] This permits banks to perform investment, commercial and other activities without the need for a new/different licence. Accordingly, banks may choose to undertake any banking services in line with their capital and risk appetite. This was meant to facilitate flexibility of doing all banking activities with just one bank and encourage banks to engage in mortgage financing, insurance business, and other banking activities enshrined in the universal banking laws. However, banks were required to adhere to new capital requirements to qualify for the universal banking license. The risk of this universal banking reform is the systemic risk – where a risk to one arm of a bank spreads to all parts and the entire financial system and the real sector of the economy.

In 2004, a new regulatory change was enacted – the Banking Act (Act 673) to replace the existing banking laws. Some of the essential modifications include the expansion of the definition of banking activities to cover insurance business, mortgage financing, securities, portfolio management, and advisory services which comprise capital restructuring, mergers and acquisitions, credit reference services, and the keeping and administration of securities. The new Act gave credence to the universal banking model of relaxing bank activity restrictions.

This new banking status represents a significant shift from the traditional functions of commercial banks mobilising savings and advancing customer-specific loans that were kept on banks' balance sheets for the duration of the loan. This has enabled universal banks to search for new fields of profitability. As Lapavitsas (2009a; 2013) argued, banks can now generate profits by mediating transactions in open markets due to their investment banking status. At the same time, banks can make profits from households by providing mortgages and other unsecured loans. He remarks that securitisation epitomises a sharp acceleration of the trend towards investment banking, widely adopted by commercial banks. Lapavitsas concludes that

---

12   The banking laws before 2003 categorised banks into commercial, merchant and development banks and therefore banks were restricted in scope- what banks could engage in, and geography- where they choose to operate.

these new ways of bank profitability are what constitute the financialisation of personal income of households/workers. Davis and Kim (2015) add that securitisation epitomises a fundamental shift in how contemporary finance is carried out. They argue that traditionally (pre-liberalisation and deregulation periods), commercial banks provide mortgage loans and hold them in their books until the maturity date of the loan; they termed this *'originate-and-hold'*.

However, in the post-liberalisation and deregulation era, mortgages provided by commercial banks are sold off to securitisation trusts, which turn them into securities and trade them to financial investors, what the authors called *'originate-and-distribute'*. Thus, securitisation changes the *'originate-and-hold' long-term* relationship between a bank and its customers (a loan taker) into an abstract *'originate-and-distribute'* relationship between households and an unknown financial investor. This new relationship makes commercial banks mere underwriters of the mortgages/loans, while the loan takers are now the de facto issuers of securities on the international financial markets. This is a fundamental shift in financial intermediation from banks to financial markets.

5.3 *Relaxation of Bank Entry Restrictions, and Abolishment of Secondary Reserve Requirements 2005–2006*

As part of the reforms, and to enhance competition and efficiency, the Bank of Ghana in 2005 relaxed bank entry restrictions. Consequently, it adopted an open but gradual licensing approach that allows the entry of new domestic and foreign private banks. This approach was expected to encourage the modernisation of banking operations and facilitate the efficiency of the industry. The central bank in July 2005 reduced the secondary reserve requirements of banks from 35% to just 15%, and further abolished the 15% in August 2006, leaving only the primary reserve requirements of 9% held in cash (the secondary reserve requirements act as additional liquidity for banks). The cancelling of the secondary reserve requirements increased the supply of loanable funds to the private sector, enhanced competition in the loan market and deepened financial intermediation. Foreign bank entry in domestic financial markets has been argued to be a decisive feature of international financialisation (Dos Santos 2009; Tabb 2013; Storm 2018).

5.4 *Recapitalising Banks*

To improve stability and enhance credit anticipated by the reforms, the Bank of Ghana occasionally revised the minimum capital requirement upwards. The more recent recapitalisation was by increasing the minimum capital requirements to Ghc 400 million from Ghc 120 million (i.e., from US$ 12.7 million to US$ 84.6 million, based on the Bank of Ghana interbank exchange rate on 17th August 2018). This has drawn mixed reactions on the likely impact on the industry (Ghana Banking Survey, 2018) (PwC 2018). While some stakeholders commended the directive, others expressed concern about the impact on the industry and the economy at large. With this recapitalisation, both local and foreign banks were expected to comply with the directives by December 2018.[13] In line with international standards and practices, the Central Bank increased the Capital Adequacy Ratio (CAR) from 6% to 10% (see appendix 1 for the various financial sector reforms).

Nigeria, like Ghana, has a history of recapitalising banks. In 2005, the Central Bank of Nigeria (CBN) raised the minimum capital requirements from N1 billion to N25 billion (i.e., from US$ 7.7 million to US$ 192.2 million based on the CBN average interbank rate for December 2005). As is currently being witnessed in Ghana, uncertainties existed over the future of the Nigerian banking sector as the destiny of many banks hung in the balance. However, during the 16 months window, banks used different methods (including mergers) to raise the necessary capital to meet the directive (PwC 2018). A similar trend is anticipated in the Ghana banking industry.

Supporters of the new capital requirement argue that few big banks will help accelerate economic growth and can underwrite big-ticket items as well as remain competitive and liquid. Besides, they believe stronger and larger banks can help decrease credit cost, improve access to credit, and reduce non-performing loans, amongst others. They also compare Ghana's economy to larger economies like Nigeria and South Africa, with few but stronger and liquid banks. Nigeria has 24 banks, while South Africa has 19 universal banks compared to 34 universal banks in Ghana (Bank of Ghana 2018).

6 Financialisation in Sub-Saharan Africa: Accounting for the Ghanaian Paradox

At the macroeconomic level and relative to the core and semi-periphery countries, Ghana's financial system is underdeveloped. Industrial enterprises are more reliant on bank credit as opposed to the core countries where capital markets development enable large firms to access debt and equity financing.

---

13   Local banks have always been given longer time than foreign banks in the previous recapitalisation of the industry. For instance, in 2008, local banks were given up to 2012 to comply while foreign already in the country were to comply by December 2009.

Besides, the numerous reforms and the privatisation of state-owned banks did not increase banking competition in the country. Banks continue to lend disproportionately to the government, which in turn crowds out the private sector. However, deregulation and the liberalisation of the financial market attracted more foreign banks into the economy with new forms of financial services, with lending and profit-making shifting towards households' income. The capital flows associated with the liberalisation of the capital account have resulted in a reversal of net capital flows.

6.1   Under-financed

Periphery countries can be assumed to have, 'all other things being equal', low levels of financial sector deepening relative to the overall size of the economic output. Besides, the financial deepening of an economy mirrors the specificities of the country's historical and institutional settings. Ghana, by international standard measures, is under-financed. Goldsmith (1969) argues that the proportion of the financial sector relative to a country's growth will rise in line with the prosperity of the country, levelling out around 3–4 times of GDP. Ghana, on the other hand, displays financial under-development even when compared to other low middle-income countries. This under-development is noticeable in the overall monetary aggregates, the ratio of broad money relative to GDP, the ratio of stock market capitalisation to GDP, total credit to the private non-financial sector, bank assets relative to GDP and ATM/Bank branches per 1000km^2. Following the financial sector reforms in the country, the domestic banking industry opened to foreign competition. The banking industry is highly diversified, comprising of 34 licensed universal banks, 17 of the foreign-owned banks accounting for almost 54% of the total industry market share in 2018. Apart from these universal banks, there are 138 Rural and Community Banks (RCBs), which account for 3.2% of total financial sector assets. There are also 63 Non-Banking Financial Institutions (NBFIS), and 503 Microfinance Institutions (Bank of Ghana 2018). The dominance of foreign-owned banks in the Ghanaian banking sector demonstrates a financial system that is vulnerable to shocks from the global financial system (table 3).

The universal banks in Ghana consist of about 85% of the total banking assets and mainly offer credit to corporate customers and concentrate on the regional capitals. Because of the high minimum deposit requirements, it is estimated that universal banks reach only about 5% of households. In contrast, RCBs extend credit to farmers, government employees and small and micro businesses and entrepreneurs and represent about 5% of total banking assets, but account for half of the total banking outlets in the country (Africa Development Bank 2012). RCBs and other informal systems offer an important

THE CASE OF GHANA 123

TABLE 3   List of universal banks in Ghana as of June 2018

Name of bank	Year bank commenced business	Majority ownership	No. of branches
Access Bank (Ghana) Limited	2008	Foreign	47
Agricultural Development Bank Limited	1965	Local	78
Bank of Africa Ghana Limited	1997	Foreign	26
Bank of Baroda Ghana Limited	2007	Foreign	3
Barclays Bank Ghana Limited	1917	Foreign	60
CalBank Limited	1990	Local	30
Ecobank Ghana limited	1990	Foreign	68
Energy Commercial Bank Limited	2011	Foreign	12
FBNBank Ghana limited	1996	Foreign	18
Fidelity Bank Ghana Limited	2006	Local	72
First Atlantic Bank Limited	1994	Foreign	31
First National Bank	2015	Foreign	7
GCB Bank Limited	1953	Local	183
GHL Bank Limited	2017	Local	4
GN Bank Limited	2014	Local	298
Guaranty Trust Bank (Ghana) Limited	2004	Foreign	32
Heritage Bank Limited	2016	Local	6
National Investment Bank Limited	1963	Local	49
OmniBank Ghana Limited	2016	Local	25
Premium Bank Ghana Limited	2016	Local	4
Prudential Bank Limited	1993	Local	40
Republic Bank Ghana Limited	1990	Foreign	43
Sahel Sahara Bank Ghana Limited	2008	Foreign	17
Societe General Ghana Limited	1975	Foreign	43
Sovereign Bank Limited	2016	Local	4
Stanbic Bank Ghana limited	1999	Foreign	39
Standard Chartered Bank Ghana Limited	1896	Foreign	27
The Biege Bank	2017	Local	70
The Construction Bank (Gh) Limited	2017	Local	1
The Royal Bank Limited	2011	Local	28
UniBank Ghana Limited	2001	Local	57

TABLE 3 List of universal banks in Ghana as of June 2018 (*cont.*)

Name of bank	Year bank commenced business	Majority ownership	No. of branches
United Bank for Africa (Ghana) Limited	2005	Foreign	28
Universal Merchant Bank Limited	1971	Local	38
Zenith Bank (Ghana) Limited	2005	Foreign	27

SOURCE: GHANA BANKING SURVEY (2018)

role in extending credit to the private sector and households to smooth out investment and consumption. These banks are particularly important in the development of rural areas.

Financial development has been measured by various financial indicators, such as the ratio of the money supply to GDP (Goldsmith 1969; Levine 2005). To measure financial depth in the periphery, the IMF has been using the ratio of broad money[14] relative to economic growth. Figure 6 below shows that Ghana's financial depth (a measure of the financial sector relative to the economic output) is relatively less than South Africa and certainly far less than the UK. The ratio of broad money relative to GDP has remained below 30% until 2011 when it increased to 32%. Since then, it has remained 32%. The ratio in South Africa has averaged 70%, more than doubled Ghana's during the period, while the UK peaked at 165% in 2009.

Another measure of financial depth is the stock market capitalisation, which is the market value of a publicly traded company's outstanding shares. Figure 7 below reveals that Ghana's stock market is underdeveloped, relative to other low middle-income countries, such as Indonesia and India. This underdevelopment of the stock markets limits firms' ability to raise capital for investment purposes. There is no available data available for Ghana from 2012, as shown in figure 7.

---

14   Broad money represents the total amount of money (notes and coins) that households and businesses can use for payments or hold as short-term instruments such as cash, bank account, gilts representing country's money supply.

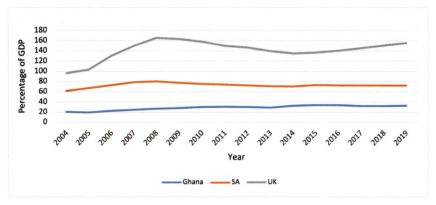

FIGURE 6   Broad money relative to GDP 2004–2018 – selected countries
SOURCE: AUTHOR'S ESTIMATES, FIGURES FROM THE FEDERAL RESERVE
HTTPS://FRED.STLOUISFED.ORG/ AND THE IMF

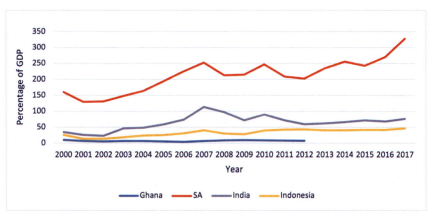

FIGURE 7   Stock market capitalisation relative to GDP – selected countries (2000–2017)
SOURCE: AUTHOR'S ESTIMATES, FIGURES FROM THE FEDERAL RESERVE
HTTPS://FRED.STLOUISFED.ORG/ AND THE IMF

In terms of market-based finance, stock market capitalisation relative to GDP in Ghana has been very low, averaging about 6% of GDP. The highest was in the year 2000 when stock market capitalisation was 9.8% of GDP, while the lowest was during 2006 at 3.4% of GDP. Ghana's stock market capitalisation has been below that of South Africa, India, and Indonesia, depicting an underfinanced economy.

It was thought that during the recent recapitalisation of banks (discussed above) the Ghana Stock Exchange would be the vehicle where banks could raise the needed capital to meet the requirements. However, it failed to raise the combined amount of GHc 4.7 billion ($530 million) needed in time. This is partly due to low investor interest in the *bourse* because of the closure of seven banks recently and high yield on government securities. The lucrative high returns on government securities coupled with its low-risk nature made them a better choice for investors. For instance, with government securities trading at 14% in the primary market, and 20% in the secondary market, investors will opt for profitable securities than to play on the stock market (PwC 2018). The low liquidity on the bourse is a challenge for fund managers to trade en bloc, hence their general aversion to the capital market.

Figure 8 shows that credit provided by domestic banks to the private non-financial sector (include corporations and households) in Ghana has been rising steadily but relatively low compared to South Africa, India, and Indonesia. This was at just 7.2% in 2000 but rose to 17.8% in 2016. Private sector credit in India rose from 62% in 2000 to 71.6% in 2016, while in South Africa it has been above 70% during the period. The figure had plateaued in Indonesia at around 38% over the period. This is another standard measure illustrating financial underdevelopment in Ghana.

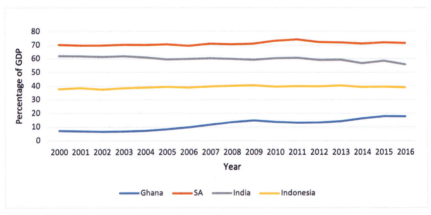

FIGURE 8   Total credit to private non-financial sector – selected countries (2000–2016)
SOURCE: AUTHOR'S ESTIMATES, FIGURES FROM THE FEDERAL RESERVE HTTPS://FRED.STLOUISFED.ORG/ AND THE IMF

Deposit Money Bank (DMB) asset is another indicator of the depth of the financial market. Figure 9 illustrates the underdevelopment of the financial sector in Ghana. Both central bank assets and deposit money bank assets started in 1973 at 8% and 7%, respectively. Central bank assets have been higher than deposit money bank assets for most of the pre-financial reform periods. However, since 2004, deposit money bank assets have been higher

THE CASE OF GHANA   127

than the central bank assets with the gap getting wider every year over the period shown. For example, in 2013, deposit money assets relative to GDP was 24% while that of the central bank was under 9%; however, in 2016 the figures were 27% and 9.5%, respectively. It should be acknowledged that financial reforms (discussed above) might have contributed to this asymmetry. The Bank of Ghana attained its independence in 2002 while the universal banking Act was enacted in 2003. Other reform issues such as recapitalisation of banks, relaxation of Bank Entry Restrictions, and Abolishment of Secondary Reserve Requirements 2005–06 may also have contributed to the increase in DMB assets relative to GDP in the economy. However, despite these increases, financial sector development in Ghana based on the evidence above is relatively weak.

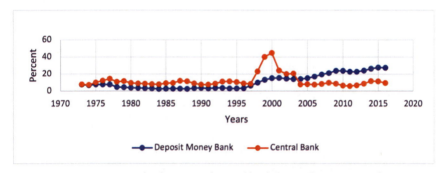

FIGURE 9   Deposit money bank assets and central bank assets relative to GDP Ghana (1973–2016)
SOURCE: AUTHOR'S ESTIMATES, FIGURES FROM THE FEDERAL RESERVE HTTPS://FRED.STLOUISFED.ORG/ AND THE BANK OF GHANA (2018)

Apart from these conventional ways of examining the size and intermediation of financial sector development in a country, this book goes beyond the traditional measures by using new indicators to examine financial access – bank branches per 1000km^2 and bank accounts for 15 years and over. Financial access demonstrates the ability of individuals and businesses to obtain financial services, including credit, deposit, payment and other financial products. Those individuals and businesses that have no or minimal access to any financial services are known as the unbanked and underserved, respectively.

Figure 10 demonstrates further a weak financial sector in Ghana. The number of adults with accounts at a formal financial institution in Ghana has been below 40% throughout the period except for 2017 when it rose to 42% of the market segment. On the other hand, South Africa and India have more than half of the adult population with an account at a formal financial institution. They peaked at 68% and 79%, respectively. Indonesia was below Ghana between 2012 and 2014 at 19%, but since 2014 has been marginally higher than Ghana and peaked at 48% in 2017. This measure of access illustrates that financial sector development in Ghana is not strong by international standards.

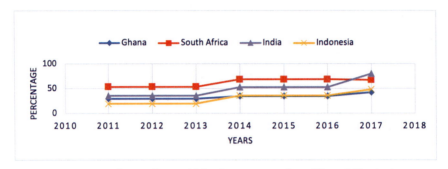

FIGURE 10   15 years of age and over with bank account at a formal financial institution – selected countries 2011–2017
SOURCE: AUTHOR'S ESTIMATES, FIGURES FROM THE FEDERAL RESERVE HTTPS://FRED.STLOUISFED.ORG/

According to the World Bank (2013) report on access to financial services in Ghana, 40% of the extremely poor, 29% of women and 27% of the youth had no access to banking services. Moreover, residents in rural regions are less likely than those in urban areas to access and use financial services. Several reasons could account for this, including the availability and proximity to a bank and the ability to offer the minimum deposit required to access and use financial services. As most poor people live in rural areas, it is not surprising that there is a lack of access and use of financial services. The report further outlines that in high-income countries such as the USA, the UK and other core economies, over 90% of adults have a bank account. This is in contrast to 57% in the upper-middle-income countries, 28% in the lower middle income and just 24% in the lower-income countries. On this account, it could be argued that 42% of financial access in Ghana, a low middle-income country, demonstrates a lower number of unbanked and underserved compared to the average low middle-income economy. Accordingly, this is the Ghana paradox.

Figure 11 shows the geographical outreach of universal/commercial bank branches per 1000km^2. This measure of financial sector access shows that only two commercial bank branches were available in 1000km^2 geographical outreach during 2006. At its peak in 2017 (with all the waves of financial sector reforms that followed SAP) the figure shows only 6.6 branches in geographical outreach of commercial/universal bank branches per 1000km² demonstrating an underdeveloped financial sector.

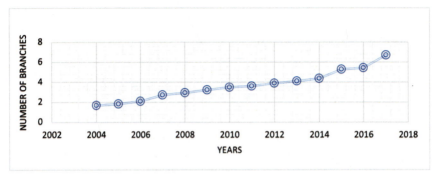

FIGURE 11   Commercial/universal bank branches per 1000km² in Ghana (2004- 2017)
SOURCE: AUTHOR'S ESTIMATES, FIGURES FROM THE FEDERAL RESERVE HTTPS://FRED.STLOUISFED.ORG/ AND THE BANK OF GHANA (2018)

The analyses presented demonstrate that Ghana is relatively under-financed by international standard measures. However, despite the under-financed position of the country, it is essential to assess if Ghana is financialising. To address this paradox, it is crucial to examine the macroeconomic picture of the country.

6.2   ... Yet Financialising

The dominance of the financial sector over the rest of the economy has been one of the crucial aspects of financialisation in the core. The rising proportion of bank assets relative to GDP indicate financial sector depth. Figure 12 depicts a sudden rise in bank assets as a share of GDP (albeit under-financed economy) during 1997 FINSAP and continues to increase every year over the period. For those economies considered as archetypes of financialisation – the UK and the US, the proportion of DMB assets relative to GDP has been intense, as shown in figure 13.

For example, in the US, DMB assets remained around 60% of GDP since 1973, while in the UK the figure peaked at 200% in 2009 and steadily declined to 1.3 times of GDP. Given this evidence, with the rate at which the financial sector is vigorously expanding, it is not difficult to present Ghana as either financialised or financialising.

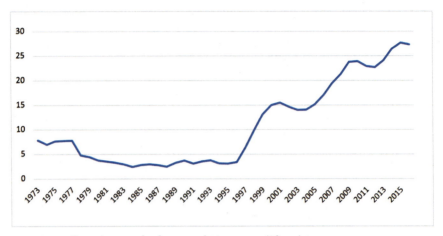

FIGURE 12 Deposit money bank assets relative to GDP (Ghana) 1975–2015
SOURCE: AUTHOR'S ESTIMATES, FIGURES FROM THE FEDERAL RESERVE HTTPS://FRED.STLOUISFED.ORG/ AND THE IMF

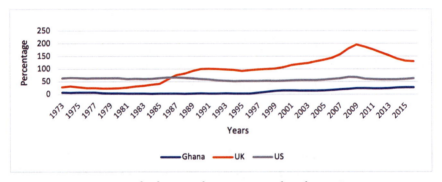

FIGURE 13 Deposit money bank assets relative to GDP – selected countries 1973–2015
SOURCE: AUTHOR'S ESTIMATES, FIGURES FROM THE FEDERAL RESERVE HTTPS://FRED.STLOUISFED.ORG/ AND THE IMF

Another measure of international financialisation is the rise of cross-border capital flows. The growth of these flows into periphery countries constitutes the global dimension of financialisation (Lapavitsas 2013; Stockhammer 2012b; Dos Santos 2013). As Gabor (2012) argued, the inflows of investment of foreign banks contribute to the financialisation of domestic financial systems. Ghana is not new to foreign banks; after all, the first two banks in the country during the colonial era were foreign-owned banks. However, Lapavitsas (2009a) argues that foreign bank entry facilitates financialisation in the periphery countries. The growth of foreign banks in the domestic financial market appears that the

THE CASE OF GHANA 131

banking sector is exceptionally profitable and thereby attracting foreign entry. Foreign banks' entry into the Ghanaian financial market has complex outcomes on the growth and performance of the sector. Advocates of financial globalisation argue the superior efficiencies in improving domestic financial systems and enhancing credit shortages for SMEs (Demirgüç-Kunt and Huizinga 2001; Clarke et al. 2003). However, there are doubts among mainstream economists on whether foreign banks have the appropriate skills to assess the *soft* information needed for lending to SMEs in the periphery countries (Detragiache, Tressel, and Gupta 2008).

Foreign bank entry in Ghana has been on the rise, and their assets accounted for 69% at the end of 2012 (see figure 14). These banks have expanded the provision of mortgages and credit cards to domestic workers facilitating the financialisation of households' income.

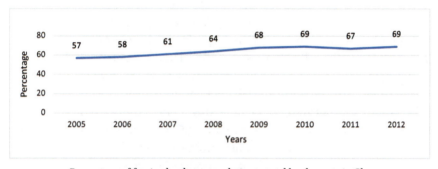

FIGURE 14   Percentage of foreign bank assets relative to total bank assets in Ghana 2005–2012
SOURCE: AUTHOR'S ESTIMATES, FIGURES FROM THE FEDERAL RESERVE HTTPS://FRED.STLOUISFED.ORG/ AND THE BANK PF GHANA (2016)

One notable consequence of foreign bank entry in Ghana has been the dynamics of lending practices. The expansion of lending aimed at personal incomes of high-income and middle-income workers, the introduction of mortgage and credit card lending as well as other financial services are noticeable. The lucrative and profitable nature of these practices has lured local banks into the field, thereby accelerating the financialisation of personal income.

P.L. Dos Santos (2013; 2012) presents evidence suggesting that foreign banks are the key agencies accelerating financialised activities; that is, making an excessive profit through practices that are unrelated to lending, such as trading, commission and assertive household lending. The key feature has been rising personal indebtedness because of these activities. He highlights credit cards and mortgage debt in Brazil as consequences of foreign bank entry. Mader (2015) remarks that the aggressive lending by foreign banks and microfinance contributed to the 2010 Indian crisis, which was marked by over-indebtedness, suicides and violence. The evidence in Ghana is still inconsistent, but the pace of change is frightening among the middle-income segment (see table 13 for the growth of credit cards issued).

Another notable thread in the literature of financialisation is the power and rising financial profit relative to the productive sector. Examining financialisation in the US, Krippner (2005; 2011) finds the dominant power of Finance, Insurance and Real Estate (FIRE) share of output. She reported that FIRE has grown from 10% of output in the post-war era to almost 25% in the early 2000s. However, the change in FIRE share of employment in the US marginally increased from 5% to 7%. Lack of data makes it challenging to estimate profitability by sectors in Ghana. However, banks profit before tax margin and Return on Equity give an indication of profitability in the industry.

Figure 15 illustrates a healthy profit before tax margin. The banking industry net profit before tax increased by 30.7% from GHc 2.54 billion ($432 million) in 2016 to GHc 3.32 billion ($565 million) in 2017, which shows a higher growth than 2016. Profit before tax margin of 36.4% in 2017 is the highest margin since 2015. Details of the Ghana Banking survey 2018 shows that the banking industry net interest income also increased from GHc 6.1 billion ($1037 million) in 2016 to GHc 6.5 billion ($1105 million) in 2017, a growth of 6%. The increase in interest income from cash and short-term funds and investment security in 2017 was significantly less than in 2016, which is primarily due to the decline in yield of government securities in 2017. The report further adds that fees and commission income grew by 10% in 2017, which was largely attributed to the strong economic growth in the country.

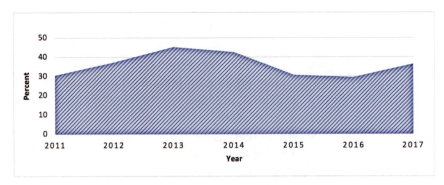

FIGURE 15　Universal banks profit before tax margin (2011–2017)
SOURCE: AUTHOR'S ESTIMATES, FIGURES FROM THE GHANA BANKING SURVEY (2012–2018)

The strong performance from trading income, fees and commissions and investment income improved the overall industry profitability despite slow growth in the industry interest income – a feature of contemporary financialised capitalism. However, it is worth noting that the top ten banks share on the average 60% net profit before tax margin, and the industry holdings of government securities increased by 43%. The data also reveals that 57% of Ghana commercial bank's (GCB) – the largest domestic bank, investment income came from government securities, a useful and secure source of income for the banking sector.

Another measure of profitability is the Return on Equity (RoE).[15] This indicates how shareholders'/investors' funds are used to generate profit/net income in a business. A sustainable and positive RoE as in the case of Ghana means the banking industry is generating shareholder value by making profitable investments, which generate returns.

Figure 16 shows that RoE in the Ghana banking industry has been higher and positive throughout the period. With an average RoE of 41.9% for Ghana, 10.4% for the UK and 9% for the US, there is no doubt as to why foreign banks are attracted to the Ghanaian financial sector. The industry RoE recovered from the decline to 11% (the lowest in the industry history in 2009 – which may be due to the global financial crisis) and recorded a healthy return of 21.9% in 2016. This is due to stronger profit performance in recent years. The industry net profit increased by 29.3% to GHc 2.3 billion ($391 million) in 2016. Thus, as long as rising financial profits could be used as a measure of financialisation (as in the literature), Ghana could be argued to be financialising.

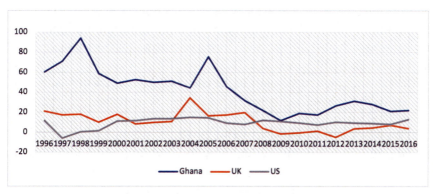

FIGURE 16   Return on equity for Ghana, the UK and the US banks
SOURCE: AUTHOR'S ESTIMATES, FIGURES FROM THE GHANA BANKING SURVEY (2000–2018) AND THE FEDERAL RESERVE HTTPS://FRED.STLOUISFED.ORG/

---

15   Return on Equity (RoE) is calculated as net income/profit divided by shareholders equity. The higher the RoE, the more efficient managers generate income from equity financing.

This increasing dominance of the financial sector relative to industry and agriculture, and the incessant short-term lending to government and households instead of long-term lending to industry suggests that the Ghanaian economy (albeit under-financed) is financialising.

Ordinary Ghanaians have been drawn into the realm of finance because the continuous economic growth has not been shared equitably; wages have been stagnant while industry and agriculture profits have been falling. Households need access to healthcare, education, housing and a variety of other needs. The state historically provided some of these needs. However, a new phenomenon emerged since the implementation of SAP, which has been a retreat of the state and introduction of private provision. As this is happening, finance has emerged as a facilitator, thus, financial markets make profits from household needs of these social amenities. Changes in institutions and ideology through waves of deregulations in both the labour market and financial markets have given rise to neoliberalism – the idea that the state is bad, and the market is good. These changes have created a profoundly unequal society. Lapavitsas (2011; 2013) and Harvey (2005) argue that financialisation is fundamentally about inequality epitomised by the changing behaviour/conduct between banks, industrial enterprises, and households. Thus, finance has acted as a critical lever in increasing inequality by creating wealth through access to financial assets and privileged ways of trading and positioning in the financial system.

Ghanaian household financialisation, like many in the periphery, is distinct from the core. Banks lend to the government while households are increasing their borrowing, predominantly the middle class of a short-term nature through hire purchase and loan advances. Microfinance, Susu schemes,[16] and mobile money platforms target the informal sector with short-term loan advances with high interest rates. However, on the macroeconomic level, financialisation is still very low.

The evidence presented points to the fact that Ghana's case of financialisation is a *subordinate/inferior* one, which is an uneven combination of the transformations that characterise inter-sectoral relations in a new era of capitalism. That is, Ghana is under-financed yet financialising. When the banking system and other financial institutions focus on making quick financial returns rather than making a real long-term investment, the economy balloons and creates a bubble that awaits bursting. Making money out of money with the capitalists eating off the hard labour of the poor, thus, the ordinary Ghanaian dream of

---

16   This is an informal means of collecting and saving money through a savings club or partnership.

sharing national prosperity has been taken by rather a few elites. For the rest of the citizens, prosperity has only been accessible on credit. The lower and middle-income households took on more debt to finance spending on education, healthcare and housing. This practice has been facilitated by the deregulation and liberalisation of the financial markets, which attract households with a modest income to borrow in order to meet their basic spending needs. Therefore, the Ghanaian economy is financialising using international standard measures. However, there are some distinct characteristics of financialisation in Ghana, due to the underdeveloped nature of the financial sector.

6.3 Reverse of Net Capital Flows – A Subordinate/Inferior Financialisation

The origin of financialisation in SSA can be found in SAP and its related liberalisation and deregulation of the financial sector in the 1980s, which abolished price and quantity control in domestic financial systems. The World Bank and the IMF steered periphery countries to adopt market-based domestic finance to open up domestic economies to global capital markets, with the view that capital would flow to the periphery countries to stimulate economic development. However, it has been shown that as periphery countries become more closely integrated with the global capital markets, capital flows in the opposite direction – from the periphery to the core countries, a trend Powell (2013), and later Lapavitsas (2013) term *subordinate financialisation*.[17]

Lapavitsas (2009b; 2013) asserts that capital flows have become negative on the net basis for the periphery countries, notably SSA. This, he argues, has been a striking feature of international financialisation, marking a profound difference with the period of imperialism. This is because the reverse flow of capital has not been initiated in actions taken by capitalist enterprises and other private agents but originated in actions taken by the monetary authorities in both core and periphery countries and reinforced by the international monetary systems through the World Bank and the IMF. He concludes that the reverse capital flows are associated with the contemporary role of the US dollar as the world quasi-money, which has affected the hierarchy among capitalist economies in the global market as well as lending a subordinate character of financialisation in the periphery. This is a process Gowan (1999) refers to as '*Dollar Wall Street Regime Theory*' (DWSR). He argues that the vast majority of countries would like to hold the US dollar as their preferred reserves because most

---

17   Jeff Powell (2013) first suggested subordinate financialisation in his analysis of Mexican non-financial corporations, and later by Costas Lapavitsas (2013:245 see footnote).

commodities are traded in US dollars. This strengthens Wall Street as an international financial centre, enhancing the supremacy of the dollar. Tabb (2013) presents that between January 1999 and July 2008 the global official reserves held in the form of US government or government agency security increased by 368% from $1.6 billion to $7.5 billion.

The key features to *subordinate financialisation* have been the flows of both international capital and international trade, particularly after the Asian crisis of 1997–98. Based on international trade, three broad sets of periphery countries stand out. The first consists of countries that have gained share in global manufacturing, most importantly the BRICs economies (semi-periphery), and thus earned large surpluses from export to the core, including consumer goods to the US and Western Europe. The second set of countries consists of hard commodities exporters such as oil and metal. Rising commodity prices have resulted in considerable trade surpluses. The third set of countries comprises producers and exporters of agricultural raw materials. Unfortunately, countries in the third category, notably in SSA operate substantial trade deficits.

However, judging by exports' relative GDP, there has been some minimal improvement, thus, the closer integration of SSA into the world market as forced policies of trade liberalisation during the 1980s has not been generally positive. Consequently, the trajectory of the current account in the era of trade liberalisation has varied considerably among periphery countries in line with trade specialisation and other historically specific factors (Lapavitsas 2013; Bortz and Kaltenbrunner 2018).

Accumulation of reserve is ultimately the reason why the net international flow of capital has been reversed, leading to capital flowing from the periphery to core economies. Bortz and Kaltenbrunner (2018) argue that periphery countries occupy lower ranks of the global currency hierarchy and thereby have to accumulate a large amount of forex reserve as a rational response to sudden capital outflows. The *subordinate* global currency hierarchy forces these countries to adopt high interest rates to maintain the domestic currency, which in turn induces hot money flows. The World Bank and the IMF monitoring the levels of reserves relating to exports and domestic monetary growth have actively prescribed *self-insurance*. In practice, Tabb (2013) and Lapavitsas (2013) reckon three rules have been used. These are: first, the ratio of reserves to imports should be enough to defend any unexpected worsening of the balance of trade, which is a crucial problem in SSA. Secondly, the ratio of reserves to short-term external debt should be sufficient to cover all short-term external debt due for a period ahead, usually twelve months (the Greenspan-Guidotti rule). Finally, the ratio of reserves to the money supply should be enough to defend any unexpected capital outflow (typically reserves should correspond to 20% of M2).

Furthermore, reserve accumulation has also been due to exchange rate policies adopted by SSA countries. Hard commodities exporting countries that have current account surpluses have attempted to keep their currency from rising to be internationally competitive. However, targeting inflation, which has been a feature in neoliberalisation, means that exchange rates were pegged against the US dollar and other major trading currencies to control imported inflation. To be able to defend the peg, central banks in SSA have to accumulate large reserves as a buffer to be able to manipulate the exchange rate. By the same token of controlling inflation, SSA has adopted high-interest rates, which have resulted in even rising exchange rates at the same time, a paradox emerges. The higher domestic interest rate has fuelled forms of *'carry trade'* where domestic residents' borrowing from abroad in order to invest in financial assets in SSA. As borrowers abroad increased, so did the pressure to hold more reserves. Investors, seeking ways to benefit from the financial market turned to currency speculation, a feature that has grown significantly. Tabb (2013) contends that the average daily trading volume rose by 20% to $4 trillion in 2010. For many SSA countries, sudden movement of speculative capital in and out of their economies characterises a clear and sustain danger. Monetary authorities are cautious in announcing policy rate changes in advance for the fear of rapid movement in currency speculation and its destabilising impact on the macroeconomy.

The costs of reserves accumulation have been high, measured either as spread between domestic and foreign interest rates or as the cost of sterilisation by central banks. Lapavitsas (2013) sees it as the periphery countries paying explicit tribute to the core countries, notably the US.

Ghana has a long, albeit modest history of capital flows. The early establishment was predominantly in import-substitution industrialisation. However, the introduction of SAP commenced a relatively successful transition to the market-based open economy. The initial surge in Foreign Direct Investment (FDI) was in response to policies adopted in 1986 to attract investment into natural resources after the new mining laws were passed. The privatisation of SOEs and most notably the partial privatisation of Ashanti Goldfields Corporation to the South African mining company *Lonmin* in 1994 attracted a total of $233 million of FDI (UNCTAD, 2011). Telekom Malaysia also acquired 30% shares in state-owned Ghana telecom. The discovery of oil and subsequent production in commercial quantities has attracted FDI to this and related sectors in the economy. The recent recapitalisation of universal banks is expected to result in mergers and acquisitions that will fuel capital inflow into the economy.

TABLE 4   Trade balance, current transfers and net capital flows to Ghana (in millions US$) 2003–2014

US$. Million

	2003	2004	2005	2006	2007	2008	2009	2010	2011	2012	2013	2014
Current transfers	1,244.9	1,579.9	1,794.2	2,248.3	2,043.2	2,211.5	2,078.0	2,322.4	2,597.4	2,405.3	1,939.4	1,878.4
Private transfers (net)	1,017.2	1,287.1	1,549.8	1,644.6	1,833.8	1,970.4	1,788.4	2,122.7	2,368.8	2,147.5	1,859.2	1,868.8
Official transfer(net)	227.7	292.9	244.5	603.7	209.4	241.1	289.6	199.7	228.7	257.8	80.3	9.6
Current account balance	325.4	-303.3	-831.0	-768.7	-1,843.4	-3,113.3	-1,687.7	-2,769.7	-3,770.1	-5,168.5	-5,704.1	-3,564.7
Capital and finance account	494.7	452.6	1,165.7	1,484.9	2,866.6	2,943.3	4,327.6	4,289.5	4,479.3	3,651.3	5,368.2	3,270.1
Financial account	340.4	201.6	834.5	1,255.0	2,678.5	2,480.0	3,763.8	3,952.1	4,034.3	3,367.9	5,018.9	3,250.2
direct investment(net)	110.0	139.3	145.0	636.0	855.4	1,211.6	2,890.2	2,527.4	3,222.2	3,293.4	3,226.3	3,363.4
Portfolio investments(net)				65.8	289.3	-49.01	-43.64	620.5	117.6	1,121.8	658.9	835.9
Loans	369.8	402.3	501.3	351.2	1,305.8	717.9	1,246.2	1,057.9	888.8	1,341.7	1,765.4	1,151.6

SOURCE: BANK OF GHANA (2015)

The passage of the Ghana Investment Promotion Council Act 1994 established the framework for investment flows. The tax holiday, import duty exemptions for foreign investors, improved remittances of dividends and profits abroad, and improved judicial processes are some of the measures adopted to attract foreign capital to the country. Besides, in 2005, Ghana obtained its first sovereign rating and then gained access to the global capital market. Furthermore, the security of investment provided by the national constitution, as well as the Multilateral Investment Guaranteed and the investment Promotion Protection Agreements, have given investors confidence and have attracted capital flows to the country (Bank of Ghana 2015).

Ghana witnessed a rise in capital flows after the 2008 global financial crisis, as well as continuous dependence on remittances from its overseas workers, which saw an increase of 50% over the period 2003–2014. The increase in the capital inflows could be due to the country's stable political-economic arrangements, and the legal protections given to foreign investors. Higher mineral prices accompanied a surge in FDI inflows in 2012 at $3,293.4 million, and a continuous rise in investment in the oil sector since the discovery of oil in 2007. Private transfers increased every year from $1,017.2 million in 2003 to $1,868.8 million in 2014, except for 2009 and 2013. Official transfer, on the other hand, has been more volatile starting at $227.7 million in 2003, rising to $603.7 million in 2006 before declining to $9.6 million in 2014 (table 4).

Figure 17 shows that most of the capital flows into the economy have remained relatively stable/stagnant. However, the overall current account balance is in deficit throughout the period, with the largest deficit being in 2013. Only direct investment (net) saw a significant increase from a few hundred million US dollars to over $3 billion a year since 2009.

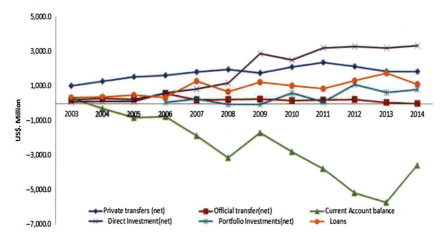

FIGURE 17   Trade balance, current transfers and capital flows to Ghana (in millions US$)
SOURCE: BANK OF GHANA (2015)

Table 5 shows that mining and quarrying (a global conglomerate multinational corporation) attracted the most FDI into the economy during the period. Investments into these sectors have more than tripled from $3,115.15 million to $9,919.02 million in 2012 due to the increase in prices of these commodities. Finance and insurance (which includes banking) activities have also attracted considerable FDIs rising from over $900 million in 2010 to almost $1.4 billion at the end of 2012. FDIs into the manufacturing sector increased from $366 million in 2010 to $590 million at the end of 2012. Agriculture, forestry and fishing, which employ most of the labour force attracted $70.43 million, an increase

TABLE 5   Sector distribution of foreign direct investment (in millions US$) 2010–2012

	2010	2011	2012
	Stock	Stock	Stock
Book value of equity as of 31st December	4,987.22	5,870.96	13,262.94
Administrative and support service activities	0.72	0.76	0.07
Agriculture, forestry and fishing	19.86	17.89	70.43
Arts, entertainment and creation	0.01	0.02	0.05
Construction	23.90	24.50	64.90
Electricity, gas and air conditioning supply	69.30	87.51	245.96
Finance and insurance activities	917.05	1,091.02	1,396.12
Information and communication	370.17	-267.16	638.87
Manufacturing	366.08	417.63	590.68
Mining and quarrying	3,115.15	4,381.08	9,919.02
Others	0.50	0.42	31.36
Professional, scientific and technical activities	0.01	0.01	0.03
Real estate activities	0.79	0.74	0.66
Transportation and storage	4.63	3.23	3.24
Wholesales & retail trade	99.03	113.28	301.55

SOURCE: BANK OF GHANA (2015)

of $50.57 million from the 2010 level. The Real Estate activities attracted a marginal and falling FDI of $0.66 million due to the underdevelopment of the sub-sector.

The development of the domestic sovereign bond market attracted net inflows of $ 620.50 million in 2010. However, the depreciation of the cedi has resulted in falling non-residence participation, despite the high yields on their investment. Ghana was the first SSA country to borrow from the international capital market when it issued a 10-year Euro bond in 2007 to raise $750 million at an interest rate of 8.5%. A second Eurobond was issued in 2013, which raised $1billion at a coupon of 8% with a maturity of 10 years. Another Eurobond was issued in 2014 to raise $1billion.

Therefore, to examine the net capital outflow from the Ghanaian economy, it is essential to analyse how the central bank addresses IMF and the World Bank *'self-insurance'* policy that may arise from increasing liquid capital inflow.

The liquid capital inflows into the country mandate the Central Bank to hold enough reserves to support the Ghana cedi and hence inflation to maintain a stable economy. To preserve the real purchasing power and maintain a high degree of liquidity of the accumulated reserve in the face of rising inflows, the Central Bank has to utilise some of the accumulated reserves in a relatively less risky but liquid asset. In a situation like this, the safest way for periphery countries to accumulate reserve has been to purchase US public debt. However, this attempt by the Bank of Ghana to address the issue of rising liquidity inflows generates colossal opportunity costs as these resources cannot be utilised for any productive domestic investment. This unintended consequence impedes economic development in the peripheries.

Thus, unintentionally, while private enterprises/individuals borrow from abroad at a rate lower than domestic interest rates, the Bank of Ghana proceeds to *insure* it by advancing/lending loan to the US at a much lower US official rate. Therefore, the beneficiaries of this *carry trade* are the US government, and the private domestic borrowers at the expense of the whole Ghanaian economy. Consequently, the social cost of holding reserves is perhaps a reduction in GDP. The higher domestic interest rate to manage inflation and strengthen the local currency fuels/induces this process while at the same time increasing the cost of capital for domestic firms. It is clear that the rising inflows of liquid capital into Ghana are not due to rising returns on productive activities but gains from exchange rate trading and interest rate arbitrage. Private enterprises, notably domestic financial institutions, borrow cheaply from abroad to capitalise on higher returns on domestic financial assets. The process has facilitated privileged private borrowers' bourgeoisie a direct appropriation of the benefit of interest spread, a process which fuels internal differentiation in the economy with dire consequences of income inequality and poverty. Thus, the practice of making more money from money or M→M¹ (*in the money circuit of capital*) mostly through carry trade and exchange rate arbitrage impedes real productive investment.

7 Conclusion

This chapter provided the country profile and the overview of Ghana's political and economic development. The review illustrates that Ghana has undergone a massive transformation in its economic and political development since independence. The political and economic contradictions that symbolised the initial years after independence have been stabilised. The economy is now the second largest in the West Africa sub-region and the 12th largest on the continent.

Nevertheless, the challenges of the initial years, which include three major problems of structural crisis, fiscal crisis, and political instability, plunged the country into the economic predicament. The confluence and the intensification of these interrelated problems reduced the efforts by successive governments to provide domestic self-reliance agenda started at independence. The predicaments forced Ghana to adopt ERP together with SAP in 1983. The ERP and SAP involved macroeconomic stabilisation, liberalisation, deregulation and privatisation of state-owned enterprises.

The shift from state intervention to market-based policies resulted in various reforms, notably, financial sector reforms, which replaced the pre-adjustment reforms. Thus, all the specialised banks created by the various governments were wholly or partially privatised, followed with abolished credit ceiling and restructuring of the distressed banks. The banking sector reforms also relaxed the entry of foreign banks, which resulted in different forms of financial products in the economy. The universal banking concept allowed banks to perform commercial, development, merchant, and investment banking activities without a new licence.

The distinctive feature of financialisation in Ghana is that the economy is under-financed by international standard measures, yet it is financialising. The underdevelopment of the capital market limits industrial enterprises' access to debt and equity financing. Consequently, firms are more reliant on bank credits as opposed to the core where large industrial firms can access a range of sources for financing. Banks continue to lend disproportionately to risk-free government securities, which crowds out the private sector.

The liberalisation and the deregulation of the financial market enabled capital flows and the ascendency of finance in Ghana. However, the initial belief that financial liberalisation will induce capital inflows to periphery countries was short-lived. As countries opened their capital market, there has been a reverse flow of capital from the periphery to the core countries. The accumulation reserves pioneered by the World Bank and the IMF have been the catalyst for this negative reversal of capital from the periphery countries. Domestic policies to attract more investment and the high interest rates in the periphery also contribute to net outflows of capital. The next chapter presents theoretical and empirical investigations to assess whether non-financial/industrial enterprises in Ghana are financialised, as presented in the literature of financialisation in the core countries.

CHAPTER 5

Dimensions of Capital Structure and Liquidity Management in Ghana

1   Introduction

The previous chapter presented Ghana's political-economic arrangements since independence and the factors that precipitated the neoliberal policy of SAP. An original analysis of the uniqueness of financialisation in SSA and its *subordinate/inferior* nature was presented. This chapter examines the dimensions of capital structure and liquidity management. A firm's capital structure comprises of its liabilities – a mix of debt-equity ratio, which is the various sources of finance employed by a firm to finance its operations, assets and the expansion of the business.

There are two primary sources of finance for a firm: internal and external financing. Internal financing relates to retained profits, and external sources of financing could be in the form of borrowing (debt) or issue of share (equity). Thus, the capital structure represents the overall risk as well as a firm's cost of capital. This is therefore significant to a firm's value and its shareholders' wealth. As argued by Baker and Martin (2011), although debt is the least costly form of capital, the impact of rising leverage through debt endangers the business to high financial risk. Thereby, borrowing may increase the chance of default as well as herald the instability of the business's earnings per share and the return on equity. Hence, the gains of a lower cost of debts erode as leverage increases due to the exposure of financial risk and its associated financial distress and bankruptcy.

A critical issue that faces firms in their external financing decision is the proportion of debt and equity to be used. These external financing options illustrate the capital structure of a firm. Abor (2008) argues that a wrong financing decision can endanger an economy due to the significant role played by firms in the provision of jobs to the people, paying wages and thereby reducing poverty, which is a vital issue facing most periphery countries, in particular Ghana. It follows that making the right and accurate financial decision can stimulate economic growth and development. This is relevant to private as well as public sector enterprises that can access external financing. Given the transformation of the financial sector in the era of neoliberalism and its associated debts and financial crises, capital structure and firms financing decisions is of paramount importance.

Section 2 of this chapter establishes the theoretical bases by reviewing theories on capital structure from the weaknesses of the traditional view to the pecking order. Sub-section 2.1 provides an empirical assessment to ascertain if industrial enterprises in Ghana are financialised, by assessing the capital structure of firms to ascertain if firms rely heavily on external financing by issuing a long-term bond or bank credit. One of the key assertions in the literature on financialisation discussed in this book is the transformation of firms' financing behaviour from long-term to short-term. Sub-section 2.2 reviews fundamental theories of capital structure. Financialisation and capital structure accumulation are examined in section 3. Section 4 presents the classification of capital structure in Ghana. The chapter ends with the original analysis of key challenges facing firms/industrial enterprises in the capital accumulation process.

2 Theories of Capital Structure

The theories of capital structure are wide and varied in the field of corporate finance and other related studies. The main thesis in capital structure studies is whether there is an optimal capital structure. That is,the level of equity and debt that minimises a firm's cost of capital but maximises its overall value. Eldomiaty (2007) and Salim and Yadav (2012) argue that various capital structure theories are based on diverse assumptions which highlight the complexity of firms' financing behaviour. Some of these theories are reviewed below.

2.1   *Capital Structure: Traditionalists' View*

Traditionalists seek to explain the capital structure of a firm based on intuition. They posit a direct relationship between the value of a firm and its capital structure. Accordingly, the liability-mix of a debt-equity ratio is significant to the value of a firm. The theory is of the view that for a firm to operate efficiently/profitably, it should have an optimal level of gearing so that the weighted average cost of capital is minimised, and the value of the firm maximised. Thereby, firms face damaging consequences of their overall performance and survival if they operate beyond the optimal level of gearing. Consequently, the optimal level is reached when the cost of capital is minimised or the value of the firm maximised (Samuels, Wilkes, and Brayshaw 1997).

The modern theory of capital structure emanates from the seminal work of Modigliani and Miller (1958), which challenged the traditionalist theory. They outlined some key limitations of the traditionalist theory. They argued that it is irrelevant to influence the capital structure by applying only debt or equity finance or a certain proportion of each. That is, a mix of the debt-equity ratio cannot influence the value of a firm. These weaknesses prompted them to propose the irrelevance theory.

2.2 Value-irrelevance Theory by Modigliani-Miller

The value-irrelevance theory pioneered by Modigliani and Miller (1958) argues that in perfect capital markets, the capital structure decision – a mix of the debt-equity ratio cannot influence the value of the firm. This theory relies heavily on several assumptions (including perfect capital market, insiders and outsiders have no information asymmetry, no transaction cost, and debt is risk-free). Advocates of this theory argue that there is no optimal capital structure, and therefore, firms can make use of as much and many debts and equity as possible. They assert that the value of a firm depends on the efficient use of its assets to generate future income. Thus, dividend and interest on debts may not influence the value of a firm. Consequently, managers should look at alternative ways of increasing the total value of a firm rather than simply manipulating a mix of debt-equity ratios.

Critiques argue that in a financialised capitalism, capital markets are not perfect, and most debts in the capital markets are risky. Besides, information asymmetry exists within investors and firms as well as between insiders and outsiders. As noted by Strebulaev (2007), a small adjustment of costs may cause considerable variations in the capital structure. In recognition of the weaknesses in the theory, Modigliani and Miller (1963, 433) acknowledged the benefits of income tax shield and introduced a new model of value-irrelevance theory to incorporate this.[1] As the proportion of debt to equity rises, the market value of the firm rises by the present value of the interest tax shield. Therefore, the cost of capital will not increase, even if the use of leverage rises disproportionately. However, Solomon (1963) and Salim and Yadav (2012) are of the view that in an excessive leverage position, the cost of capital must increase. They argue that extreme levels of debt will prompt the market to demand a higher rate of return. Thereby, it follows that to minimise the weighted average cost of capital, firms should avoid a pure debt position and seek an optimal mix of debt-equity ratio.

However, as recognised by Miller (1988, 102), the theory was not intended to suggest that '… the debt-equity ratio was indeterminate …' given this position,

---

[1] Interest on the debt is a tax-deductible expense, this means that a firm tax bill will decrease as it employs more debt.

Myers (2001) asserts that Modigliani and Miller (1958) model should be seen as a benchmark and not the ideal result. The prepositions are merely illuminating that financing does not matter, except for specific transaction costs.

As the literature on capital structure evolves, it is clear that there is no consensus on a particular/precise capital structure model. However, the common view is that the value-irrelevance theory provides the foundation for contemporary studies of capital structure (Salim and Yadav 2012). These include the popular trade-off model and the pecking order theory.

2.3   Capital Structure: Trade-off Theory

The traditional trade-off theory proposes that there is an optimal level of leverage – debt to equity ratio for all firms. This optimal debt ratio is determined by the point where costs of financial distress offset the advantages of tax shield, that is the trade-off between the losses and gains of borrowing (Brennan and Schwartz 1978; DeAngelo and Masulis 1980). This theory presupposed cost and benefit associated with debt and equity mix. Consequently, there must be an optimal capital structure that trades off the marginal benefits and marginal cost of debts after considering the imperfections in the market (such as, agency costs, taxes and bankruptcy costs). As the debt level falls, the marginal benefit rises; however, the marginal cost of debt falls as debt falls. Thereby, a rational firm will seek to finance its operations by maximising the trade-off point of the debt-equity mix.

Despite its popularity, some limitations have been identified in the trade-off theory. Chen (2004) argues that the theory fails to account for corporate behaviour regarding stock market changes, which continuously cause stock prices to rise and fall. Furthermore, the theory assumes that profitability and leverage are positively related; therefore, firms will borrow more to benefit from tax to shield their income. However, some empirical evidence available points to the contrary (Chakraborty 2010; Sheikh and Wang 2011). The competing theory to trade-off hypothesis is the pecking order theory.

2.4   Capital Structure: Pecking-order Theory

One of the prominent theories of capital structure is the pecking-order model which seeks to explain various options of financing among firms, something which was entirely ignored by other theories. Myers and Majluf (1984) and Myers (2001) suggest that capital structure is driven by a firm's desire to finance new investment, in order, by first looking internally before seeking external financing. External financing should start with low-risk debt, and if these attempts fail or not enough capital is raised, then equity finance can be sort. Internally generated funds such as retained earnings have the least issue cost compared to equity finance. Unlike the trade-off theory, pecking-order does not suggest an optimal capital structure. It, however, demonstrates the preference for internal financing as opposed to external financing. Advocates of pecking order theory remark that transaction costs, asymmetric information and tax reasons are the central themes in favour of using retained earnings compared to external financing of debt and equity

Despite the popularity of pecking-order theory, a more significant proportion of it has been on the core countries with very few studies based on the periphery countries (Seifert and Gonenc 2008; Lemmon and Zender 2010). The differences in the institutional structures in these regions limit the usefulness of the theory worldwide. Other empirical evidence also points to the contrary with firms opting for external funds even though they have access to retain profit. A study conducted by Minton and Wruck (2001) concludes that firms pursue credit from the capital market to fund investment at the time that they have not fully utilised retained profit. This argument contradicts pecking order theory where firms would expect to exploit all internally generated funds before seeking external funds. Seifert and Gonenc (2010) point out that pecking order financing is dominant only in those emerging economies where there are issues of asymmetric information and high agency costs. Their findings lend support to the theory that financing decisions are a function of the prevailing market conditions firms operate.

From the discussion above, it is clear that the pecking order theory is inconsistent. This may be either due to the methodology employed or that the financing decisions are subject to other factors that may affect capital structure differently.

3   Financialisation and Capital Structure Accumulation in Ghana

The recent increase in financial activities in Ghana has been caused by many factors, notably the liberalisation and deregulation of the financial sector. These factors, primarily (maybe unintentionally) exacerbated the already high cost of capital in Ghana, bearing in mind that there are high returns on financial assets than a real productive asset. Consequently, the financial sector has attracted the most excellent human capital as well as capital from the economy.

Ghana witnessed accelerated economic growth in the last three decades of implementing neoliberal policy prescriptions. Indeed, this economic growth promoted Ghana to a low middle-income status. Paradoxically, the well-being of most Ghanaians, including those in the rural areas, the peasants, and the working classes have not improved meaningfully, and they still suffer relentless poverty. I argue that neoliberal policy prescriptions undermined Ghana's ability to diversify its economy into industrialisation, particularly manufacturing.

The work of Hilferding, Keynes and Marx, to mention but a few, suggests that profit is the magnate that attracts capital to a capitalist production process. Consequently, if sufficient profit could not be earned from a particular productive venture, capital will migrate to seek refuge in profitable ventures, especially in financial speculation. Accordingly, it is argued in this book that to understand the paradox of Ghana's accelerated economic growth without sufficient development, it is essential to examine why there is low profitability in the real sector of the economy. Given that, capital migrates to sectors where maximum profit could be earned.

In line with Hilferding's (1981[1910]) observation that the prerequisite for the export of capital (FDI)[2] is the changes in the rate of return on capital, sufficient profit should be earned in a venture in order to entice long-term capital to that sector. The low rate of profitability in the real productive sector could be the crucial reason why the economy has failed to attract substantial long-term capital to accelerate the real capital accumulation process for sustainable development.

Additionally, it is contended that the neoliberal policies implemented in the 1980s undermined rather than resolved capital accumulation constraints in the country. This is because the neoliberal policies intentionally (maybe unintentionally) encouraged factors that undermined the possibility of the real productive assets to earn commensurate returns to facilitate the flow of capital to these sectors to ensure the survival of industrial enterprises. Rising profit in the financial sector incentivised managers to divert funds into financial assets at the expense of productive investment. Thus, the pace of real capital accumulation has been disappointing in the era of financialisation due to rising financial profit.

4 Classification of Capital Accumulation Process in Ghana

It is essential to classify Ghana's capital accumulation process and then investigate the impact of neoliberal reforms on the pace of real capital accumulation in the country.

The importance of SMEs in sustainable development cannot be underestimated. Hall, Hutchinson, and Michaelas (2004) and Ayyagari, Beck, and

---

2 Foreign Direct Investment, which is intended to earn sufficient profit abroad.

Demirguc-Kunt (2007) reckon that SMEs account for about 20% to 50% of global GDP. Ahiawodzi and Adade (2012) argue that SMEs are most vital in accelerating growth and livelihoods in the peripheries. They assert that about 90% of all enterprises in Africa are SMEs and they account for an average of 50% to 60% of all employment on the continent. In Ghana, Quartey (2008) and Abor and Quartey (2010) presented the significance of SMEs in the country. They remarked that about 90% of all firms are SMEs and account for about 70% of GDP, and over 80% of manufacturing jobs in the economy.

However, despite the significance of SMEs in accelerating economic growth, creating employment, increasing income and development, access to affordable capital remains a challenge to their very survival.

Many scholars have contended that profit is the carrot that induces certainly most entrepreneurs to go into business. For example, Luxembourg (1913) argues that profit motive is what directs/dictates the mode of capitalist production. Minsky (1986) remarks that the price mechanism must facilitate sufficient rewards to encourage present and future production. Consequently, the present income must certify the past debt obligation. In other words, today's profit must certify the previous debt obligation. Therefore, an entrepreneur should be able to validate today's debt obligation from future income before they can embark on any investment. In short, no profitable entrepreneur would invest without sufficient return on the investment to ensure continuous survival.

In order to extract profit, a firm has to ensure that the cost-price margin is sufficient to guarantee the returns to the production process, to replace the initial investment, compensate its cost and other related costs associated with the production process. These related costs such as wages for labour time and compensation for the entrepreneur, should be less than the revenue generated to have a leftover for further accumulation (Smith 2006[1776]; Marx 2019[1867]; Keynes 2018[1936]; Minsky 1986). Thereby, to guarantee sufficient profit, a firm has to maintain a high enough cost-price margin.

However, most industrial enterprises in Ghana do not have sufficient market (global) power to sustain a high enough profit margin. The price-taking firms, according to Minsky (1986), alter their marginal costs to respond to variations in demand. In such a competitive market environment, a sudden fall in demand might cause cash flow problems to enable the industrial enterprises to satisfy all of their cost commitments and debt. Therefore, the options available are to reduce the production cost or embark on product differentiation to maintain high-profit margins.

The challenges for these options are the lack of technology and expertise, particularly amongst SMEs in Ghana to exploit this benefit to gain some competitive advantage in a competitive global market.

Furthermore, the lack of and inadequate human capital development in Ghana makes it difficult for SMEs to produce high-tech goods. The inability to produce differentiated and high-quality products limits their ability to command high prices in the global market. Another option that firms in Ghana could exploit is the cheap labour-power available in the country. After all, semi-periphery economies such as China, India and others started their industrial revolution based on cheap labour-power, which gave them a comparative cost advantage (Schuman 2009). However, capitalists in SSA in general and Ghana in particular, are constrained by distinct problems, which hinder their ability to emulate these semi-periphery countries' developmental trajectories.

This book uncovers the critical factors obstructing industrial enterprises' ability to make sufficient profit to ensure their continual existence. These factors have undermined the real capital accumulation process, together with sustainable economic development in Ghana. The key factors that will be addressed include lack of affordable capital (due to high interest charged by moneylenders) and government policies. The consequences of the government of Ghana forced adopted neoliberal policies have resulted in lack of exposure due to the uneven competition in the global economy, that is unfair competition between Ghanaian capitalists and those from the core (mainly UK, Europe and the US) and semi-peripheries (mainly South Africa, China, and Dubai). This has led to ineffective appetite and demand for domestic products.

The confluence of these obstructive factors hinders industrial enterprises' ability to reproduce commensurate profit and thereby causing the decline in the pace of real capital accumulation. Although these factors are individually distinctive, this book will demonstrate how these inhibiting factors complement each other to stagnate the pace of real capital accumulation in Ghana. Accordingly, this study will recommend that, to solve Ghana's economic predicaments and to alleviate poverty, these constraints should be addressed collectively. Although Ghana has moved up on ranking in the recent World Bank ease of doing business, the country still needs to do more to support SMEs. According to the 2018 Ease of Doing Business Report,[3] Ghana ranked 114 out of 189, an improvement from

---

3   Ease of doing business ranks economies from 1 to 189, with first-place being the best. A high ranking (a low numerical figure) means that the regulatory environment is conducive to business operation. The index averages the country's percentile rankings on ten topics covered in the World Bank's Doing Business. The ranking on each topic is the simple average of the percentile rankings on its component indicators.

the 120th position ranked in the previous report. The indicators as described in the report include getting electricity (improved from 122 in 2016 to 120 in 2017), resolving insolvency (improved from 158 in 2016 to 155 in 2017) and trading across borders (improved from 167 in 2016 to 154) (Bank of Ghana 2018).

5 Contradictions in Political-Economic Arrangements in Ghana

Access to finance is one of the major constraints facing firms in Ghana. The World Bank Enterprise Survey (2013) shows that almost 60% of firms (irrespective of the size of the firm) complain lack of finance is a significant problem. This constraint (lack of finance) is predominant in Ghana than SSA and disproportionately on small firms than medium and large firms. The factors impeding real capital accumulation are examined below.

5.1 *Financing Challenges*

The financial system in Ghana before the 1980s was severely fragmented and limited by restrictive government-controlled policies that direct interest rates, control commercial banks and allocate credit to specific priority sectors. SAP and FINSAP signify the removal of these restrictions and the empowerment of market competition in the banking industry. Government subsidies previously given to certain priority firms were removed. These had a massive impact on the performance of many small manufacturing firms. Access to credit is paramount to the success of any firm, as it assists the start-up of new ventures, enables investment in equipment, stock, staff and labour. Yet, the acquisition of credit can be challenging for firms. As discussed in chapter 4, Ghana's financial sector is relatively underdeveloped, with a lack of institutional and legal structures that facilitates the management of firms, particularly SMEs risk.

According to PricewaterhouseCoopers (PwC 2018), banks are aware of the strategic importance of the SME market but are unwilling to adopt traditional approaches to access the market. Meanwhile, SMEs remark that banks do not understand and value them. This misalliance in perceptions can often be linked to the types of financing provided by the banks. In particular, banks are reluctant to offer both long-term lending and working capital facilities that SMEs require for development.

A developed financial industry provides mobilised savings, payment systems, and eases investment opportunities. Efficient financial markets offer a range of sources of finance for firms by linking firms to various lenders and investors. This connection reduces firms' dependence on unreliable sources of finance such as family and friends and retained profit. It is clear from figure 18 that enterprises in Ghana, SSA and low middle-income countries, rely heavily on internal sources of finance for investment. In Ghana, 76% of firms' investment comes from their internally generated funds. This is, however, higher than the SSA average of 74.8% and low middle-income countries 68.9%. Bank sources of finance for investment account for just 12.6% in Ghana, 9.9% in SSA, and 15.5% in low middle-income countries. Equity (sale of stock) financing for investment is lower in SSA and low middle-income, compared with their trade credit financing.

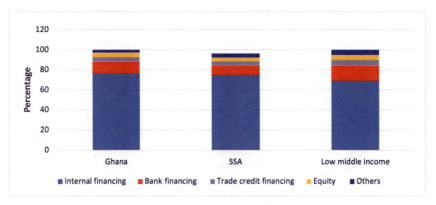

FIGURE 18   Various sources of finance for long term investment
SOURCE: AUTHOR'S ESTIMATES USING FIGURES FROM THE WORLD BANK ENTERPRISE SURVEY FOR GHANA (2013)

The underdevelopment of Ghana's stock market is evident, with just 4.7% of firms' sources of finance for investment coming from equity finance. Thus, the capital structure of firms in Ghana is composed of mainly internal financing. This evidence contradicts the literature on financialisation discussed above. It however, supports a geographical investigation into financialisation in the periphery, and Ghana in particular. Although banks' source of finance for investment is low, firms in Ghana may be argued to follow pecking order capital structure theory. However, it is essential to note that the World Bank Enterprise Survey remarked that access to finance constraints was the primary issue among all firms surveyed. The over-reliance on internal funds signifies potentially ineffective financial markets and intermediaries. Beck and Demirguc-Kunt (2006) contend that firms that have access to credit can expand faster and achieve optimum size, enhance performance and are more able to exploit other investment opportunities. The access to finance constraints will impede firms' success and expansion and therefore limit their ability to make sufficient profit to ensure continuous existence.

There is limited access to alternative sources of finance in the economy. The role of other financial intermediaries like venture capital, lease companies, and the bond market, in terms of connecting firms with investors and lenders, remains narrow, underdeveloped and considered insignificant sources of finance for industrial enterprises in Ghana. As a result, firms have narrow access to long-term funds required for meaningful investment. As pointed by Mu, Phelps, and Stotsky (2013), the average market capitalisation (as a proportion of GDP) of the bond market in SSA from 2001 to 2010 was just 1.2%. This signifies the illiquid capital market in SSA and the financing constraints in the region. With 76% of firms' investment coming from retained profit, it highlights the importance of retained profits as a vital source of funds for firms. However, the inhibiting factors restrain firms from making sufficient profit to retain for long- term investment opportunities. The consequences have been low wages, unemployment and poverty.

The sustainability of firms is crucial to the firms' working capital.[4] Figure 19 shows the proportion of working capital that is financed by external sources. The survey shows that in Ghana, 26.8% of firms' working capital comes from external sources. The figures for SSA and low middle-income countries are 22.3% and 27.2%, respectively. Adequate working capital provides a cushion for a firm when extra cash is needed.

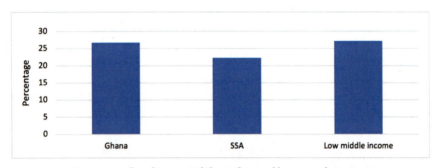

FIGURE 19 Percentage of working capital that is financed by external sources
SOURCE: AUTHOR'S ESTIMATES USING FIGURES FROM THE WORLD BANK ENTERPRISE SURVEY FOR GHANA (2013)

A glance at figure 20 illustrates the percentage of working capital financed by firms' size and shows that a higher proportion of firms' working capital,

---

4 Working capital is the capital of a business that is used in its day-to-day trading operations, calculated as the current assets minus the current liabilities. The benefit of working capital is that firms have more flexibility, enabling them to meet their customers' orders, expand their business, and invest in new products and services.

irrespective of size, comes from internal sources. With only 31% of large firms' working capital coming from external sources, the rest is generated internally.

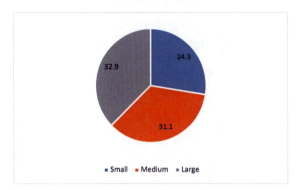

FIGURE 20   Percentage of working capital across firm size
SOURCE: AUTHOR'S ESTIMATES USING FIGURES FROM THE WORLD BANK ENTERPRISE SURVEY FOR GHANA (2013)

The inefficient and underdeveloped financial markets in Ghana are signs of potentially insufficient financial intermediaries connecting firms with lenders. However, other factors also deter firms from applying for credit. Out of the 76.7% of firms who did not have access to bank credit, only a few cited that they have enough capital to carry on their daily activities. Other reasons for not applying for credit include unfavourable interest rates, high collateral requirements and bureaucratic procedures, among other things.

Another dominant constraint regarding access to finance in Ghana and other periphery economies is the problem of high collateral security (figure 21). Lenders (due to high default rates) usually demand high collateral in their contractual agreements. The value of collateral required to access a bank loan is 240% in Ghana – 2.4 times the value of loan needed, 213% in SSA, and 190% in low middle-income countries. Almost 80% of bank loans require some form of collateral. These inhibiting factors deter firms from accessing credit from the formal financial sector and increase the cost of firms that can get some form of bank credit. When borrowers cannot meet the collateral requirements of lenders, they are likely to go for short-term credit, which requires less collateral, but limits firms' ability to acquire fixed assets, and to exploit long-term investment opportunities. Abor (2008) and Ramlall (2009) highlight the significance of collateral in securing debt in SSA. They argue that firms without sufficient collateral are unlikely to be accepted for financial assistance by lenders. Thus, an industrial capitalist with profitable investment opportunities but who lacks adequate collateral may not be able to secure financial assistance for investment projects.

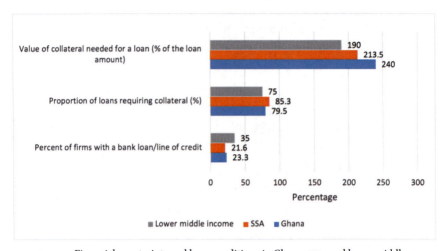

FIGURE 21   Financial constraints and loan conditions in Ghana, SSA, and lower middle-income countries
SOURCE: AUTHOR'S ESTIMATES USING FIGURES FROM THE WORLD BANK ENTERPRISE SURVEY FOR GHANA (2013)

Small firms are disproportionately impeded by access to finance constraints compared to their counterparts. The value of collateral needed to acquire a loan is disproportionately higher for small firms' 259.8% than large firms' 215.8% (figure 22). This is likely to impede the development of small firms and deter them from applying for a bank loan.

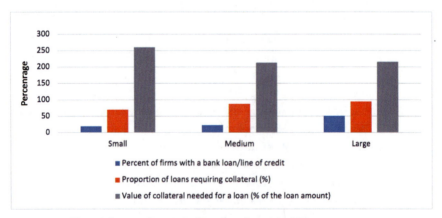

FIGURE 22   Financial constraints across firms based on size of firm
SOURCE: AUTHOR'S ESTIMATES USING FIGURES FROM THE WORLD BANK ENTERPRISE SURVEY FOR GHANA (2013)

One key determinant of loan repayment is the interest rate. A high interest rate remains a severe obstruction of firms accessing bank credit. Since the deregulation of financial markets in the late 1980s, and the neoliberal agenda of controlling inflation as the main objective of governments, the interest rate has risen massively. Although Ghana has made a tremendous improvement in reducing the inflation rate recently, higher inflation has been persistent for many years. High inflation leads to a high lending rate. This high lending rate limits firms' ability to access a substantial loan, as they will find it challenging to repay the principal plus the interest. The persistent fall in the rate of profit coupled with the rising cost of production makes it difficult for industrial enterprises to afford the higher cost of external capital. The Bank of Ghana (2016) presented that the cost of borrowing for firms in Ghana ranges from 25% to 40%. These high lending rates obstruct the private sector to finance investment by borrowing.

Consequently, their capacity to expand, create employment and pay higher wages is limited. Thus, in the Ghanaian case, real capital investment yields minimal returns, yet much is still anticipated to service the debt due to higher interest rates. Essentially, firms are burdened with exorbitant interest charges and high production costs, which decimate their ability to earn enough profit. Thus, while interest on a loan has been in double digits, the rate of profits made from using the capital has been in single digits.

Figure 23 illustrates the monetary policy rate, inflation rate and Treasury bill rate in Ghana. Bank of Ghana's monetary policy rates has moved in tandem with the trend of inflation over the period shown. The policy rate declined

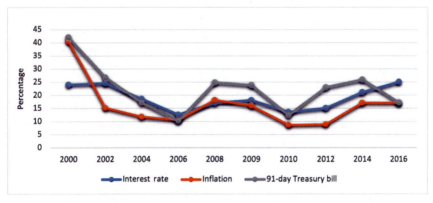

FIGURE 23   Monetary policy rate, inflation (end of the year), and 91-day treasury bill rates 2000–2016
SOURCE: AUTHOR'S ESTIMATES USING FIGURES FROM THE BANK OF GHANA DATASET (VARIOUS)

from 24% in 2000 to 12.5% in 2006 and increased to 25% in 2016 to curb rising inflation. The rising inflation and subsequent increase in policy rates impede firms' ability to access funds for long-term investment. Other market rates have followed a similar pattern with a steady fall from 2000 to 2006 and a rise afterward. Interest rates on government securities have followed the trend. The high fiscal deficits in 2008 and 2012 and the subsequent rising of domestic borrowing by the government to finance the deficits caused interest rates on government security to rise sharply in 2008 and 2012. The high interest in government securities also crowds out the private sector of the needed capital for any meaningful long-term investment. Since the government default rate is less or unlikely, investors and lenders are more comfortable lending to the government that gives higher returns on their secured investments. If investors can earn quick and generous returns on secure government securities, then there is no incentive for them to invest in riskier productive sectors. Any investor willing to lend to the private sector is likely to demand high collateral (as seen in figure 21) and high returns on their risky investment.

The Bank of Ghana publishes Annual Percentage Rates (APR), and Average Interest (AI) paid on deposit for the public. This publication promotes transparency in the provision of banking services. The table below shows the cost of credits to households and industrial enterprises.

Table 6 depicts a high average annual cost of borrowing for households at 33.7% for vehicle loans and other credits, and 33.2% for mortgages. GCB and Royal Bank charge as high as 40% on all forms of household credit, although the average policy rate has been 26%. It is difficult to predict with precision the exact amount of banks' revenue that originates from the household sector. However, an approximate picture can be used to assess those categories in which households account for most of the debtors. About 85% of mortgage debt and almost 90% of other consumer credit debt (such as credit card, education loan and other credits) is consistently held by households. What is worrying is that other consumer credit (including credit cards) is unsecured, but banks are increasingly confident to provide.

On this evidence, it is not difficult to conclude that households have been a significant source of income for banks. Industrial enterprises also face high costs of credit with agriculture 32.6%, manufacturing 33.0%, commerce 32.6% and 32.6% for construction. Omnibank and Royal Bank charge more than 38% for credit to all industrial enterprises. On this evidence, it could be argued that financial liberalisation and the various waves of financial reforms promised to bring about efficient and competitive financial markets and hence lower costs of credit, did not live up to the expectation. It has resulted in high costs of capital for both households and industrial enterprises. This has obstructed firms' ability to

TABLE 6   Universal bank lending and deposit annual percentage rates as of 31st January 2018

Banks	Deposits Average interest rate	Base rate	Households Vehicle loans Percent Annual percentage rate	Mortgage Annual percentage rate	Other consumer credit Annual percentage rate	Enterprises Agriculture Annual percentage rate	Manufacturing Annual percentage rate	Commerce Annual percentage rate	Construction Annual percentage rate
Access Bank	16.4	27.3	N/A	N/A	31.8	N/A	29.5	N/A	N/A
ADB	6.2	22.9	31.8	N/A	29.2	27.8	29.8	29.8	29.2
Bank of Africa	13	26.9	35.6	36.6	N/A	35.6	35.6	36.6	35.6
Bank of Baroda	15.4	17.6	22.28	32.28	22.28	22.28	22.28	22.28	22.28
Barclays Bank	10.4	19.2	34.2-38.5	34.2-38.5	34.2-38.5	26.2-32.9	26.2-35.9	26.2-35.9	26.2-35.9
Cal Bank	9	28.3	35.3	35.3	35.3	N/A	35.3	35.3	35.3
Ecobank	9.2	25.9	34.1	34.1	N/A	26.5	26.5	28.7	26.5

TABLE 6 Universal bank lending and deposit annual percentage rates as of 31st January 2018 (*cont.*)

		Households				Enterprises			
Energy Bank	6	30.6	N/A	N/A	35.6	35.6	35.6	35.6	35.6
First Atlantic Bank	13.8	25	N/A	N/A	41.2	37.6	37.6	37.6	37.6
FBN Ghana	9.8	28.4	32.8	32.8	32.8	31.7	31.7	31.7	31.7
Capital Bank	17.4	33.3	N/A	N/A	36.1	N/A	N/A	N/A	N/A
Fidelity Bank	12.7	23.2	N/A	N/A	35	33.9	33.9	33.9	33.9
First National Bank	11.1	23.5	N/A	N/A	N/A	N/A	N/A	23.8	N/A
GCB Bank	8.3	25	40.3	40.3	40.3	31.8	31.8	31.8	31.8
GN Bank	13.2	22.2	32.0	N/A	32	32	29.9	27	32
GT Bank	7.4	25.8	N/A	N/A	33.3	N/A	31.5	31.5	31
HFC	11.4	29.7	36.7	31.1	38.1	39.5	35.2	37.1	36.3
NIB	11.4	30.5	N/A	N/A	N/A	37.2	37.2	37.2	38.2
Omnibank	-	29.8	36.9	N/A	36	38	38.5	38	38.9
Prudential Bank	10.9	26.7	33.6	33.6	33.4	33.3	34.5	33.6	34.5

DIMENSIONS OF CAPITAL STRUCTURE AND LIQUIDITY MANAGEMENT

Sahel Sahara (BSIC)	10.9	29.7	29.5	29.5	29.5	29.5	29.5	29.5	29.5
Sovereign Bank	12.9	34.1	N/A	N/A	N/A	N/A	N/A	N/A	38
Standard Chartered Bank	3.4	16.1	N/A	N/A	27.5-33.0	24-32	24-32	24-32	N/A
SG Bank	9.7	20.3	N/A	25.3	N/A	27.7	28.7	28.2	29.7
Stanbic Bank	14.1	19	25.3	35.5-40.5	25.3	25.3	25.3	25.3	25.3
The Royal Bank	15.5	35.5	35.5-40.5	N/A	35.5-40.5	35.5-40.5	35.5-40.5	35.5-40.5	35.5-40.5
UBA	13.6	27.5	33.1	N/A	31	32.9	30.4	32.6	31.7
Universal Merchant Bank	10.2	31.3	N/A	N/A	37.4	33.4	38.9	38.5	42.5
Unibank	12.5	39.9	39.8	N/A	32.8	N/A	37.9	36.9	37.9
UT Bank	11.6	30.6	33.6	33.6	33.6	33.6	33.6	33.6	33.6
Zenith Bank	11.8	23.8	29	N/A	29	29	32.9	29	29.9
Industry average	11.3	26.8	33.7	33.2	33.7	32.6	33	32.6	33.6

SOURCE: BANK OF GHANA (2018)

invest, expand and employ new workforce. The high cost of household credit has also reduced aggregate demand with negative consequences for multiplier and accelerator processes in the economy. This limits firms' ability to make enough retained profits for long-term investments. Despite the high cost of credit, banks are reluctant to lend to firms due to high returns on government securities.

Surprisingly, only a handful of studies have given enough attention to low access to affordable funds as a major cause of underdevelopment in Ghana. Although the more recent World Bank Enterprise Survey for Ghana recognises lack of finance as the critical obstacle hampering the potential development of firms in Ghana, it fails to examine the rising cost of capital with the rate of profit that could be made in the country. The survey only compares the cost of capital in Ghana to other periphery countries but fails to compare the cost of capital in the economy to the average rate of return obtainable elsewhere in the country.

Banks constrict their credit position on loans due to rising defaults. Non-performing loans in Ghana account for 19.7% of gross loans and advances as of December 2017. PricewaterhouseCoopers' report on banking survey 2018 reveals that the industry loans and advances fell by Ghc 3.0 billion ($510 million) constituting a 10% fall from 2016, despite a fall in the average base rate from 25.5% to 20% in 2017. Table 7 below depicts that between 2013 and 2016, loans and advances generally declined for most sectors. However, commerce and finance continue to be significant to the banking industry as it maintains the position as the leading recipient of bank loans and advances. Even though banks tightened their credit stance on loans and advances, commerce and finance sectors have generally maintained the 24% shares of the overall loans and advances.

The service sector, which comprises the telecommunication network providers is the second-biggest recipient of bank loans and advances, which ranges from 26% in 2013 to 19.2% in 2017. The housing sector receives the lowest credit, and although it has been increased by 200% between 2013 and 2017, it remains less than 1% of loans and advances from banks. This further signifies the paradox of financialisation in Ghana. The housing market is underdeveloped, and as a result, mortgage debt is not a significant problem in the economy. The data shows that Ghanaian households have not had the same paradigm as those households in the core countries, which experienced a congruence increase in debts and housing prices in the era of financialised capitalism.

The mining and quarrying sectors also saw a decline in loans and advances from 2.7% in 2013 to 2.5% in 2017 after rising from 2014 to 2016. The sharp fall between December 2016 and December 2017 was mainly due to the fall in gold prices on the global market, which forced mining companies to adjust their operational strategies and cut down production. This sub-sector (mining and quarrying) also has access to the international capital market because of its global

TABLE 7 Composition of bank loans and advances (percentage) 2013–2017

	2013	2014	2015	2016	2017
Commerce & finance	23.3%	24.4%	24.9%	24.5%	24.0%
Services	26.0%	19.7%	19.2%	19.5%	19.2%
Miscellaneous	8.3%	11.5%	9.7%	9.5%	13.9%
Manufacturing	11.6%	11.4%	10.0%	8.8%	10.7%
Transport, storage & communication	4.7%	4.3%	4.3%	8.5%	7.9%
Construction	9.2%	8.7%	9.5%	8.9%	7.8%
Electricity, gas & water	8.6%	12.5%	14.1%	12.4%	7.4%
Agriculture, forestry & fishing	5.2%	4.2%	3.9%	4.1%	5.7%
Mining and quarrying	2.7%	3.1%	3.6%	3.1%	2.5%
Housing	0.3%	0.2%	0.9%	0.8%	0.9%
Total	**100.0%**	**100.0%**	**100.0%**	**100.0%**	**100.0%**

SOURCE: GHANA BANKING SURVEY (2018)

ownership. The conversion of energy sector loans to bonds accounted for the decline in the energy sector loans and advances. The restructuring of energy sector loans under the Energy Sector Levy Act (ESLA) bond contributed to a 41% decline in loans and advances and enabled the energy sector to have alternative sources of finance. This phenomenon is synonymous with financialisation in the core economies, where large firms do not depend on bank credit for investment.

The agricultural sector accounts for most of the employment in the informal sector in Ghana and contributes about 22% to the GDP. However, bank loans and advances to the sector fell from 5.2% in 2013 to 2.9% in 2015. The decline in bank credit to the sector is attributed to high risk and uncertainty. Despite this uncertainty, bank credit to the sector grew by 39% between December 2016 and December 2017 (Table 7). This is due to the recent government initiative such as *Planting for Food and Jobs*[5] and the introduction of the Government Incentive-Based Risk-Sharing System for Agricultural Lending (GIRSAL). This is a guarantee fund that seeks to underwrite the risk exposure in the agricultural sector and is expected to promote lending by commercial/universal banks to the sector.

---

5 This is Government of Ghana initiative designed to facilitate growth in food production to address the falling output in the agricultural sector as well as providing jobs for the youth.

The significance of access to finance cannot be ignored if these firms are to participate meaningfully in the growth and development of Ghana. However, despite various initiatives that have been adopted by the government of Ghana, many firms, in particular SMEs, continue to face challenges in accessing financing, particularly from formal financial institutions. The financial system in Ghana remains relatively underdeveloped despite the numerous reforms since FINSAP. Andrianaivo and Yartey (2010) assert that the bond markets in many SSA are profoundly underdeveloped as governments continue to be the primary issuer of bonds in these countries, and conclude that the role of the corporate sector in the bond market is minimal. Lack of finance limits firms' ability to invest, employ and pay decent wages, which are key determinants to end both monetary and non-monetary aspects of poverty.

5.2   *Government Policies*

Ghana still depends on the Western legacy bestowed to it by British colonial rule. According to Boateng (2004), the 1963 Companies Act is still being applied to all companies in the country. However, the Act only recognises large corporations and not SMEs, which now contribute the most to the economy in terms of employment, income and GDP. He describes the legal system in SSA as *shaky* and the business environment as unregulated. Many markets in Ghana are isolated and underdeveloped. These markets include market vendors, food processing, handicrafts, garment (e.g., tie and dye) and other service sectors. They are subject to a long channel of distribution with many intermediaries between the producer and the consumer, resulting in a high cost of production or services. The long supply chain blurs the distinction between the suppliers and retailers.

Good economic governance in areas such as taxation, regulation, and enterprise licencing and registration are essential pillars for the creation of enabling the business environment. Ineffective regulations fail to address market imperfections that limit productive investment and reconcile private and public interests. According to the (World Bank Enterprise Survey 2013), the number of permits and approvals that firms need to obtain and the time it takes to obtain them are expensive and time-consuming. This adds to the bureaucratic costs of doing business in the country. The report further argues that the prevailing legislation of the country also determines the mix of legal forms/ownerships private firms take, and this determines the level of protection for investors, thereby affecting the incentive to invest. Other obstructive factors to business growth are addressed below.

5.2.1 Corruption

One of the inhibiting factors to business growth in Ghana is corruption. Corruption by public officials is a significant administrative and financial burden on businesses. Corruption creates a hostile business environment by discouraging the operational efficiency of businesses and increasing the costs and risks related to doing business. Inefficient regulations impede firms' overall efficiency as they present occasions for soliciting bribes where businesses are asked for bribes by a public official to complete a specified set of business transactions. Gonzalez, Lopez-Cordova, and Valladares (2007) argue that on average, two out of every five firms in the periphery (Africa and Latin America) reported paying bribes in order to get things done; and one in six firms described that they were expected to offer gifts when meeting public officials. The report concludes that African firms are three times as likely to be asked for unofficial payment to a public official *to get things done* than Latin American.

Figure 24 measures the composite index of corruption, the Graft Index.[6] The index shows a higher possibility of paying bribes and informal gifts in Ghana at 29.7% than the SSA average of 19.4% and low middle-income countries at 14.2%. González et al. (2007) contend that bribes and informal gifts in SSA represent about 2.7% of sales. More worrisome is that the incidence of corruption and bribes are higher in the periphery, where there are pressing needs for development. For instance, whereas only 9% of firms in Chile argue that informal gifts are required *to get things done*, 87% of firms in Burkina Faso believe

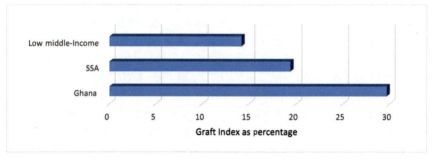

FIGURE 24 Graft Index of corruption: Ghana, Sub-Saharan Africa and low middle-income countries
SOURCE: AUTHOR'S ESTIMATES USING FIGURES FROM THE WORLD BANK ENTERPRISE SURVEY FOR GHANA (2013)

---

6 Measures the proportion of times a firm is asked or expected to make *unofficial* payment when soliciting six different public services, permits or licences. The World Bank uses it in its Enterprise Survey.

that informal gifts are required to complete business transactions. These unofficial payments add to firms' costs and thereby constraint profitability.

Government policies can affect the performance of firms in an economy. In as much as taxes are vital for the development of any nation, the level of tax rates and the complexity need to be carefully chosen. In countries where it is more difficult and costly to pay taxes, large shares of economic activity end up in the informal sector where businesses pay no taxes at all (Doing Business data). Corporation tax rates in Ghana have been 25% since 2006, with an all-time high of 32.5% in 2004 before dropping to 25% in 2006. This is higher than in the UK (19%), and the US (21%). Personal income tax for SMEs also stands at 25%. However, the income tax applicable to non-resident individuals is only 20% (Ghana Statistical Service 2018).

The Local Government Act, 1993 (Act 462), empowers district assemblies to levy rates, tolls, poll taxes and licences on businesses and households in their localities. However, according to the National Board for Small Scale Industries (https://nbssi.gov.gh/) report on taxation and small-scale business operations, there is no consensus in the rates applied by districts, and the rates are rarely predictable, thereby, making SMEs less secure. The report remarked that the frequent complaints from SMEs were the overburden of taxes, impeding business growth and expansion.

The Government of Ghana's trade liberalisation policies of the 1980s have exposed many local firms to global competition due to the cheap importation of goods and has impeded their growth. SAP opened up the domestic economy to foreign competition. This put pressure on domestic firms to compete with their global counterparts/monopolies whose superior resources and technological advancement enable them to produce higher quality products at lower costs. Furthermore, the weakening of the local currency against the major international currencies (see figure 25 below) increases the cost of equipment and raw materials, which adds to the already high cost of production. Consequently, poor quality locally made products tend to be more expensive than high-quality imported goods and services. This diverts demand away from locally made goods to the imported ones. These issues have had a damaging effect on the performance of domestic firms.

Falling exchange rates should have been beneficial for exporting firms. However, only 18.9% of firms in the country engage in some forms of exporting activities, and most of the products that they export tend to be price inelastic, and therefore do not benefit from the depreciation of the Ghana cedi. These factors increase firms' costs, causing their profit margins to fall and therefore, unattractive for investors to invest.

Figure 25 depicts the trend the exchange rates of the Ghana cedi have had against the major trading currencies. The Ghanaian cedi depreciated by 63% against the sterling over the period 2013–2017 and continued to depreciate in 2018 against the major trading currencies. Against the US dollar, the Ghana cedi recorded a depreciation of 100% and fell by 71% against the euro over the period. Except for the fall in the pound sterling between 2015 and 2016, which could be attributed to the Brexit campaign/vote, all the major trading currencies appreciated against the Ghana cedi throughout the period. The uncertainty and the *'dollarisation'* of the Ghanaian economy make it more burdensome for firms to be profitable. The continuous depreciation means that external investors (foreigners) will require a higher return on investment to cater for the depreciation. These external costs constrain firms' ability to expand and employ workers to help to reduce poverty in the country sustainably.

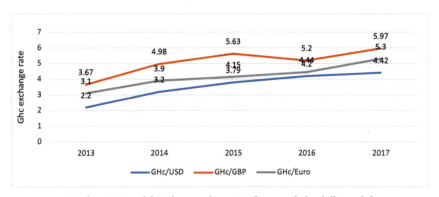

FIGURE 25   Exchange rate of the Ghana cedi against the pound, the dollar and the euro 2013–2017
SOURCE: AUTHOR'S ESTIMATES USING FIGURES FROM THE BANK OF GHANA (VARIOUS)

5.2.2   State of Infrastructural Development

Infrastructural development plays a crucial role in contributing to the cost of doing business, deepening trade and FDI. However, empirical evidence shows acute and dilapidated infrastructure in the sub-region. The European Investment Bank (2013) presented that infrastructure development in SSA lags far behind other periphery economies. The report remarked areas of concern as electricity, irrigation, water and sanitation, information and communication technologies and transport networks. It is estimated that chronic power shortage alone costs the region 1–2% of its economic growth. The provision and accessibility of social amenities such as electricity, clean water, good roads and appropriate office spaces pose a challenge to the development of firms. The dilapidated infrastructure facilities in Ghana impede the ability of firms to remain productive and profitable.

Deficiencies in infrastructure impede the competitiveness of an economy, which obstructs business opportunities as well as increasing costs. Suitable infrastructure effectively links businesses to various stakeholders and facilitates contemporary production methods to reduce long-run average and marginal costs. For example, the chronic power supply will add to the already high cost of production and limit the ability of the firm to earn sufficient profit. Table 8 shows that on average, the number of power outages in a typical month in Ghana is 8.4, which is higher than SSA (7.8) and low middle-income countries (4.8). This means that Ghanaian firms face more disruption in a typical month than their competitors elsewhere do. The use of generators to supplement electricity supply adds high costs to firms' cost of production, therefore reducing their profitability. The value lost due to power outage is 11.5% of sales

TABLE 8 Selected infrastructure indicators for Ghana, Sub-Saharan Africa and low middle-income countries

Indicators	Ghana	Small firms	Medium firms	Large firms	SSA	Lower middle income
Number of a power outage in a typical month	8.4	7.9	9	10.1	7.8	4.8
Value lost due to a power outage (% of sales)	11.5	11.3	11.3	12.7	4.9	2.5
Number of water shortage in a typical month	2.7	2.7	2.2	3.6	2	1.5
The average duration of water shortage (hours)	6.9	6.1	6.2	10.8	3.5	2.7
Delays in obtaining an electrical connection	44.7	44.9	54.2	17.9	32.8	22.1
Delays in obtaining a water connection	57.7	56.8	60.5	56	33.5	21.2

SOURCE: AUTHOR'S ESTIMATES USING FIGURES FROM THE WORLD BANK ENTERPRISE SURVEY FOR GHANA (2013)

in Ghana, while the SSA average is just 4.9% and 2.5% in low middle-income economies. The greater loss in value due to power outages coupled with delays in obtaining electrical connections in Ghana imposes high costs on enterprises and may act as barriers to entry and investment.

An efficient and reliable water supply is vital for many businesses, especially the manufacturing sector. Many manufacturing firms depend on reliable and efficient water supply for their survival. Table 8 shows that the number of water shortages in a typical month in Ghana (2.7) is higher than SSA (2.0) and low middle-income economies (1.5). On average, the duration of water shortage in Ghana is 6.9 longer than SSA (3.5), and low middle-income economies (2.7). These add further costs to firms in Ghana and lower their profitability. (Frimpong 2020) reveals that more than 50% of perishable foods produced in the country get destroyed without reaching the consumer due to either bad roads or lack of storage facilities.

6   Conclusion

This chapter reviewed the key theories of capital structure from the traditionalists' view to the Modigliani and Miller (1958) irrelevance theory and provided original analysis of financialisation, albeit rising financial investments and profits and stagnating real economic sector. The traditional trade-off theory proposes an optimal level of debt relative to equity for all firms but does not explain the contemporary corporate behaviour concerning the stock market. Pecking-order theory, on the other hand, does not suggest optimal capital structure but favours internal financing to external financing; and on the external financing, preference should be given to low-risk debt before equity financing is considered.

Thus, the key limitation of the capital structure argument is that it assumed firms would use both internally-generated funds as well as external funds (debts and equity) towards productive investment. However, as it has been presented throughout this book and consistent with the heterodox economics understanding of the firm, it is uncertain whether firms will invest in real productive or financial assets; bearing in mind that returns on financial assets and government securities are lucrative and less risky. This is in line with the theory of financialisation presented in this book.

However, the distinctive characteristic of the financialised corporation in Ghana (periphery), and the archetypical financialised corporation in the core (for example, the US and the UK) is that firms in Ghana (large and small) are forced to rely on internally-generated funds due to contradictions in the political-economic arrangements. The forced liberalisation has resulted in high interest rates, which divert funds away from productive assets to financial assets and government securities. Thus, the lack of affordable capital for domestic industrial enterprises in Ghana due to high interest rates charged by moneylenders and demand for high collateral security coupled with limited alternative sources of finance, have resulted in stagnant profit in the productive sector in favour of rising financial profits. To a large extent, firms in Ghana still rely on the high-cost non-existing bank credit. Thus, industrial enterprises make little or no profit from their capital investment but are burdened with high interest charges and high production costs.

The subordinate nature of the Ghanaian economy also impacts costs on firms resulting in deficient capital accumulation. This is due to the contradictions of the political-economic arrangements. This is consistent with the heterodox economics view of financialisation discussed above (see, for instance, Crotty 2005; Epstein 2005; Krippner 2005; Orhangazi 2008; Stockhammer 2012a; Lapavitsas 2013; Storm 2018). These factors have impeded firms' ability to expand, employ and pay decent wages to their workers. The inability to do these has made it a challenge for poverty alleviation in the country. The next chapter considers issues surrounding the meaning of poverty and argues that the inappropriate definition of poverty has resulted in wrong approaches to poverty alleviation, consequently mass and chronic poverty in SSA.

CHAPTER 6

The Issue of Poverty

1   Introduction

The previous chapter presented a detailed original analysis of firms' capital structure and the key challenges facing firms in Ghana. Lack of finance and government political and economic policies were identified as the major factors inhibiting the capital accumulation process in the country. This part of the book considers issues surrounding the definition of poverty, how poverty is measured at both national and international levels, and highlights the drawbacks associated with some of these measurements. Stiglitz (2015) remarks that one of the greatest challenging issues facing the world today is poverty and inequality. He argues that national and international governments have a responsibility to battle the vicious-circle dynamics of poverty and inequality. Thus, without governments' intervention, human talent, which is the most valuable thing we possess in the world, will go to waste. Besides, just as worryingly, the social divisions that poverty and inequality produce will eat away the trust on which a prosperous economy depends. Section 2 examines poverty and its challenging measurements. Sections 3 and 4 investigate absolute and relative poverty issues. The chapter ends with the long-standing debate on the impact of neoliberal globalisation/financialisation on poverty, by addressing the issues supporting the debate as well as the concerns of the critics.

The extent of world poverty and inequality in recent times has been highlighted by Oxfam in Davos 2014 (World Economic Forum). Oxfam pointed out that the wealthiest 85 individuals in the world are as wealthy as the poorest half of the global population- '*3.5 billion people own less than a tiny elite whose number can be fitted into a double-decker bus*'. The report added that those classed as the super-rich have a combined wealth of over £1 trillion. The research further showed that the share of the world wealth owned by the wealthiest 1% increased by 4% to 48% between 2009 and 2014, and that the wealthiest 1% were on track to own more than the rest of the 99% of the global population (www.oxfam.org).

It is essential to recognise that poverty is not the same as inequality. Whereas poverty is concerned with the inability to maintain the basic standard of living, inequality deals with the relative standard of living across the whole society. However, there are some strong arguments about the importance of inequality in the poverty debate. It is obvious that inequality means some people have less money and resources than others do. Those with fewer resources are referred to as relatively poor, but sometimes questions are asked whether these people are absolutely poor (Stiglitz 2015; Piketty 2013).

Since the 1990s, poverty reduction became the dominant development agenda. The World Bank and the UN took poverty as the central theme to increase the awareness of the seriousness of global poverty (World Bank 1997; UNDP 2010). It was meant to facilitate strategies to fight and eradicate global poverty.

According to the World Bank Report, global extreme poverty declined substantially in the previous three decades. In 1981, more than half of people in the periphery countries lived on less than $1.25 a day. This rate has since decreased drastically to 21% in 2010 from 52% in 1981. Besides, despite population increases of about 60% in the periphery, fewer people were living below the threshold of $1.25 a day in 2010 (1.2 billion) compared with (1.9 billion) three decades ago (World Bank 2010).

Figure 26 shows that China has been able to reduce its extreme poverty rates drastically from 84% in 1981 to just over 10% in 2010. Extreme poverty in Europe and Central Asia has been stable over the period but rising in the 1990s. India's extreme poverty has been halved in the three decades, from 60% to 33%. However, it is essential to recognise that despite falling extreme poverty rates across continents, SSA witnessed an increase in the number of poor individuals between 1981 and 2010. The extreme poverty rates increased from 51% to 58% between 1981 and 1999 and fell to 48% in 2010. However, because of the increase in population, the absolute number of impoverished people actually increased (see figure 27). More than twice as many impoverished individuals lived in SSA in 2010 (414 million) than there were in 1981 (205 million). The number of poor individuals in SSA has increased throughout the period.

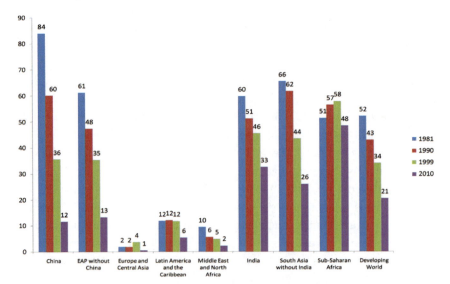

FIGURE 26 The evolution of extreme poverty rates by region 1981–2010
SOURCE: WORLD BANK STAFF ESTIMATES (2010)

In the case of poverty reduction in China, Ang (2016) presents a cyclical process that cuts through the usual debate about whether economic growth or strong institutions should come first in the process of economic development. She asserts that strong institutions and good governance allow markets to emerge. Emerging markets activity may generate problems that require the state to build further stronger institutions to deal with markets' inefficiencies. Good governance will further stimulate and preserve market development. However, China's recent developmental trajectory cannot be attributed to a single cause of action but a somewhat contingent interactive process, which Ang calls *'directed improvisation.'* She concludes that the creative adaptation, which has been remarkably agile in the Chinese system, may be difficult for others to follow. However, Ang's assessment illustrates the significance of government and influential institutions in the fight against poverty.

Heavy reliance on neoliberal market-based policies to reduce poverty has been unsuccessful in sub-Saharan Africa. Kiely (2005) remarks that the developmental successes in China and other East Asian countries that became apparent in the late 1970s and 1980s originated from the state policies carried in the 1960s. He argues that the state-directed capital investment through credit allocation, state planning, capital controls and public-sector investment were the key factors to the successes of China and other East Asian countries. In his view, successful capital development requires state regulation of the capitalists. SAP and its associated deregulation and liberalisation policies in SSA prevent state intervention to allocate credit to the most needed sectors of the economy. Neoliberals argue that capital control and credit allocation will distort the efficiency of the free market.

Figures 27 and 28 shows that in 1981, extreme poverty in SSA accounted for just 11% of the global poverty; by 2010, the region alone represented more than a third of the extreme global poverty. India's contribution also went up from 22% to 33% while China's contribution fell from 43% in 1981 to 13% in 2010. The Middle East and North Africa (MENA) contribution has been stable, ranging from 7 to 10%.

Figure 29 further illustrates the significance of chronic poverty rates in SSA. The gap between absolute poverty rates in East Asia and SSA has widened over the period shown. The two regions had the same absolute poverty rates in 1992 at about 56%, but since then, East Asia poverty has declined sharply to 3.5% while SSA remained at 41% in 2012. Strong institutions and good governance to control market inefficiencies (a feature of ordoliberal) are argued to be the main reason for such sustainable economic development in East Asia.

Figure 30 presents the recent global extreme poverty rates (incidence) and poverty headcount (number of poor) over the period. The global extreme

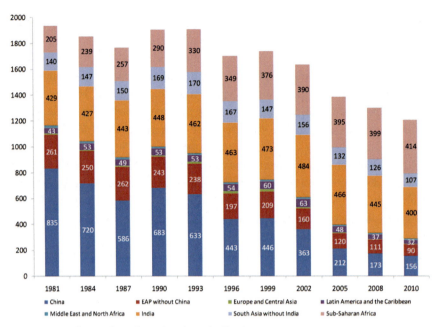

FIGURE 27   The number of poor by region (million) 1981–2010
SOURCE: WORLD BANK REPORT (2010)

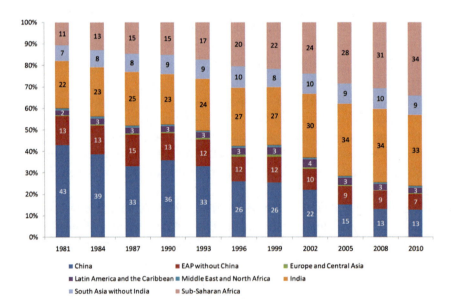

FIGURE 28   Regional share of the world's extreme poor population (%) 1981–2010
SOURCE: WORLD BANK STAFF ESTIMATE (2010)

THE ISSUE OF POVERTY 175

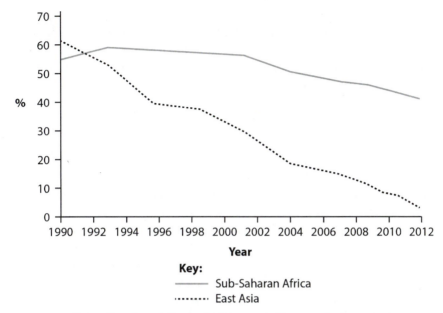

FIGURE 29   Proportion of population in absolute poverty ($1.90 per day in 2011 PPP)
SOURCE: HTTPS://OPENKNOWLEDGE.WORLDBANK.ORG/BITSTREAM/
HANDLE/10986/25078/9781464809583.PDF

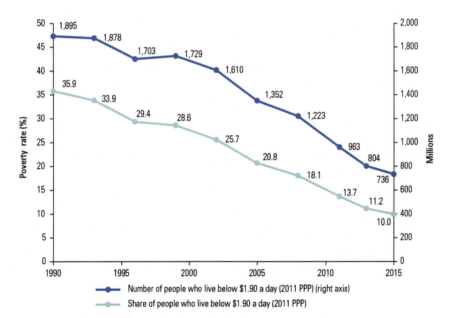

FIGURE 30   Global extreme poverty rate and headcount, 1990–2015
SOURCE: POVCALNET (ONLINE ANALYSIS TOOL), WORLD BANK,
WASHINGTON, DC, HTTP://IRESEARCH.WORLDBANK.ORG/POVCALNET/

poverty rate has decreased from 35.9% in 1990 to 10% in 2015. At the same time, the number of extremely poor individuals also fell from 1.895 billion in 1990 to 736 million in 2015. However, as shown in figure 29, the overall figure masks the uneven development across continents. SSA deviates significantly from the global picture presented.

2   Poverty Measurement Conundrum

Regardless of the policy focus to alleviate extreme global poverty, there are still debates on the definition, measurement, method and data used to determine poverty lines. The major theme in the debate is the difficulty in comparing the standard of living of people consuming a variety of products at various price levels using different currencies. Ferreira et al. (2012; 2015) and Ravallion (2014; 2018) argue that the challenge is to define a uniform threshold that represents a common standard of living across the world; below that threshold an individual will be regarded as poor. Since early 1990, the World Bank adopted the national poverty lines of some of the poorest countries as the threshold for the International Poverty Line (IPL) – the World Bank poverty line. This threshold is expressed in US dollars converted into local currency using the Purchasing Power Parity (PPP)[1] exchange rates for international comparison. The first World Bank poverty line (threshold) was set at $1.01 using 1985 PPPs and used in the World Development Report. This was later updated to $1.08 per day using the 1993 PPPs. A new national poverty line was later proposed in 2005 and set at $1.25 in 2005 PPPs (Ravallion, Chen, and Sangraula 2009). With the release of 2011 PPP conversion factors in 2014, a new international poverty line was set at $1.90 (in 2011 PPP) per person per day.

The World Bank's recent aim of reducing the global extreme poverty rate to less than 3% has adopted Ferreira et al.'s (2015) proposal of new poverty rates at two higher thresholds. These are $3.20 per day and $5.50 per person per day for the lower and upper thresholds, respectively. It has been argued that a substantial number of the world's poor now reside in middle-income countries where economies usually have a more demanding assessment of poverty. The new threshold, therefore, represents typical standards in low-income as well as middle-income countries. Furthermore, it recognises that the issue of poverty is

---

[1] The specific PPP conversion factors used for this exercise are those for private consumption, which come from the International Comparison Program (ICP). www.worldbank.org/data/ICP for information on ICP. See Reddy and Pogge (2008). *How Not to Count the Poor?* Oxford University Press.

THE ISSUE OF POVERTY

dependent on social circumstances (World Bank 2018). This prompted the World Bank to incorporate monetary measurement – income/consumption as well as non-monetary indicators – low educational attainment, access to health and other essential services and environmental issues in the definition of poverty.

Figure 31 shows the projections of extreme poverty by 2030 with a target of less than 3%. With the 2018 poverty rate of 8.6%, the World Bank was on course to achieve the 2020 target of less than 8% before the outbreak of COVID-19, which resulted in a rise of global extreme poverty to 8.2%. Nevertheless, the pace slowed since 2013. The figure shows that between 2013 and 2015, the extreme poverty rate only fell by 0.6% annually. This represents the slowest decline for the previous 25 years average, where poverty rates declined by one percentage point every year. The four growth assumptions demonstrate scenarios where countries projected growth rates from 2018–2030 are (from top to bottom): 1. a country's average growth from 2005–2015; 2. the historical average for the region between 2005 and 2015; 3. twice the historical regional growth average; 4. if growth is pro-poor, that is if the bottom 40% on the average grows faster than the rest of the country (World Bank 2018). Thus, by 2030, the global extreme poverty rate will depend on the particular growth assumption realised. What should be recognised is that in a financialised capitalism, economic growth could be induced by household spending financed by debt, which may

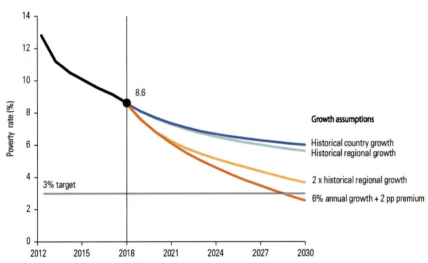

FIGURE 31   Projections to 2030 of global extreme poverty
SOURCE: POVCALNET (ONLINE ANALYSIS TOOL), WORLD BANK, WASHINGTON, DC, HTTP://IRESEARCH.WORLDBANK.ORG/POVCALNET/; WORLD DEVELOPMENT INDICATORS; WORLD ECONOMIC OUTLOOK; GLOBAL ECONOMIC PROSPECTS; ECONOMIST INTELLIGENCE UNIT

not be sustainable when the debt bubble bursts. The slow decline of poverty rates between 2013 and 2015 is partly due to the reverberation of the financial sector meltdown in 2007/8, which caused the global economic recession. A recession normally has disproportionate effects on the vulnerable and the poor in society.

Many governments have pursued poverty reduction programmes in recent years in many parts of the world, particularly in SSA. National governments and policymakers, international donor agencies, and non-governmental organisations have all devoted a lot of attention, effort and resources towards achieving poverty reduction. The goal of achieving poverty reduction drove the United Nations at the turn of the 21st century to establish a set of milestones popularly known as the Millennium Development Goals (MDGs) for periphery countries to reach by 2015. These goals represented a partnership between the core and periphery countries 'to create an environment at both national and international levels, which is conducive to development and elimination of poverty (UNDP 2010).

Ghana, under the IMF, has implemented various programmes over the last four decades to eradicate poverty. These programmes include Structural Adjustment Programme (SAP) in 1983, Ghana Poverty Reduction Strategy, 2002–2004 (GPRS I), Growth and Poverty Reduction Strategy, 2005–2009 (GPRS II) and the recent medium-term development policy framework. Ghana Shared Growth and Development Agenda, 2009–2013 (GSGDA) also focuses on accelerated economic growth with the ultimate aim of alleviating poverty (Government of Ghana 2009; 2010).

It should be recognised that what is perceived as poverty sets out the basis on which strategies are formulated to fight poverty alleviation. However, lack of consensus in the literature has led to many proposed measures (Atkinson 1987; Ferreira et al. 2012; Ravallion 2014).

Poverty in Ghana is on a downward trajectory (see figure 32); however, the number is still high. The poverty measurement used in Ghana reflects the minimum income/expenditure required to satisfy the basic needs. When income/expenditure falls below this threshold, a person is classified as poor. The $1.90 a day poverty line for extreme poverty has been the standard adopted by the international organisation and the World Bank to reflect the minimum consumption/income level necessary to meet one's basic needs. Although this minimum requirement differs over time and across countries, it allows governments and other agencies to compare poverty across regions/countries with a common reference point (Harrison 2007; Ferreira et al. 2015; Ravallion 2018). The poverty headcount measurement could be presented as a percentage (the incidence of poverty) or as the number of people who are poor. However, the headcount measurement does not indicate the extent of poverty, that is how poor the poor are.

The poverty gap is another significant measurement of poverty. This measures the distance below the threshold as a percentage of the poverty line, that is how far individuals fall below the poverty line. It indicates the extent of poverty in an economy (Atkinson 1987; Harrison 2007). The poverty gap, however, does not consider inequality amongst the poor but instead measures the intensity to which people on the average fall below the threshold. World development report (1990), stated that the poverty line could be thought of as comparing two elements; firstly, the income required to afford a minimum standard of nutrition and other basic necessities and, secondly, the necessary income that differs across countries, representing the cost of engaging in the daily life of that community.

Ghana has periodically conducted several surveys known as the Ghana Living Standard Survey (GLSS) since 1980 to determine the incidence of poverty across localities and socio-economic groups in the country. From these surveys, consumption/expenditure-based poverty measurement is used to ascertain a poverty line, which indicates the levels of consumption below which one is classified as poor. The more recent survey conducted by Ghana Statistical Service, 2018 – GLSS7 outlines two key poverty lines based on the January 2013 price level expressed in the constant prices of Greater Accra. This is because food items are more expensive in Greater Accra than in other regions, whereas, for non-food items, other regions (except the three northern regions) are more expensive than the capital. The poverty lines are:

- A lower poverty line of Ghc 792.05 per adult per year: this focuses on what is required to meet the nutritional intake of an individual. Individuals whose total expenditure falls below this threshold are classified to be in extreme poverty. This is because even if they allocate the whole household budget to food, they would not be able to meet the minimum nutrition requirements (if they consume the average consumption basket). This threshold is 27.1% of the mean consumption level in 2012/2013.
- An upper poverty line of Ghc 1314.00 per adult per year: this considers essential food and non-food consumption. Individuals consuming above this threshold can be considered able to purchase enough food to meet the nutritional requirements and the essential non-food intake. This threshold is 44.9% of the mean consumption level in 2012/2013.

The lower poverty line indicates an individual expenditure of Ghc 2.17 per adult per day or $1.10 per day for the extreme poverty line; and Ghc 3.6 per adult per day or $1.80 per day for the upper poverty line (based on the January 2012 exchange rate). It is interesting to note that the domestic currency has since depreciated against the dollar and other major currencies on the foreign exchange market. The Ghana cedi has depreciated 100% against the US dollar between 2013 and 2017 (see figure 25). However, both poverty lines remain the same. Therefore, the Ghana Statistical Service and other agencies should appreciate the links between exchange rates and other macroeconomic variables such as inflation, interest rate, poverty and unemployment in the country. They should go beyond using the GLSS to identify the basket and engage all ten regions to validate further the basket and the weight associated with determining the incidence of poverty. Local people should be involved in determining the basket as well as the weight associated.

It is challenging to set a fixed poverty line using the value of consumption needed to satisfy minimum subsistence needs. Calorie or nutritional requirements may also give a misleading picture because it depends on which food basket is chosen. Townsend (1962) argues that there are many gaps in the existing knowledge of the quantitative aspects of a man's needs. He criticises the British Medical Association (BMA) committee report that 'a man requires 1750 calories or more a day depending on his daily activity' (p.216).

In his later work, Townsend (2010; 2014) remarks that there is little evidence to suggest that any individual fatty acids are requisite for the nutrition of a man. He argues that doubts exist concerning the necessary intake of calcium, iron, protein and other vitamins, especially vitamin C. It is also important to acknowledge that in the era of neoliberalism where cut-throat competition is prevalent, some individuals make their purchases not only by the tastes and nutrition, but by the way the product is advertised and packaged. That is, brand loyalty has a significant influence on what some people consume. These individuals may not be aware of the nutritional content of the food they consume.

Another conundrum in poverty measurement is how poverty numbers should be presented. While the incidence of poverty (the percentage of the poor) has been falling over the years, the absolute number of individuals has not changed (with increases in some regions) over the same period. Advocates of neoliberal globalisation frequently use the incidence of poverty to prove a positive relationship between increasing globalisation/financialisation and poverty alleviation. Critics, on the other hand, point to the absolute number of poor individuals in regions such as SSA to argue their case (Harrison 2007).

Poverty in Africa has a disproportionate effect on women. Women use most of their time nurturing and rearing children, working on the farm, fetching firewood and water, and also doing almost all the household chores with little or no income in return. Women lack access to education and better employment opportunities. These make it difficult for women in periphery countries to escape poverty (Kyei 2000).

One other significant problem of poverty measurement is that those who define and measure poverty have no living experience of what poverty entails. These are usually the elite of the World Bank, IMF, OECD, UN, statisticians, economists, and other international agencies. They rely on data extracted from large-scale demographic and income surveys at the household level and subject these to econometric/quantitative analysis. These elites can only have an outsider's view of what it is to be poor, a view which is entirely distorted (Chambers 1995; Kyei 2000) . Some might argue that one should not have a living experience in poverty to be able to define poverty, but it is essential to recognise that inappropriate measurement of poverty will lead to a wrong policy to alleviate poverty.

Owusi and Yankson (2007) remark that methods used in measuring poverty are very crucial because it affects the approaches that policymakers approve to alleviate poverty and form the basis on which the analyses of the poor are administered. Agbenyega (1998) points out that primarily, statistics and qualitative analysis of the poor are used in the same way as a *drunken man* uses a lamp post, not for its primary purpose of illumination but for supporting their preconceived notions. This presents a conundrum to draw up an appropriate programme to alleviate poverty. If the problem has been defined or measured by an outsider who has no experience in what the problem (poverty) is; and as this book will outline later, the poor must be involved in designing programmes that will help alleviate poverty. Chambers (1995, 180) argues that poor people's criteria differ from those assumed for them by professionals and outlines the reasons why income poverty, though flawed, has been widely used.

In the first place, he argues, economics concepts, methods, and measures dominate the development discourse and have been accepted as the norm of development practices and policymaking. It is essential to acknowledge that this is not in any way to underestimate the importance of economic concepts and methods. However, economists' view of poverty tends to become the standard and dominant meaning and measurement for other disciplines and professions.

Furthermore, the poor in the core countries have been mainly urban and have tended to rely on and receive some form of income support, such as welfare benefits in the United Kingdom. Consequently, the economic status of the poor is easily captured in income/consumption. Transplant this measure in the periphery assumes that similar conditions prevail. Poverty in Ghana is a rural phenomenon (see table 9) characterised by hardship, suffering, lack of opportunities and hopelessness.

Moreover, income or consumption poverty is measurable. Thus, non-monetary aspects of poverty can also be measured by given shadow prices and combined into a single scale. These make it possible for poverty lines to be measured and drawn to facilitate international comparisons. Consequently, governments and other agencies could be assessed on how well they are presumed to be working to alleviate poverty. This, therefore, gives professionals supremacy and pride, which tend to go unchallenged. Thus, the measurable then become measured, which becomes a reality and what matters, standardising the diverse, and excluding the divergence and difference.

Besides, it is erroneously assumed that poor households are mostly concerned with income/consumption to meet the basic needs to survive. Therefore, the more deprived the poor find themselves, the more acceptable economic reductionism income/consumption poverty becomes. Consequently, income/consumption poverty becomes pro-poor. This, however, does not eradicate poverty but rather postpones the problem.

Chambers concludes that these point to the reasons why income-consumption poverty has some dominance as a measure of world poverty. Kabeer (1996) remarks that the principal concern of the majority of economists is with income/consumption poverty; with the quantifiable and the merchandisable. The equation of poverty with the household income, he argues, demonstrates the measurement and the institutional flaws of mainstream economics.

It is essential to recognise that there is a lack of consensus regarding a precise definition of poverty. Within the Social Sciences, many attempts have been made to have a coherent definition within numerous poverty research and studies (Townsend 1962; Atkinson 1987; Chambers 1995; Kyei 2000; Ravallion 2001; Harrison 2007). However, no agreed definition unites the various approaches available to Social Sciences. But, unless local people have standards to define and recognise the poor, it will be challenging to design and administer programmes to alleviate poverty (Harrison 2007; Ferreira et al. 2015).

Lack of, and deficiency, are the common themes held in most definitions of poverty. Beyond this general view, nothing unites the various disciplines on what represents poverty. Besides, this notion only constitutes the simple relativity of the concept. This narrow definition colonises the general usage. Income/consumption poverty is used as a proxy for other deprivations and then subsumes them. It has been common to view poverty as more than a monetary problem but then allowing the quantifiable and measurable to seize control and dominate (Chambers 1995; Ferreira et al. 2012; 2015). Chambers argues that income poverty, though significant, is only one aspect of deprivation, and maintains that poverty includes lack of physical necessities, assets, and income.

Chambers (1995, 180) outlines the following characteristics as the reality of the rural poor, which is a phenomenon in the periphery, and Ghana in particular:
- Physical weakness, which includes disability, sickness, pain and suffering.
- Powerlessness – the poor are powerless and lack influence. Some easily ignore them and are exploited by others.
- Isolated in communication and lacking contact and information.
- Humiliation – this is often overlooked because it does not lend itself to measurement. Lack of self-respect and independence.
- Social inferiority – this includes gender, race and ethnic origin or being referred to as low in society in terms of occupation, social class, tribe, or even caste.

Thus, poverty is more than just income and consumption as it includes the lack of what is necessary for well-being, and its scope should encompass social, economic and other forms of disadvantages outlined above – powerlessness, isolation, humiliation and physical weakness.

The measurement and analysis of poverty in Ghana have focused on consumption poverty, comprising food and non-food items. Since GLSS was conducted, seven rounds of data have been collected. However, this book will focus on the recent rounds of data collected from 2005/06, 2012/13, and 2016/17. This is due to the similarities of the questionnaires used, thereby making it viable to compare their results.

Figure 32 illustrates a downward trend in poverty in Ghana. It is also clear that poverty is predominantly a rural phenomenon. For example, the Greater Accra Metropolitan Area (GAMA) has consistently recorded the lowest poverty incidence in the last two rounds of the survey. In percentage terms, the number of people classified as poor has decreased from 51.7% in 1991 to just over 24% in 2013. This means that Ghana attained the Millennium Development Goal target 1, which seeks to halve poverty incidence by 2015 from the 1990 rate. Since 2013, there has been a marginal decline in the poverty rate from 24.2% to 23.4% in 2017. However, during the same period, economic growth has averaged 5%, while the average annual per capita income for 2014–2017 was GHc 5,540.8, which is double the 2010–2013 average per capita income of GHc 2,672.2. This paradox explains the myth of finance-growth-poverty alleviation nexus in Ghana. The expansion of the economy impacts marginally on the poor.

It is also essential to recognise that the general picture of falling poverty rate conceals significant differences across localities, administrative regions, economic activity and even gender. Although poverty rates in urban areas such as Accra (GAMA) have decreased from 12% in 2005 to just 2% in 2017, some pockets of these urban centres are characterised by overcrowding, poor sanitation,

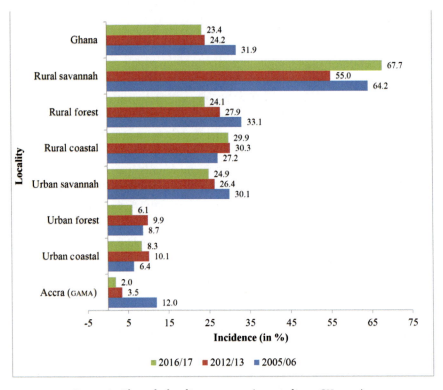

FIGURE 32   Poverty incidence by locality 2005–2017 (poverty line = GHc 1,314)
SOURCE: GHANA STATISTICAL SERVICE (2018) – GLSS7

and an occasional outbreak of diseases (for instance the cholera outbreak in Accra in July-August 2014). Poverty rates in urban coastal have actually increased from 6.4% in 2005 to 8.3% in 2017. A similar trend in rural savannah where the highest poverty headcount is found, saw poverty rates increase from 64.2% in 2005 to 67.7% in 2017 after falling to 55% in 2013. Rural forest and urban savannah, however, witnessed gradual falls in poverty rates from 33.1% and 30.1% in 2005 to 24.1% and 24.9% in 2017, respectively. The most recent improved national poverty rate of 23.4% indicates that roughly one in four Ghanaians is living in poverty and over two million are in extreme poverty.

Table 9 shows that even though just about half of Ghana's population resides in rural areas, it contributes more than 80% consistently to the overall poverty incidence. Rural savannah accounted for almost 50% of poverty incidence in 2016/17 and has consistently contributed the most to the poverty incidence in the country. The persistent poverty in this region is worrying, and it will, therefore, be vital to analyse the principal causes of this (which is beyond the scope of this book) to inform future policies and programmes.

TABLE 9 Poverty incidence and poverty gap by localities- 2005–2017 (poverty line = Ghc 1,314)

Locality	2016/17 Poverty incidence (P0)	2016/17 Contribution to total poverty (C0)	2016/17 Poverty gap (P1)	2016/17 Contribution to total poverty gap (C1)	2012/13 Poverty incidence (P0)	2012/13 Contribution to total poverty (C0)	2012/13 Poverty gap (P1)	2012/13 Contribution to total poverty gap (C1)	2005/06 Poverty incidence (P0)	2005/06 Contribution to total poverty (C0)	2005/06 Poverty gap (P1)	2005/06 Contribution to total poverty gap (C1)
Accra (GAMA)	2.0	1.3	0.3	0.6	3.5	2.2	0.9	1.8	12.0	4.4	3.4	3.7
Urban Coastal	8.3	2.6	1.9	1.6	10.1	2.1	2.3	1.5	6.4	1.2	1.3	0.7
Urban Forest	6.1	5.8	1.2	3.1	9.9	9.0	2.0	5.8	8.7	4.0	2.2	3.0
Urban Savannah	24.9	7.2	7.0	5.6	26.4	8.6	6.6	6.8	30.1	5.1	10.7	5.3
Rural Coastal	29.9	8.2	8.9	6.8	30.3	6.9	8.7	6.3	27.2	9.3	6.7	6.7
Rural Forest	24.1	25.3	6.3	18.4	27.9	30.3	7.9	26.8	33.1	29.1	8.4	21.4
Rural Savannah	67.7	49.6	31.2	63.7	55.0	40.8	22.0	51.1	64.2	46.9	28.0	59.4
Urban	7.8	16.8	1.8	11.0	10.6	22.0	2.5	15.9	12.4	14.7	3.7	12.6
Rural	39.5	83.2	15.1	89.0	37.9	78.0	13.1	84.1	43.7	85.3	15.4	87.5
All Ghana	23.4	100.0	8.4	100.0	24.2	100.0	7.8	100.0	31.9	100.0	11.0	100.0

SOURCE: GHANA STATISTICAL SERVICE (2018) - GLSS7 REPORT

Extreme poverty in Ghana is classified as where a person's income is not sufficient to meet the necessary nutritional needs even if they spend the total consumption budget on food (Ghana Statistical Service 2018, *GLSS7 Report*).

Figure 33 illustrates that extreme poverty has declined from 16.5% in 2005/06 to 8.2% in 2016/17 (a decline by 8.3%). However, between 2013 and 2017, extreme poverty reduced by just 0.2%. This demonstrates that the reduction in the incidence of extreme poverty has slowed down. Based on the 2010 Population and Housing Census (PHC) (estimates for 2017), about 2.4 million Ghanaians predominantly in the rural areas are unable to consume the minimum daily requirements of calories per adult per equivalent of food per day. That is, even if they devote their total spending on food. What is surprising is that this figure is up by 200,000 from 2012/13 levels. Within these same periods, financial activities in the country are on the rise with the introduction of financial inclusion and its mobile money as a way of reducing poverty (detailed

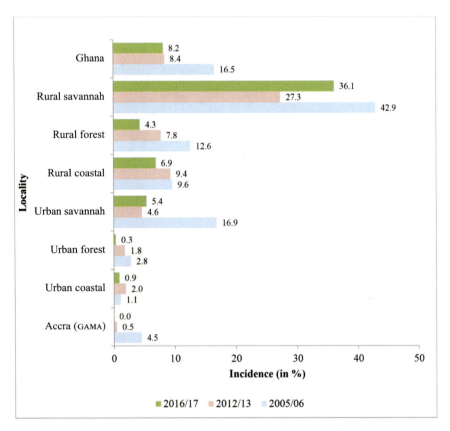

FIGURE 33   Extreme poverty incidence by locality 2005–2017 (poverty line = GHc 792.05)
SOURCE: GHANA STATISTICAL SERVICE (2018)- GLSS7 REPORT

analysis in chapter 7). This paradox of rising financial activities and financial interests and rising poverty headcounts demonstrates that financialisation in Ghana is not having meaningful impacts on the living standards of the poor, especially those in the rural areas.

Table 10 demonstrates that the incidence of extreme poverty is a rural phenomenon. Over 2 million rural inhabitants are in extreme poverty (2010 Population and Housing Census (PHC) estimates for 2017). Extreme poverty is more pronounced on the local level than the overall poverty incidence. The rural-urban divide is more noticeable with rural savannah, again recording an 8.8% increase from the 2012/13 levels to 36.1% in 2016/17, which is more than four times the national average, and contributes over 75% to the incidence of extreme poverty. However, except for rural savannah, all regions recorded some decline in extreme poverty. GAMA contributes nothing to the extreme poverty incidence. With an estimated urban population of 14.7 million (based on 2010 PHC projections for 2017), only 1% of this figure is impoverished and accounts for just 6.2% of the national incidence. However, 15.6% of the rural population (estimated at 14.2 million) are extremely poor and account for 93.8 of the overall extreme poverty indicators. It is clear that the World Bank and the IMF financial inclusion programmes aimed at the poor are not having the desired impact in rural Ghana. Drawing these poor people into the realms of finance is causing the incidence of extreme poverty to increase in places like rural savannah.

Poverty is a rural phenomenon in Africa characterised by lack of opportunities, hardship, illiteracy, diseases, hunger and low life expectancy. The underlying goal of development enshrined in the constitution of Ghana is to improve the well-being of all citizens by alleviating poverty through a sustained increase in the wealth of the nation and more equitable distribution of income and wealth – 1992 constitution (Government of Ghana 1992).

The Structural Adjustment Programme (SAP) and its associated liberalisation and the more recent financial inclusion policy initiated by the Bretton Wood Institutions have brought a renewed interest in the impact of liberalisation on sustainable economic development at the local levels. There is a growing consensus that the local people, NGOs, local governments and even the poor have a role to play in the fight against poverty. Economic development and poverty alleviation are participatory processes and thus require the active involvement of the poor in decision-making.

Poverty exists when individuals cannot maintain the necessary level of well-being that is considered minimum standards by that community (Ravallion 2001; 2018; Ferreira et al. 2015). As argued by Gaiha (1993) and Ravallion (2018), it is not enough for policy purposes to know that poverty exists, but also

TABLE 10   Extreme poverty incidence and poverty gap by locality 2005–2017 (extreme poverty line = GHc 792.05)

Locality	2016/17 Poverty incidence (P0)	2016/17 Contribution to total poverty (C0)	2016/17 Poverty gap (P1)	2016/17 Contribution to total poverty gap (C1)	2012/13 Poverty incidence (P0)	2012/13 Contribution to total poverty (C0)	2012/13 Poverty gap (P1)	2012/13 Contribution to total poverty gap (C1)	2005/06 Poverty incidence (P0)	2005/06 Contribution to total poverty (C0)	2005/06 Poverty gap (P1)	2005/06 Contribution to total poverty gap (C1)
Accra (GAMA)	0.0	0.0	0.0	0.0	0.5	0.9	0.1	0.5	4.5	3.2	1.1	2.5
Urban Coastal	0.9	0.8	0.3	0.9	2.0	1.2	0.4	0.9	1.1	0.4	0.1	0.1
Urban Forest	0.3	0.9	0.1	0.5	1.8	4.8	0.2	2.1	2.8	2.5	0.8	2.3
Urban Savannah	5.4	4.4	1.1	2.7	4.6	4.4	1.0	3.3	16.9	5.5	5.1	5.5
Rural Coastal	6.9	5.4	1.4	3.3	9.4	6.2	1.8	4.4	9.6	6.4	1.6	3.4
Rural Forest	4.3	13.0	0.9	8.2	7.8	24.3	1.8	20.2	12.6	21.4	2.1	11.9
Rural Savannah	36.1	75.4	13.6	84.3	27.3	58.3	8.7	68.5	42.9	60.6	16.0	74.3
Urban	1.0	6.2	0.2	4.2	1.9	11.2	0.3	6.9	5.1	11.6	1.4	10.4
Rural	15.6	93.8	5.4	95.8	15.0	88.8	4.3	93.1	23.4	88.4	7.2	89.6
All Ghana	8.2	100.0	2.8	100.0	8.4	100.0	2.3	100.0	16.5	100.0	5.0	100.0

SOURCE: (GHANA STATISTICAL SERVICE (2018) – GLSS7 REPORT

essential to know how much poverty exists. The authors argue that much of the theoretical literature is mainly concerned with the aggregation problem; however, several problems exist relating to the identification issue.

3 Absolute Poverty

Absolute poverty is when a household is unable to afford the basic needs of life, thus, having the bare minimum food to survive on. This is someone who struggles to make ends meet – lack of food, shelter and clothing. This poverty line is determined by using the standard of living measure, which is fixed for the whole period and accepted across countries. This makes it relatively easier to compare poverty levels across countries and regions. The threshold, however, fails to consider differences in income across countries. Ferreira et al. (2015) contend that absolute poverty comparison considers two or more households of the same income budget to be either poor or not poor, regardless of when or where they were assessed.

3.1 *Poverty in Administrative Regions*

There is a wide disparity in the incidence of poverty and poverty gap in the ten regions of Ghana.[2] The northern half of the country (Upper West, Northern Region, and Upper East) has consistently accounted for the highest incidence of poverty in the country since records began. GAMA area contributes the least incidence of poverty, with just 2.5% in 2016/17, which is 20.9 % lower compared with the national figure of 23.4%. However, half of the regions (five regions) in the country recorded an increase in the poverty level in 2016/17 – worsening poverty conditions. These regions consist of the three regions in the north, which recorded the top three highest poverty rates in the country – Upper West 70.9%, Northern region 61.1%, and Upper East 54.8%. Even among the top three poverty regions, the variation is pronounced. Western 21.1% and Volta 37.3% are the other two that experienced worsening rates in 2016/17 from 2012/13 levels. The rest of the regions, including the GAMA area, experienced a decline in poverty rates (Figure 34).

---

2 There are now 16 regions in Ghana. However, the recent GLSS7 (2018) was conducted before the new regions were created. Thus the analysis is based on the old ten regions as the newly created regions do not have any poverty data.

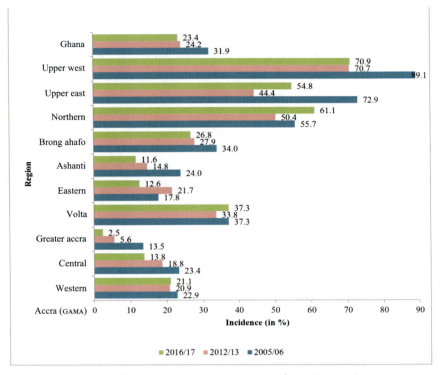

FIGURE 34　Poverty incidence by region 2005–2017 (poverty line = GHc 1,314)
SOURCE: (GHANA STATISTICAL SERVICE (2018) – GLSS7 REPORT

Although the Upper West region recorded the highest poverty rate in the country, it contributes just 8.5% of the national figure. This is because the region has the smallest population in the country and adds 574,794.9 (based on 2010 PHC projections for 2017) to the 6.8 million individuals regarded as poor in 2016/17. The Northern region of Ghana has been the largest contributor since 2005 and accounts for about 1.8 million poor people to the overall figure (Table 11).

About a quarter of Ghanaians are deemed poor, and there is a wide regional variation. Since records began, poverty has been very much a rural phenomenon. The majority of the residents in the three regions in the north are deemed poor or extremely poor. Rural savannah accounts for most of the poor people in the country. Therefore, poverty reduction in these regions will help to reduce the overall national figure. Many of the rural population work tirelessly and depend on farming for their livelihoods and to support their family, but poor harvest and other unfavourable market conditions mean that they hardly earn enough to provide for themselves and their families. Some struggle to pay their hospital bills as well as sending their children to school. However, what is worrying is that

TABLE 11   Poverty incidence and poverty gap by region (%) 2006–2017 (poverty line = GHc 1,314)

Region	2016/17 Poverty incidence (P0)	2016/17 Contribution to total poverty (C0)	2016/17 Poverty gap (P1)	2016/17 Contribution to total poverty gap (C1)	2012/13 Poverty incidence (P0)	2012/13 Contribution to total poverty (C0)	2012/13 Poverty gap (P1)	2012/13 Contribution to total poverty gap (C1)	2005/06 Poverty incidence (P0)	2005/06 Contribution to total poverty (C0)	2005/06 Poverty gap (P1)	2005/06 Contribution to total poverty gap (C1)
Western	21.1	9.1	4.9	5.9	20.9	7.9	5.7	6.8	22.9	7.3	5.4	5.0
Central	13.8	5.0	3.6	3.6	18.8	6.9	5.6	6.4	23.4	6.4	5.6	4.4
Greater Accra	2.5	1.7	0.5	0.9	5.6	3.8	1.6	3.5	13.5	5.9	3.7	4.7
Volta	37.3	13.6	13.0	13.3	33.8	12.1	9.8	11.0	37.3	8.7	9.2	6.2
Eastern	12.6	5.8	3.1	3.9	21.7	9.3	5.8	7.8	17.8	7.5	4.2	5.2
Ashanti	11.6	9.5	2.7	6.1	14.8	12.0	3.5	9.0	24.0	12.6	6.4	9.8
Brong Ahafo	26.8	10.8	8.8	9.9	27.9	11.4	7.4	9.4	34.0	9.8	9.5	7.9
Northern	61.1	26.1	26.7	31.9	50.4	20.8	19.3	24.9	55.7	21.0	23.0	25.2
Upper East	54.8	9.8	23.8	11.9	44.4	7.4	17.2	9.0	72.9	10.9	35.3	15.3
Upper West	70.9	8.5	37.6	12.6	70.7	8.4	33.2	12.3	89.1	10.0	50.7	16.4
All Ghana	23.4	100.0	8.4	100.0	24.2	100.0	7.8	100.0	31.9	100.0	11.0	100.0

SOURCE: (GHANA STATISTICAL SERVICE (2018) – GLSS7 REPORT

the accepted neoliberal policy prescriptions of liberalisation and deregulation seem to be causing worsening living standards rather than improving them for those in rural areas. The reduction in government subsidies to poor rural farmers has negatively affected farm yields and incomes. This has made it difficult to achieve a sustainable rural livelihood and food security in those regions, especially for rural women and those who rely on marginal lands for farming.

Absolute poverty is measured using a basket of goods considered to ensure the basic consumption needs of a household. The challenge of this measure is the constituents of these basic needs against which the line would be drawn. For many periphery countries, as Gaiha (1993) pointed out, basic food expenditure forms the essential component of the recommended nutritional consumption. A small allowance of non-food expenditure is then added to determine the threshold.

However, it is crucial to recognise that what is consumed in most poor households in rural Ghana comes from their subsistence farms and therefore not purchased from the market/shop, giving severe measurement issues of valuing home production. Kyei (2000) argues that there is a lack of consensus on the choice of food energy needed to meet the recommended nutritional intake. Thus, the computations of the recommended nutritional intake are based on an estimate which is subject to a margin of error. Townsend (2014) and Ferreira et al. (2015) argue that the nutritional content of certain products varies depending on where and when the product is produced, and the value society places on the product. For instance, yam is more valuable in Ghanaian society than cocoyam. This makes it difficult to rely on certain nutritional intake as an indicator of poverty.

Furthermore, the level of poverty line set is influenced by how food costs are analysed and whether they are based on experts' opinion of the cheapest way of meeting foods' needs or based on actual food that the poor people eat. The differences can be caused by whether the definition and measurement of poverty include some basic services or not. Thus, despite the agreement that poverty exists, there is a disagreement on how best to define and measure it. Different methodologies, the goods included as needs, price estimate techniques and proxy value estimates all lead to different results (Mitlin and Satterthwaite 2013).

4 Relative Poverty

Relative poverty is when income falls below a certain percentage of the mean income in a society. It does not compare a household to a fixed cut-off income/consumption, but relative to the rest of the society. When all levels of income in the economy increase, absolute poverty will fall; however, for relative poverty to fall, the rate of growth of low income must be above the rate of growth of average income. Thus, relative poverty is when a household cannot acquire adequately the common standard of living which is the customary behaviour in the society they live (Townsend 2014; Ravallion 2018).

It is challenging to translate the relative poverty concept into a concrete measure. This measure ignores essential aspects of deprivation, such as the quality of goods and services, and relies heavily on income measurement of poverty. According to Townsend (1962, 2010), households are deemed rich or poor depending on their share of the available resources. In his view, households that command fewer resources than the average in their society are classified as living in poverty, irrespective of where they live.

4.1 Using Non-monetary Deprivation

It is contended that poverty is not just about lack of money, but lack of physical necessities, assets and command over resources (Chambers 1995; Townsend 2010; Ferreira et al. 2015). The variety of problems related to the quantifiable income and monetary measurement of poverty justifies the inclusion of non-monetary means of poverty measurement. It is, however, essential to use both approaches in tandem to enable a proper assessment of the poor. Researchers and policymakers should give much attention and effort towards a more accurate definition of poverty that encompasses all aspects of poverty, that is monetary and non-monetary or income and non-income aspects of poverty. In support of Chambers (1985) and Ferreira et al. (2015), poverty is multi-dimensional, and a household is poor when their income and other resources fall short of the average household, and as a result, excluded from society and are unable to meet the basic needs of the society. Townsend (2010) argues that individuals and families in a society can be classified as poor when they cannot participate in the activities of the society because they lack the necessary resources and the living condition to do so.

Clearly, this definition of poverty goes beyond the *economics of income* and includes both the psychological and social aspects of well-being. It highlights the multi-dimensional features of poverty. Human Development Index (HDI) recognises that there is much more to human development and well-being than just economic growth and GDP per capita. HDI indicators include quality of life indicators such as access to health and education, safe drinking water, life expectancy rate, infant mortality rate, illiteracy rate and happiness. Since the early 1990s, the World Bank's measurement of global poverty using national poverty lines has been expressed in US dollars (discussed above). Thus, consumption or income information has been the benchmark to estimate poverty lines.

However, poverty is multidimensional, and the monetary measurement of poverty does not capture many important aspects of human well-being. Poverty encompasses lack of income and shortfall in consumption, but also powerlessness, isolation, which refer to being inferior and unable to access education, health and lack of social and economic support as well as living in a hazardous environment. Without a comprehensive definition of poverty – monetary as well as non-monetary indicators, a homeless person living on $3.50 a day will not be regarded as being poor. A family on an income of $4 per person per day, but lacks access to adequate sanitation, electricity, spends much time fetching firewood for cooking, and draws water directly from the river/well will not be captured in the poverty line. In short, the monetary-based measurement would not encompass all aspects of well-being, because not all goods and services that households consume have a market value (World Bank 2018). For instance, common non-market goods without market prices such as public goods, clean environment and secure community may not be captured in the income definition of poverty. The prices of these public goods do not exist and therefore may not be accurately reflected consumption values.

The monetary measurement of poverty illustrates Chambers' (1985) argument that poverty becomes what has been measured. The World Bank and the IMF's financial inclusion policy, that the poor need access to finance to fulfill their potentials, signifies that a lack of access to finance is deemed as the primary cause of poverty, and therefore other social problems are less important. Financial inclusion as a way of empowering the poor makes poverty a financial problem, which requires new credit relation – the financialisation of poverty. This exemplifies Mader's (2015) point that in the era of financialised capitalism, poverty has come to mean a lack of decent finance, hence neoliberal economic policy has come to produce more financial relations, that is a new institution to manage the poor.

5 The Paradox of Sub-Saharan Africa's Middle Class

The high economic growth rates and increased Foreign Direct Investment (FDI) in sub-Saharan Africa (SSA) has prompted many to argue that the continent is the next East Asia Miracle where the next global economic growth will come from. However, many have questioned whether the wealth created by ten years of economic growth has been evenly shared or has been concentrated in the hands of the few rich individuals. The argument is that, if decades of economic growth has been shared growth, the evidence should be a rising middle class on the continent. Nevertheless, there is controversy surrounding the definition of SSA's middle class.

The question as to who qualifies as middle class, and the actual size of Africa's middle class has been the subject of fierce debate in recent times. *The Economist* published an article on 24th October 2015 arguing that *'Africans are mainly rich or poor, but not a middle class; this should worry democrats'.* This brings the question as to how big is Africa's middle class and more importantly how is it measured?

Different studies offered different interpretations depending on the standards used to measure. Credit Suisse believes the size of Africa's middle class is just 3.3% which equates to about 19 million Africans. The standards used include households having between $50,000- $500,000 (using 2005 purchasing power parity) in wealth. This purchasing power parity is the equivalent of $50,000 in different countries; thus, about $22,000 in South Africa and $18,000 in Ghana. It is important to recognise that the standard of living differs within and across countries and therefore using the same benchmark across states and continents seems an unfair comparison.

Another study by the Pew Research Centre, Kochhar (2015), an American outfit, using a narrower and what they call a more internationally acceptable definition – using consumption expenditure of $10-$20 per person per day, reckons just 6% of sub-Saharan Africans qualify as middle class. Using this consumption expenditure, most Africans, that is about 90% will fall below the minimum threshold of $10 per person per day and will not be classified as middle class. Based on Pew Research Centre estimates, the number of the middle class in Africa barely changed in over a decade to 2014. They argue that although African economic growth had benefited many citizens and lifted many out of poverty; it does not mean that many have made it to the middle-class level. It concludes that over a decade to 2011, Nigeria's poverty rate fell by 18% and the share of low-income earners grew by 17%, while the share of middle-income earners rose by only 1% over the time. There were similar results in many African countries; the poverty rate fell in Ghana from 52% in the 1990s to 23.4 % in 2017 with limited improvement in the middle class (Ghana Statistical Service 2018).

The puzzling question from the above analysis is why is Africa's middle class so skinny and stagnated after a decade of rapid economic growth and substantial FDI on the continent? *The Economist* argues that the benefits of economic growth have not been evenly distributed and that only relatively small urban consumers have benefited from the transient commodity boom. According to Credit Suisse, African super-rich individuals have been the main beneficiaries of the continent's economic boom with just 0.2% of the population owning 30.6% of the wealth. Although inequality is visible on the continent of Africa, it is not a peculiar problem to Africa but a worldwide issue in the era of neoliberalism.

Another reason could be that poverty on the continent had been so extreme that although millions may have benefited from the economic growth with rising incomes, these people are now actually poor rather than extremely poor. An American think tank, the Brookings Institute points out that the average person in extreme poverty in Africa lives on just $0.74 a day compared with the average of $0.98 a day in the developing world (Isaacs et al. 2011). Another issue has been the rapid population growth in Africa – many more people to feed on the scarce resources available. The rising population outpaces income and GDP growth.

Africa Development Bank (AfDB), however, presents a different picture of Africa's middle class. According to AfDB, Africa's middle class has tripled over the last three decades from 111 million or 26% of the population in 1980 to 313 million or 34.3% of the population in 2010 and expected to rise to 1.1 billion or 42% of the population by 2060 (Africa Development Bank 2012). AfDB defines middle class by using African household expenditure as individuals who spend between $2- $20 a day. This makes one in three Africans qualify as middle class. This definition is based on the average cost of living in Africa, and it should be acknowledged that there are some criticisms of the sub-categories of AfDB's description of Africa's middle class. By using the conditions of Africans to determine who qualifies as a middle class no doubt shows a robust reflection of Africa's middle class.

AfDB and the South African based Standard Bank, the biggest lenders in the sub-region, reckon the structural change on the continent has brought about real improvements in the last decade, which has resulted in the surge of the middle class (Figure 35).

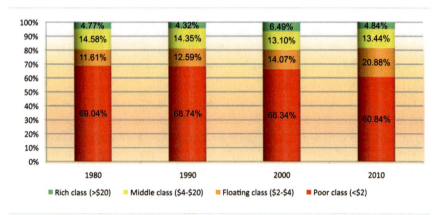

FIGURE 35   Distribution of African population by classes
Notes: *Floating class (US$2-$4), ** Lower-middle class (US$4-$10), *** Upper-middle class (US$10-$20)
SOURCE: AFDB STATISTICS DEPARTMENT ESTIMATES

According to AfDB, there are three sub-categories of Africa's middle class. The first group represents those whose consumption expenditure falls between $2- $4, and account for about 60% of the whole of Africa's middle class – the floating group. This group is just above the international poverty line of less than $2 per day and is vulnerable and may struggle to withstand any economic shock or a sharp rise in the cost of living, loss of income, or multiple effects of climate change. It is therefore difficult to accept this floating group as representative middle class. This subgroup is just above the extreme poverty level and should be classified as poverty or subsistence. MNCs might not be persuaded to invest based on people's consumption expenditure of $2- $4 a day.

The second category according to AfDB is the lower middle class and are those who live just above the subsistence level and with consumption expenditure of between $4- $10 a day. This subgroup accounts for 25% and can meet basic expenditures and save for some necessities. This lower-middle-class group can have sufficient nutrition and somehow enough consumption expenditure to live a relatively comfortable life. The upper-middle-class comprises 14% with consumption levels of between $10- $20 a day. The upper-middle-class as described by AfDB is in line with what Pew Research Centre called an internationally acceptable definition of a middle class. Thus, AfDB (2011) estimates that about 123 million Africans earned or consumed between $4- $20 per day and are in a category of the stable middle class. This secure middle class is what this book believes to be the true reflection of the middle class in the sub-Saharan African context. Critics argue that considering the World Bank's absolute poverty line of $1.90 per day, the minimum consumption ($2- $4) level defined by AfDB to qualify as middle income is too low. The graph, however, shows that the majority of Africans are still below the poor line.

The World Bank classifies a middle class at an income level of $12 to $15 per person per day. According to David Cowan, a senior economist for Africa at financial service group Citi, someone earning $13.70 per person per day is a more widely accepted definition of an emerging market middle class; and argues that it is at this level of and above that people really increase their purchases of consumer durable goods. Kings College put forward an alternative approach based on four consumption layers. The first layer they called global absolute poor consuming between $0- $2 per person per day; the second layer – global insecure $2- $10 per person per day; global secure is the third layer with consumption level $10- $50; and the final level global prosperous earning above $50 a day. Kings College alternatively argues that the global secure or the third layer is what qualifies someone as middle class. The upper-middle-class could be classified as global prosperous. Debates concerning the definition of the middle class are not unique to Africa. Ernst & Young (2013) argue that depending on the standards used to measure the size of the middle class, India's middle class could range from 30 million to 300 million people.

It has been argued in this book that classifying poverty or a middle class with a fixed income threshold is prone to higher error rates. The one size fits all model is difficult to implement. This is because a fixed income cut-off ignores income fluctuations and emergencies. The over quantification will miss the key issue it tries to measure. A middle class should be segmented to incorporate all aspects of quality of life. Thus, a middle class should encompass someone who has enough resources, be it income/asset/socio-economic networks to comfortably afford sufficient nutrition and comfortable accommodation with running water and electricity, ability to send children to good education from nursery to tertiary levels and have access to good health care when needed. This makes the description of the middle class both relative and absolute in the sense that different resources are required within and across countries for someone to live comfortably. These resources could be provided by the state as well as the private sector. Access to these resources should be included in the measurement of a middle-class grouping. It also addresses the question of whether a financial resource is the only measure of the quality of life. The United Nations outlines many indicators such as life expectancy, literacy rate and access to quality health care, amongst others.

It is argued that while there may be disagreement over whether Africa's middle class is rising or not, what is certain is that there is a rise in consumer spending power on the continent, even if it is at the lower end. The rising consumption has been fuelled by borrowing from both formal and informal financial institutions. Kingombe (2014) believes that more and more are now convinced that the opportunities are now inside Africa and indicates that middle-class households spend more on consumer durables, education, and health and are more likely to be optimistic about the future than the poor. The rise of the middle class has attracted MNCs to the region. Although Africa accounts for just about 3% of global consumption, the prospect is rising. This positive outlook is also good for domestic businesses, which stimulate a cycle of rising economic growth and development. McKinsey Global Institute (2016) argues that emerging markets will be changing where and how the world does business, and points out that for the last three decades emerging markets have been the source of cheap but skilled labour. It concludes that consumer spending in Africa is likely to reach over $2.1 trillion by 2025. The continent is also predicted to have the largest workforce by 2034, overtaking China and India.

The number of Africans living in urban areas continues to increase above the current 40% of the population. Likewise, households with discretionary income are expected to reach 128 million in the next decade, a rise of 50%.

Nevertheless, governments have a huge role to play if these predictions would be realised. Governments should focus more on local resources, diversifying the economy from raw material production to industrialisation, deepening infrastructure development and facilitating regional integration. Thus, transforming public leadership and governance will stimulate shared economic growth to the benefit of all citizens. However, neoliberal restructuring impedes governments to be actively involved in the production of goods and services other than providing the enabling environment for the private sector to flourish.

5.1 *The Two Competing Narratives on Africa*

At present, there are two competing narratives on Africa. Firstly, some commentators see Africa as a success story of growth, modernisation and a genuine global player in economic development. *The Economist* (2015) reckons the financial district of most African cities are well resourced with high tech computers, tablets and smartphones, glassy skyscrapers with multinational western companies. However, few metres away are the slums and street vendors. This highlights the two poles/divides of the economies, the haves and have-nots, with no middle ground/class (www.economist.com).

Critics argue that economic growth based on primary products and commodities is unsustainable due to global fluctuation in demand and is unlikely to withstand economic shocks such as a sudden fall in commodity prices, which is currently going on in the global commodity market. According to Moghalu (2014), economies that engage in extractive activities are more likely to generate high inequality with a few very wealthy, and the rest of the population stuck in extreme poverty. However, good governance and strong institutions could promote shared prosperity within and across countries. This promotes economic development with a rising middle class. This is because improving the income of the poorest in society stimulates the growth of average household income. However, if inequality exists coupled with limited life opportunities for the poor, average household income will decrease in real terms. Goldman Sachs (2013) reckons Africa's potential includes more than natural resources. They believe Africa is ascending on the same or similar curves that the BRIC (Brazil, Russia, India and China) economies climbed some decades ago in areas such as urbanisation, industrialisation and consumption. It concludes that some household consumption in parts of Africa has overtaken that of the BRICS. Middle-class consumption is vital to the development of any nation.

The second narrative on Africa is a story of poor governance, war, famine and poverty. The supporters of this narrative see sub-Saharan Africa as a passenger in the world economy and still have images of the old Africa. *The*

Economist once branded sub-Saharan Africa as the world's most war-torn region, with conflicts in West Africa; Liberia and Sierra Leone, East Africa; Burundi, Rwanda and Uganda, Central Africa; Democratic Republic of Congo and Southern Africa; Mozambique. It is worth noting that longstanding wars, conflicts and violence in some parts of Africa such as Rwanda, Mozambique and other places have ended and in most cases these countries have returned to growth and are now doing well economically. However, there are still some pockets of violence and conflict in places such as South Sudan,[3] Mali and recently in Burundi.[4] Many international institutions and donor agencies have shifted from a narrative that portrays the continent as desperate; poverty riddled and has embraced the rising story of Africa.

None of the narratives above can describe SSA's many trajectories across the continent. However, it is important to acknowledge that both sides of the debate can gather enough evidence in support of their case. Kingombe (2014) reckons Africa is an optimistic continent and argues that Africans are optimistic than Western countries that their children will be better off than them. For Keating, the improved living standard is visible in most African countries. However, he also acknowledges that inequality within and between countries is rising. Jerven on the other hand questions the quality of statistical underpinnings of an alleged Africa economic boom. He argues that basic African economic statistics cannot be trusted and concludes that Africa's rising story is a myth (Jerven 2013).

6   Neoliberal Globalisation and Poverty

The impact of neoliberal globalisation on inequality and poverty reduction has attracted the attention of governments and other international organisations. International trade is one of the standard measures of globalisation to ascertain the proportion of export relative to economic growth to determine the integration of the domestic economy into the global economy. Supporters

---

3 In Sudan (North), the violence was only demonstrations to remove the former president, Omar Al Bashir, which were successful. it is in South Sudan where the president and vice president have two opposing factions, keep agreeing to divide power and then disagreeing all over again.
4 The violence in Burundi ended a long time ago, and only came back six years ago when Pierre Nkurunziza was running for the third time. The country doesn't have any real violence at the moment, and has a new president who is trying to unite all Burundians and call refugees back home.

of globalisation remark that the neoliberal policy of trade liberalisation has facilitated poverty reduction. They argue that international trade stimulates export-led growth, which fosters poverty alleviation (Sachs et al. 1995; Dollar and Kraay 2002; Ravallion 2018). However, Kiely (2005) questions the evidence and asserts that liberalisation policies have contributed to rising inequality and poverty. He argues that increasing economic growth and falling poverty rates are the successes of anti-globalisation policies. Although the percentage of global trade measured by export relative to GDP has increased, the gains are uneven across regions. He remarks that by 1995, the share of SSA export had decreased from 5.5% to 1.5%. The more recent figure shows Africa's share of global trade at 2.4% (World Trade Organisation 2018). Advocates of neoliberal globalisation point to the increased interdependence and integration as a sign of countries benefiting from comparative advantage with the declining cost of production, resulting in competitive advantage in the global market.

Figure 36 shows that despite Ghana's greater integration into the global market, the economy has not reaped the benefit of globalisation as expressed by the neoliberals. The country has not benefited from the perceived cheap labour to exploit the comparative advantage. As the economy gets more integrated into the global economy, the trade deficit has not improved. The value of exports and imports have moved in tandem until 2011. Despite the rise in export, it was always accompanied by a rise in imports from 1995–2010. Exports rose after 2010 but saw a sharp decline to increase the trade deficit again. On this evidence, it is not difficult to argue that SAP and its associated liberalisation policies are a myth to poverty alleviation in Ghana. Kiely (2018) argues that only a handful of countries can meet the quality standards to export manufactured products to the core countries.

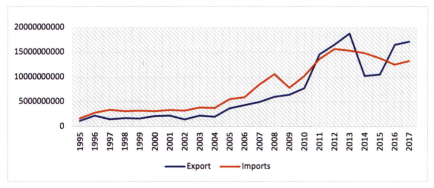

FIGURE 36   Trade balance for Ghana (1995–2017 in $billion)
SOURCE: AUTHOR'S ESTIMATES USING FIGURES FROM WTO (2018)

In a primary commodity-dependent region like SSA, the comparative advantage in some of the labour-intensive agriculture products could lead to oversupply resulting in falling prices, hence lower wages for workers. For example, Ghana and Ivory Coast produce the larger quantity of the world's cocoa (more than 75%) and get approximately $20 billion, while companies processing and adding value to cocoa beans make more than $200 billion annually. The chocolate industry alone was worth reported to be $107bn in 2020, this is partly due to the COVID-19 pandemic and restrictions. However, Ghana the second largest producer of cocoa only earned $2bn from the industry. There is a lot of money generated from cocoa beans but the producing countries receive very little of this income. This is a familiar pattern for many periphery economies where trade relationship is shaped by imperial order in which they export commodities to be processed by the core (Ndukwe 2021). Thus, neoliberal policies facilitate divergence and unevenness, contrary to their convergence and equilibrium expectations. The rising import relative to export threatens domestic employment, particularly in the already declining manufacturing sector. It has been argued that globalisation process facilitates free trade in products significant to the core countries.

The proportion of exports relative to GDP is a significant measure of the benefits of globalisation to an economy. Figure 37 illustrates that the value of exports as a proportion of GDP has been stagnant from 1995–2010. The rise in the value of exports between 2011 and 2013 is due to the exploration of oil in commercial quantities. The value of export relative to GDP has actually declined since 2014. The forced liberalisation processes with the hope of facilitating export-led growth have not delivered the expected growth. This

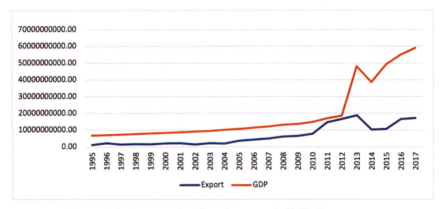

FIGURE 37   Exports relative to GDP for Ghana (1995–2017 in $billion)
SOURCE: AUTHOR'S ESTIMATES USING FIGURES FROM WTO (2018)

illustrates the weaknesses in the neoliberal policies in achieving sustainable economic development. Even the UNCTAD (2018) report raised concern about the declining share of manufacturing relative to GDP in most SSA economies. Manufacturing is the sector that can provide substantial employment to facilitate poverty alleviation.

However, the inability to compete on the world market has resulted in SSA as a dumping ground for global manufacturing products, which continues to hurt local manufacturers. Thus, neoliberal globalisation has opened up SSA economies to imports and dumping, while Africa has very little to sell/export to the core economies. New trade barriers hinder African exports. Just as the global tariffs and quotas agreements negotiated at the WTO are starting to pave the way for SSA to expand its share of global trade/export, other trade restrictions emerge. These domestic technical requirements[5] inhibit products from entering the core markets if they fail certain standards. These restrictions become more complicated when different nations adhere to a different degree of risk tolerance. The European Union is noted for its protective trade policies, which makes it difficult for many developing countries to access the EU market for goods and services. Thus, international trade per se is not a bad thing for the development of the periphery countries, but the rule makers benefit at the expense of everyone else.

There is overwhelming evidence to support that international trade (export) plays a leading role in China's economic development. However, internal trade and other robust domestic policy reforms cannot be underestimated. China, for instance, liberalised imports very slowly and still maintains some forms of restrictive trade barriers (Ang 2016; Kiely 2018).

Another measure of neoliberal globalisation is foreign investment – FDI. Capital movement, like global trade, is confined to a few core countries with minimal benefits to periphery countries. The UNCTAD (2018) argues that global FDI, which was down 23% on the 2016 level concentrated in a few countries with a 26% decline in FDI to SSA. With the $42 billion FDI to SSA, a significant proportion of it was confined to the commodity-exporting countries. Harvey (2005) maintain that FDI (in the neoliberal era) to periphery economies usually does not result in new ventures but rather benefits from undervalued privatisation of State-Owned-Enterprises (SOEs) (see chapter 4 for

---

5 These restriction include sanitary and phytosanitary (SPS) measures (Gumisai Mutume, 2006 https://www.un.org/africarenewal/magazine/january-2006/new-barriers-hinder-african-trade). These are imposed to protect domestic citizens, animals and plants from any hazards.

the consequences of capital inflows to Ghana). However, Ackah and Aryeetey (2012) remark that the capital inflows into the mining and the financial sectors stimulated the performance of the Ghanaian economy. Nevertheless, they argue that globalisation has not provided any meaningful impact on domestic income and employment in the primary sector.

Nsowah-Nuamah, Teal, and Awoonor-Williams (2012) contend that from 1991–2010, growth in domestic income was primarily due to increases in the level of education and training in all sectors. Thus, there is little evidence to conclude whether neoliberal policies had any impact on rising domestic income. FDI has been a significant source of external finance for periphery countries, accounting for 39% of total capital inflows (UNCTAD 2018). The declining FDI limits SSA's ability to grow and improve the living conditions of the people. It is worth noting that financial liberalisation has precipitated financial instability across the world with negative impacts on employment, income and the real economy.

The growth of MNCs has been another driving force of globalisation. Tandon (1999) reckons MNCs have seized control of national borders with the primary motive of satisfying shareholders. He asserts that these MNCs are not interested in providing job security and poverty alleviation. Stiglitz (2006) posits that many countries associate MNCs with the destruction of the globalisation process. He argues that some of these MNCs control revenues that are larger than the GDP of most periphery countries. He explains that 'Wal-Mart revenue of $285.2 billion was larger than the combined GDP of SSA' (p.186). This illuminates the power of these companies and how it can be difficult for smaller countries like Ghana to control the operations of these giant corporations. Consequently, MNCs pay low wages, destroy the environment and repatriate their profit without any challenges. Local businesses are essential to every economy; however, these SMEs are unable to compete with the global MNCs and therefore forced out of business, breaking the backbone of the economy.

In his analysis of global inequality, Bourguignon (2017) argues that the gap between the core and periphery countries has narrowed due to the expansion of international trade, the rapid mobility of capital and skilled labour and the spread and transfer of technological innovation. However, he contends that at the same time, income distribution within countries has widened. The globalisation of capital means that the income stream from capital has been rising faster than from labour (particularly the less skilled workforce). This argument is shared by Stiglitz (2015) and Piketty (2013), who remarked that since the inception of neoliberal ideologies, wealth has been growing faster at the top than economic output, resulting in widespread inequality within and across countries. However, it is essential to acknowledge that other factors can influence inequality such as technological progress, the domestic capacity for economic growth as well as policies of redistribution of income.

Advocates of neoliberalism argue that globalisation encourages international trade as well as investments which facilitate competition and efficiency, therefore leading to growth and poverty alleviation. However, there is a lack of consensus regarding the positive relationship between economic growth and poverty alleviation in a financialised capitalism. When inequality is higher, the most impoverished household may not share the benefit of economic growth (Holden and Prokopenko 2001; Odhiambo 2009; Ho and Odhiambo 2011).

Milanovic (2016) views neoliberal globalisation as a threat to social protection. He argues that the losers of globalisation are the lower middle class in the core countries, and the winners are the poor and middle-class in the periphery countries. Thus, in his view, the power shift of low-skilled manufacturing jobs from the core to the semi-periphery economies is a crucial factor accounting for winners-losers of neoliberal globalisation. Thus, neoliberal globalisation generates uneven global outcomes.

It is difficult to rely on cross-sectional data to make a generalisation. Using cross-section data, Dollar and Kraay (2004) argue that there is no relationship between increasing trade volumes and inequality on average. However, Lundberg and Squire (2003) maintain that increasing trade volume has a minimal positive effect on inequality. The OECD (2011) report that neither financial liberalisation nor trade interconnectedness have accounted for rising inequality. This paradox illustrates that even if neoliberal globalisation has any benefit to those that are globalised, the gains that materialised seem to be at best quite modest. As argued by Bardhan (2005), there is a perverse degree of causation on both sides concerning neoliberal policies and poverty/inequality indicators. Nevertheless, the forced liberalisation policies that opened SSA economies to global competition have made it difficult for the region to achieve sustainable economic development. It is difficult to understand how the local SMEs will be able to compete fairly (on quality and price) with the global MNCs even on the domestic market, let alone the international market.

Chang (2010) debunks the free trade myth. He argues that core countries favour free trade and globalisation on the grounds that their economies face little or no competition from periphery countries. As soon as developing countries improve their market share of global trade using their comparative advantage of cheap labour, the core countries pull up the drawbridge favouring protectionism with the argument that they face unfair competition from developing countries. The fact is that core countries' development trajectory was on the basis of protectionism and subsidies, which is contrary to the policies and institutions they now recommend to periphery countries. The core countries used tariff protection and subsidies to develop their industrial base, and once they become developed, they began to recommend and in some cases force developing countries to adopt free trade, deregulation and open their capital market. Paul Krugman, an advocate of strategic growth theory, has argued that periphery countries can promote faster economic development by identifying and protecting key industries that are significant to their economic growth and development. This means that periphery countries should not bow to pressure from core countries to open up industries and institutions vital for successful economic growth.

As argued by Stiglitz (2002), almost everyone knows something has gone wrong with neoliberal globalisation. He questions why a force that offered so much gains has now become so contentious. International trade drives economic development when a nation's exports stimulate its economic growth. After all, export-led growth was key to much of Asia's economic progress, which took many people out of poverty. Globalisation has increased international interconnectedness, which has enabled access to knowledge beyond domestic borders. MNCs move across the globe with new technologies, markets and new industries. Nevertheless, for many in the periphery economies, globalisation has not delivered what was promised by the neoliberals.

A growing divide between the rich and poor has plunged many in the developing countries into extreme poverty with dire consequences. In SSA, the aspirations of economic prosperity in the 1950s and 60s, following independence have been largely unachieved. Many of these countries were forced or promised to accept neoliberal policies to accelerate poverty alleviation effectively. Now the region has plunged deeper into misery with falling incomes, falling standard of living and rising extreme poverty. Thus, neoliberal globalisation and its open market economy have neither succeeded in alleviating extreme poverty nor facilitating economic stability.

Globalisation, in particular financial globalization, means that a meltdown in one region spreads like bush fire to other parts of the world. Anti-globalisers accuse the core countries of forcing periphery countries to remove trade barriers only for the core to erect new hurdles to prevent developing economies to access their markets, thus denying them valuable export revenues for development. This hypocrisy only hurts developing countries, which further exacerbates the living conditions of many people. Stiglitz asserts that Western countries have driven the globalisation agenda to ensure that most of the benefits accrue to them at the expense of poor countries. Western governments continue to subsidies agriculture and other industries, protect other industries with tariffs, quotas and other administrative restrictions, yet they put pressure on developing countries to open their economies with a promise

THE ISSUE OF POVERTY 207

that liberalisation will facilitate poverty alleviation. Consequently, the poorest countries are made worse off under neoliberal restructuring.

Financial globalisation and the relaxation of capital controls in the periphery countries have resulted in inflows of speculative hot money in search of interest rates arbitrage. The sudden outflows of such money have had negative consequences on the real economy. Thus, in most aspects, if not all aspects of globalisation even ostensibly well envisioned have produced ill outcomes. The proposed benefits of globalisation are yet to be seen by many developing countries, as the environment has been destroyed, governments have been corrupted and forced to cut spending in the name of neoliberalisation/globalisation. These have resulted in unemployment and underemployment, low wages, poverty and social dislocation in many SSA countries. Stiglitz stresses that globalisation problems are hardly new, but the rising global reaction against the policies that facilitate globalisation is an important transformation. There is no wonder mass protests welcomed WTO meetings on the streets of Prague, Seattle, Washington and other cities demanding change to the unfair, unbalanced global trade. These protestors, the supposed beneficiaries view globalisation differently from that of finance and trade ministers in the Western countries.

7 Conclusion

Poverty reduction has become a dominant development agenda since the 1990s when the World Bank Development report took poverty reduction as the central theme, and thus, increased the drive for poverty alleviation. However, as the global extreme poverty declined to 8.6%, the World Bank forecast extreme poverty in SSA to remain in double digits by 2030 unless there is a significant shift in policy. The Bank advocates for pro-poor investment to end extreme poverty by 2030.

There is a long-standing debate about the measurement of poverty. This book argues that the inaccurate definition of poverty is a hindrance to the ineffective solutions that have been implemented to address the problem. Poverty should be defined to incorporate the dimensions of poverty, which include monetary as well as non-monetary aspects of poverty.

Poverty alleviation is a complex endeavour and needs time, effort, patience, and commitment, which requires a multifaceted approach. Poverty reduction programmes in the past have been guilty of compounding the problem instead of solving it. Previous programmes have provided aid in places when development and rehabilitation programmes are needed. Most commonly, organisers have failed to listen to the needs of the local communities who have living experience. Even though the rural population represents just about half of the population in Ghana, it contributes 83.2% to the national poverty incidence. In short, rural residents in Ghana are more likely to live in poverty.

The globalisation and trade liberalisation only resulted in an open economy for imports/dumping. The subsistence nature of the Ghanaian agricultural sector means that domestic subsistence farmers cannot benefit from globalisation. On the macroeconomic level, the exports of primary raw materials with price inelastic demand also limit any benefit associated with globalisation.

This book presents that the ascendency of financial activities and financial motives on the one hand, and the rising poverty headcounts on the other, illustrate that financialisation in Ghana has not improved living standards for the poor, especially the rural population. I argue that the neoliberal policy of economic liberalisation has not served the Ghanaian economy well. Thus, although the incidence of poverty has declined, there is no improvement in the poverty headcounts, and in some cases, worsened. The next chapter examines the financialisation of households by critically investigating financial inclusion policy and mobile money in Ghana.

CHAPTER 7

Financialisation and Households

From Theory to the Context of Ghana

1   Introduction

The previous chapter discussed the issues surrounding the definition of poverty and the financialisation of poverty – when poverty is defined as a lack of decent finance. The chapter argued that the inaccurate definition of poverty has been the major hindrance to the poverty alleviation programmes.

Two main objectives drive chapter seven. The first part is to establish the theoretical bases by reviewing the literature on household finance and to assess the importance of political economy in addressing household finance/debt. The second part provides an empirical assessment of financialisation of households in Ghana using Bank of Ghana and National Communication Authority data on financial inclusion policy pioneered by the World Bank and the IMF to measure/assess the transformation of households' finance. Section 2 examines household debt through Modigliani's *Life Cycle* and Friedman's *Permanent Income Hypotheses*. The theories assume that a rational household will smooth out consumption over time by taking on debts. Section 3 investigates the political economy of household finance and argues that household assets and liabilities are managed by financial agents, financial actors and financial institutions with their idiosyncratic interests. Section 4 provides an overview of the payment systems in Ghana. The chapter ends with financialisation, financial inclusion and Mobile Money, providing the specificities of financialisation in Ghana.

2   Theory of Consumption Function: Household Debt and the Life Cycle and Permanent Income Hypotheses

The Life Cycle Hypothesis (LCH) pioneered by Modigliani and Brumberg (1954) assumes that a rational individual chooses their spending as they grow. The only constraint to this is the resources available to them over their lifetime. Consequently, individuals can take out debt to smooth out consumption when current income is insufficient to satisfy consumption needs. Thus, future income will validate the current debt stock. The theory also assumes that individuals' debt levels will reduce in their middle age so that they can prepare for retirement. As a result, indebtedness in this context is the transfer of the wealth of the nation from one generation to another. This is because as one generation reduces debt, another starts to accumulate it. Thereby, debt is a natural occurrence among rational consumers to meet current consumption needs to be validated by future income stream.

However, the theory does not account for the household's ability to access debt and the need for collateral in securing the debt. This theory will be at odds with household financing behaviour in the periphery (notably in Ghana) where lenders require a substantial amount of collateral to secure credit. Even in the mainstream framework, it is doubtful if it can provide a robust theoretical account of contemporary household debt.

The *Permanent Income Hypothesis* (PIH) is an alternative mainstream theory that explains household debt. The theory developed by Friedman (1953) is based on the premise that short-term changes in income could be compensated for by debt to facilitate smooth consumption. Meghir (2004) argues that the theory provides an empirical fact of why volatility in income does not affect consumption. He remarks why the long-run marginal propensity to consume from income is higher than the short-run. The theory posits that households consume a fraction of their permanent income in each period and that the marginal and average propensity to consume will be the same. The propensity to smooth consumption may differ depending on the interest rate, preferences and uncertainty.

Unlike LCH, PIH is not restricted to brief stages of life to accumulate debt. However, as pointed out by Lapavitsas (2009b; 2013), the theory has little explanatory power to account for the complexity of rising household debt accompanied by stagnant consumption and the recent spiralling house prices in the UK and elsewhere. Besides, if a household debt is a result of predictable future income, debt should be sustainable. Conversely, the recent financial crisis illuminates the weaknesses in the theory. Moreover, if household debt is due to rising house prices, then the theory offers a limited explanation on the contemporary misuse of other forms of credit like credit cards, Mobile Money (in low-income countries), pay-day loans, and other shadow banking activities.

The assumption that individuals can borrow as much as they want to limit the variations in consumption creates challenges for internal consistency for both theories. This contradicts the introduction of liquidity constraints and adverse selection. Kehoe and Levine (2001) argue that individuals may be restricted as to how much they can borrow, and some may not even access credit if they are uncertain about future income. Thus, the equilibrium quantity of borrowing depends on certain factors such as the terms on which one can obtain credit, the type of credit, and the value of collateral available to the individual.[1] Bunker (2015) remarks that rational individuals may not borrow if they are uncertain about validating payments when due. Thus, even if their expectations of future income rise, they will keep to their current consumption in line with their current earnings. Such behaviour contradicts the critical principle of the LCH theory that consumption profile could be isolated from the income profile. Very much the same outcome can be obtained in a theoretical model in which individuals want to borrow, but constraint. A household may need to save a fraction of current income to smoothing out future consumption, because they may be constrained to have consumption higher than their current income. This is often known as 'high frequency' smoothing of income, as opposed to 'low frequency' of income smoothing that was hypothesised by Modigliani and Brumberg (Deaton 2005).

Behavioural economics poses a theoretical challenge to the central principle of the LCH/PIH theory. One of the key pillars in behavioural economics theory is the work of Kahneman and Tversky (2013b). This tradition rejects the mainstream argument of a rational individual who assesses the costs and benefits of their actions and inactions. The behavioural theory argues that individuals' economic behaviour depends on the present context, where lack of self-control impacts decision-making. This bounded self-control suggests that individuals have limited control over their decision-making and thus make decisions that are not in their best interest. They contend that individuals exhibit time-inconsistent behaviour and focus on current consumption than future consumption (Deaton 2005; Kahneman and Tversky 2013a).[2] The theory supports the argument that financial liberalisation provides excessive liquidity and therefore reduces welfare.

The paradox of choice indicates that sometimes people make bad choices when they have too much to choose from, leaving them feeling overwhelmed. Restricted choice remedies this, providing less scope but allowing individuals to make more informed decisions. The tradition also predicts that over-indebtedness is due to myopic behaviour on the part of the individuals, who could not anticipate the future consequences of their actions. Thus, bounded

---

1   As empirically examined in chapter five, the value of collateral to secure/obtain bank credit is considerably higher in low-middle income countries, and firms and households without sufficient collateral are unlikely to be granted bank credit. High-interest rate is another constraint to access credit in Ghana.
2   Kahneman and Tversky (2013) demonstrate a variety of ways in which household behaviour violate the axioms of expected utility theory. however, behavioural economics ignores the class implication.

rationality suggests that when people make decisions, they are limited by factors such as the availability of information, their intellectual capabilities, and how much time they have to make decisions. Therefore, by knowing that individuals have limited control when making decisions, different strategies could be adopted to help people to maximise their welfare as well as improving social welfare.

The behavioural theory provides realistic insights into household behaviour, but it fails to incorporate the dominant role of the current financial system in household debt. The choice to enter into a credit agreement, according to Nelson (2018) is a consequence of impediment in current affairs rather than an assertion of a preferred future. Rodrigues Teles Sampaio (2014) argues that these reductionist theories should be rejected when investigating household finance in favour of a wide-ranging systemic approach; an approach that identifies the structural transformation of the world market in the last four decades and caters for changes in diverse social and geographical settings. Dos Santos (2013) and Lapavitsas (2013) reckon that only a method grounded in political-economic tradition can explain the changing conduct of banks, industrial enterprises and more importantly, household finance and consumer debt in contemporary financialised capitalism.

3   The Political Economy of Household Finance

Other disciplines such as sociology and culture economy[3] have recently opened new avenues for research on household finance. For example, Erturk et al. (2007), Krippner (2011) and Mader (2015) present various techniques that financial systems have facilitated households in the core, in particular, to participate in financial assets and liabilities. Since individuals lack the necessary financial knowledge to make an informed decision, a paradox emerges. Households play a minimal role in their financial dealings with the financial sector; thus, both sides of the household balance sheet are controlled and managed by financial agents, financial actors, and financial institutions with their idiosyncratic interests.

The securitisation of assets and liabilities has become a trademark of the contemporary financial market, where households know very little about the transactions facilitated by different forms of securities. Central

---

3 See for instance, Sum and Jessop (2013) *Towards a Cultural Political Economy: Putting Culture in its Place in Political Economy* for a critique of contemporary institutional and cultural turns in heterodox economics and political economy.

to financialisation is securitisation – where illiquid assets are transformed through financial innovation into financial security (Leyshon and Thrift 2007; Storm 2018).

However, a more comprehensive and inclusive work that offers a better understanding within the realms of political economy could be attributed to Lapavitsas (2009b, 2013), P.L. Dos Santos (2012), and Lapavitsas and Dos Santos (2008). These studies offer a more robust and realistic insight into the relationship between households and finance by bringing together the various findings of household financial behaviour through a thorough investigation of Marxist class analysis and power asymmetry. The study does not simply provide a comprehensive insight into the increasing household financial engagement as a consequence of financial liberalisation, but incorporates the activities of industrial enterprises and banks. Lapavitsas (2009b, 2013) postulates against the background of a profound historical transformation of modern capitalism since the triumphant neoliberalism in the mid-1970s. He outlines vital changes associated with this transformation. First, industrial enterprises (in the core countries) are increasingly capable of financing investment out of retained profit, and this has given them some degree of autonomy from commercial banks. Leyshon and Thrift (2007) reckon large blue-chip borrowers find it cheaper to access capital from the capital market through the securitisation of their assets rather than borrowing from banks. Since big businesses can now play financial games and engage in financial activities on their account, this has changed the structure of their organisation. This suggests that banks profit-making from lending to large corporations will fall.

In Marxist terms, monopolies have become self-sufficient and do not require bank credit for fixed capital; thus, large corporations have become financialised. Secondly, banks' responses to falling profit opportunities have been many. Banks have lent less to blue-chip borrowers and have now become financial *transactors* in the financial markets, and thus make profits from fees, commissions and trading. Leyshon and Thrift (2007) argue that banks were able to meet the borrowing needs of their customers through securitisation to circumvent global baking regulations, which could otherwise have restricted how much loans banks could give relative to their capital requirements. Lapavitsas (2009b; 2013) further contends that banks have also turned to households' income to generate profit, together with trading in the open market as well as mobilising savings and lending to households. Thirdly, households have been drawn into the home of the financial systems to facilitate access to necessities. Individual savings have also been increasingly mobilised by the formal and informal financial systems. As presented by Dos Santos (2013), the continuous rising interest payment on credit cards and other forms of credit together with the usurious money dealing fees that banks earn out of consumers' income account for between a third and half of the total profit of major US banks. The consequence of this unequal relationship is the rising household over-indebtedness during the last four decades.

This new relation has been conceptualised by Lapavitsas (2009b; 2013) as 'financial expropriation' – a source of profit that has transpired systematically in the last four decades, and argues that this expropriation should be separated from exploitation that occurs in production and remains the cornerstone of contemporary capitalist economies. He concludes that this source of profit primarily comes from the sphere of circulation. Insofar as it originates from household earnings, it comprises current flows of money. Although originating in the sphere of circulation, it embodies an exploitative nature because it involves economic processes.

One significant feature of Lapavitsas and Dos Santos' work, which needs acknowledging, is the power relation, which is ignored in mainstream theory. As households engage with the financial system to acquire the basic needs of life, such as a pension, housing, consumption, insurance and others, they have few options to circumvent the mechanisms of financial systems. Therefore, households' earnings become a source of financial expropriation. This differs qualitatively from finance directed to industrial enterprises, who are relatively of equal standing to the financial institutions in terms of social and economic powers. The financial products industrial enterprises obtain are used for the production and circulation of value and use-value. Households, on the other hand, are interested in acquiring use-value. Thus, diverse information and power enable financial institutions to engage separately with these economic agents. Consequently, as households increasingly engage with the financial system, the inherent disadvantage in information, power, and innovation have allowed financial institutions to exploit them. The superior and subordinate relation in this context is different from the exploitation in the production process. This financial expropriation originates from the power asymmetry between financial institutions and households' need to access necessities such as pension and housing.

One of the appropriate ways to examine exploitation between capital and labour is through the money circuit of capital developed by Marx. The general form of the circuit of industrial capital is $M \rightarrow C \rightarrow P \rightarrow C^1 \rightarrow M^1$.

In this circuit, the industrial capitalist advanced money capital (M) to acquire commodity inputs (C) which include labour-power (LP) and means of production (MP) which will then enter the means of production (P), and producing finished products (C^1), which include the surplus-value created by labour-power over and above the value of advanced capital (M). This is shown by the sale of the output for more money capital (M¹) -M¹>M. This can be expressed as $M \rightarrow C < \frac{MP}{LP} \rightarrow P \rightarrow C^1 \rightarrow M^1$ (Fine and Saad-Filho 2004, 52).

The money circuit of capital demonstrates that financial expropriation could be located in the sphere of exchange, since this source of profits originates primarily from labourers' income. This is partially at odds with the classical position of exploitation in production, what Marx (2019) terms as *secondary exploitation*, taken from profit from alienation, which is grounded in pre-capitalist modes of production as shown in Marx's *Grundrisse* (1857, 853):

> What takes place is the exploitation by capital without the mode of production of capital. The rate of interest appears very high because it includes profit and even a part of wages. This form of usury, in which capital does not seize possession of production, hence is capital only formally, presupposes the pre-dominance of pre-bourgeois modes of production.

Although financial expropriation is qualitatively different from the exploitation in production, the consequence of dispossessing household and the power asymmetry that emerges is not necessary as a wage labourer in itself, but positioned in the sphere of circulation at the hands of usurers. Thus, this type of profit directly from workers' income resonates usurer's profit. Lapavitsas (2009b; 2013) argues that financial expropriation normally emerges because of commercialised production, which induces households to depend on money as a means of exchange. Therefore, the interests earned by the usurer derived from the incomes of households and industrial enterprises could potentially affect the minimum needed for reproduction.

Financial expropriation has attained a new level in the era of financialisation due to the marketisation of social provision. This has resulted in rising financial profit coming directly from households and continuous vulnerability and exploitation of the working class, leading to rising inequality within and across countries. This analysis contains specific social elements/content and goes beyond the simple transfer of income, which must be acknowledged in the study of household finance in contemporary capitalism. Thus, in a financialised capitalism, profits derived from households become the money capital, which acts as a significant source of demand for products and in turn enables the circuit of the industrial capital accumulation process. This type of expropriation forms the basis of regulationists' 'wage-labour-nexus' concerning contemporary financialised capitalism.

This sheds light on tensions between the two poles of capitalism presented by Gowan (1999), money-dealing capitalism and productive sector capitalism. These forms of capitalism possess unique kinds of concerns because of the unique circuits of their capitals. In productive capitalism, capital starts as money, some of which could be borrowed from the money-capitalist. This fund/capital is then transformed in the production process into plant, material and labour. The process then climaxes with mass production of commodities for sale, and when the sale is completed, capital then emerges out the circuit with extra surplus. This process enables money-capitalist to receive the money advanced and royalties from the productive processes.

The circuit of a money-dealing capitalist takes a different form. The process starts with a fund of money, which is locked into a project for a period of time. At the maturity date, the money-dealing capitalist expects to receive the fund invested with interest/royalty. The key feature of this process is that the money-dealing capitalist looks for any project that will provide a future royalty. Thus, for a money-capitalist, capitalism is not limited to the productive process but any venture where future royalties could be earned. If trading in shares, bonds, or any other financial asset provides higher royalty, that is where the money will be channelled to. The uncertainty or certainty of the future royalty is given minimal consideration compared to the rate of royalties that could be earned. There is a tendency for the financial market and thus the money-capitalist to search for projects that offer quick returns and thereby keep capital as liquid as possible. This could be homeowners borrowing against their property in which future royalties emerge from homeowners' income earned in the production processor trading on the stock market. This undermines the long-term capital needed by the productive capitalist for fixed capital investment.

The analysis above shows that the money-dealing capitalist can pick and choose where to advance money capital. This makes the money-capitalist dominant over the productive capitalist. This is because the financial sector decides which sector in the economy to channel savings from the past and the new fictitious credit money to. Nevertheless, the productive capitalist is the determinant in this process because it provides the real stream of value out of which the money-dealing capitalist receives their future royalties. Gowan contends that the money-capitalist generates volatile hot money flows, which are very sensitive to changes in the economy. The productive capitalist, on the other hand, provides cold and long flows that are robust to any changes in the economy.

4   Payment Systems in Ghana: A Route towards Financialisation

The payment system remains one of the fastest-growing components of the financial services industry in Ghana. Economic, financial, public policy, as well as improvements in local Financial Technology (FinTech) industry and global trends in payment systems development, have engineered the recent trend in payment systems improvement.

The passage of the Electronic-Money and Agent Guidelines Act (Act 662) prompted financial and non-financial institutions to provide various financial products and services to promote financial engagement. The overall objective has been to encourage financial inclusion and sustaining price stability. These financial products have been designed to promote digital savings, lending, and investment for the underserved and unbanked segments of society. Various mobile money services in Ghana have attracted international attention.

Ecobank (Ghana) Limited in partnership with Mobile Telecommunications Network (MNT) Ghana, introduced treasury bills on the MNT mobile platform. It was aimed to mobilise funds from the informal sector and to engender financial inclusion. Mobile money subscribers can purchase treasury bills as low as Ghc 1.00 (about $0.17) using a mobile money wallet. The *'TBILL4ALL'* also allows the public, particularly the unbanked and underserved[4] to buy Government domestic fixed income bonds using mobile money wallets at any time of the day. The interest earned at the time of launch (in 2018) was between 13–17% per annum.

This is the first of its kind in the world, and consequently attracted international attention, particularly those in the sub-region. For example, the Central Bank of Tanzania organised study tours to Ghana to study the design and roll out the product. Ecobank, in addition, provides *Xpress* microloan products using customers' mobile wallets. The loan product provides customers with secure and instant access to credit in emergency cases and the promotion of a cash-lite economy as well as financial inclusion effort in the country.

4.1   *Background-Mobile Money Services in Ghana*
Mobile payments have been adopted in many SSA countries to enhance financial inclusion promoted by the World Bank. Recent data shows rising usage of Mobile

---

[4] The unbanked are those who do not possess any form of financial account with the formal financial sectors; underserved represents those with partial engagement with the formal financial institutions.

Money[5] (MM) accounts in the region from 200,000 in 2006 to 277 million in 2016. MM was introduced in Ghana in 2009 (Bank of Ghana 2018). The rise in the usage of MM as a means of payment has been attributed to the recent improvements in the mobile handset as well as the penetration and applicability of mobile phones amongst the underserved and unbanked segments of the population. The improvements in Point-of-Sale (POS) infrastructures coupled with convenience, speed, flexibility, and affordability could not be underestimated in the surge of MM usage.

By the end of December 2018, three mobile phone operators were providing MM services in Ghana – MTN *Momo*, AirtelTigo Money, and Vodafone Cash. This follows the merger between Airtel and Tigo in November 2017. The primary use of MM wallets in the country is transferring value between users (P2P), payment for goods and services such as mobile top-up, utility bills, television subscription, micro-credit and savings. Users receive quarterly payments of interest on float balances. The total float balance at the end of December 2017 was Ghc 2,321.07 million ($396 million), compared with a float of GHc 1,257.40 ($214 million) in December 2016, an increase of 84.59%, but a growth of 1,1748% since 2012 (figure 38). The arrangement for payment of interest on e-money float requires 80% of which should be accrued to customers and 20% to the electronic money issuer.

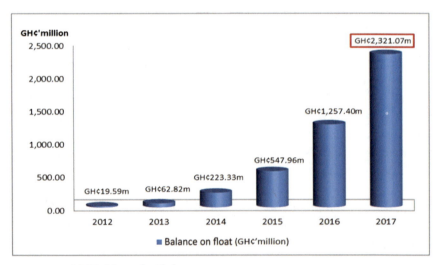

FIGURE 38   Mobile Money float balance 2012–2017
SOURCE: BANK OF GHANA (2018)

---

5   Mobile Money is electronic cash backed by an equivalent amount of the Central Bank notes and coins stored using the Subscriber Identification Module (SIM) in a mobile phone as an account identifier. The Mobile Money operators who issue the SIM cards keep the electronic account in the mobile phone for the users of Mobile Money.

The MM industry provides employment for agents, service providers, and users, including financial technology companies, merchants, retailers, and aggregators. Table 12 shows a 48% increase in registered agents between 2016 and 2017, but the exponential growth of 2148% since 2012. The total volume and value of transactions increased from 18,042,241 and Ghc 594.12 (million) ($102 million), respectively in 2012 to 981,564,563 and Ghc 155,844.84 (million) ($26,549 million), respectively in 2017. Thus, a growth of 5,340% and 26,131%, respectively. This demonstrates an increase in the value of each transaction made.

The growth of MM transactions and volume since 2012 marked an improvement in MM usage. However, this is not exclusive to Ghana. Other SSA countries such as Nigeria, Kenya, Uganda, and South Africa also recorded significant growth in MM transactions (Diniz, Porto de Albuquerque, and Cernev 2011).

Figure 39 shows increased activities of MM services in both volume and value of transactions since 2012. The excitement of MM when it was introduced in 2009 was short-lived in the first few years. After three years of the launch, only a handful of Ghanaians were actively using the service[6]. Both universal banks and community banks were not happy with the Central Bank and NCA circular because of the indirect competition and intrusion in their territory. The new agent and e-money regulatory reform by the Bank of Ghana in 2013 seemed to be mostly responsible for the growth of MM usage from 2013 onwards. By 2017, there were over 11 million active MM accounts from the registered accounts of over 23 million.

The MM agents act as liquidity managers that convert cash to and from the electronic form on demand. The prepaid nature of MM and the link to other financial services such as microloans and payment schemes explicitly designed to suit the poor, the unbanked and the underserved in the society, especially in the rural areas, has been remarkable. This has benefited the demand-side as well as the supply-side of the financial system. There is greater opportunity for the underserved, unbanked, and the poor in the rural areas to be engaged in financial services. Financial institutions also deliver bespoke financial services to these segments of the population who otherwise could not have been reached profitably.

---

[6] The first three years saw only 350,000 Ghanaians actively using MM. To put it into perspective, Jack and Suri (2011), and Martinez and Mckee (2011) examined growth trend of M-PESA (a mobile service operator in Kenya) and found that the operator (M-PESA) gained 2.37 million subscribers in the first year of implementation.

TABLE 12 Mobile Money transactions 2012-2017

Indicators	2012	2013	2014	2015	2016	2017	2017 Growth (%)
Total number of mobile voice subscription (Cumulative)	25,618,427	28,026,482	30,360,771	35,008,387	38,305,078	37,445,048*	(2.25)
Registered mobile money accounts (Cumulative)	3,778,374	4,393,721	7,167,542	13,120,367	19,735,098	23,947,437	21.34
Active mobile money accounts	345,434	991,780	2,526,588	4,868,569	8,313,283	11,119,376	33.75
Registered agents (Cumulative)	8,660	17,492	26,889	79,747	136,769	194,688	42.35
Active agents	5,900	10,404	20,722	56,270	107,415	151,745	41.27
Total volume of transactions	18,042,241	40,853,559	113,179,738	266,246,537	550,218,427	981,564,563	78.40
Total value of transactions (GH¢million)	594.12	2,652.47	12,123.89	35,444.38	78,508.90	155,844.84	98.51
Balance on float (GH¢million)	19.59	62.82	223.33	547.96	1,257.40	2,321.07	84.59

SOURCE: AUTHOR'S ESTIMATES USING FIGURES FROM THE BANK OF GHANA

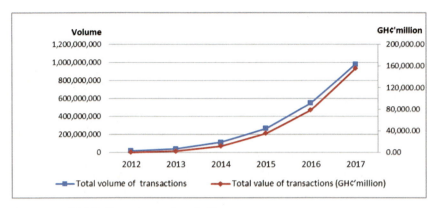

FIGURE 39   Mobile Money transactions in Ghana 2012–2017
SOURCE: BANK OF GHANA (2018)

Despite the effort by the government to incorporate all adults into the financial sector, a report by the World Bank in April 2018 shows that over 7 million people do not engage with the financial system. This includes the much talked about MM and formal bank accounts to engage in financial services. These people excluded from any benefits of financial inclusion may not be significantly engaging with the economy since the World Bank sees financial inclusion as a crucial factor in economic development. The report argues that financial inclusion translates into other potential development benefits such as the ease of receiving and transferring money, getting insurance, investing in education and health, and smoothing out consumption through easy access to credit to withstand financial shocks. Overall, the report points out that 1.7 billion adults worldwide do not have financial accounts down from 2.5 billion since the World Bank launched Global Findex – a database that tracks financial inclusion efforts around the world in 2011.

The importance of MM as the dominant non-cash payment method as of the end of 2017 with a volume of 981.6 million transactions more than debit cards (60.4 million) and cheques (7.3 million) can be seen in table 13. Nevertheless, cheques continue to be the significant non-cash retail instrument with GHc 179.6 billion ($30.49 billion) compared with GHc 155.8 billion ($26.54 billion) mobile money. The number of cheques cleared as a proportion of total non-cash payments fell from 60.21% to just 49.33% over the period. At the same time, the value of mobile money increased from 31.02% to 42.81% in 2017. The significance of MM financial services in the economy is depicted by the exponential growth in both the volume and value of 78.40% and 98.51%, respectively in 2017.

TABLE 13 Retail payment instruments in Ghana

	2016			2017		
Instrument	Issued	Volume	Value (m)	Issued	Volume	Value (m)
Cash						
Cheque	5,446,030.00	7,309,406	152,390.42	5,953,484.00	7,334,460	179,555.47
Direct credit transfer		5,242,610	19,245.65		6,061,093	24,327.26
Direct debit transfer		874,846	127.01		940,649	126.28
Debit card	9,217.00	46,456,021.00	13,582.67	14,698	60,382,177.00	17,785.18
Credit card	58,907.00	138,037.00	70.09	86,017	185,101	100
Prepaid card	1,878,044	312,143.00	103.26	2,364,456	472,071	256
E-zwich	136,769	5,365,085	2,362.97	194,688	8,367,017	3,431.49
e-money (mobile money)		550,218,427	78,508.90		981,564,563	155,844.84
Grand total	7,528,967.00	615,916,575.00	266,390.96	8,613,343.00	1,065,307,131.00	381,426.38

SOURCE: BANK OF GHANA (2018)

Historically, credit cards have not been a popular payment instrument in Ghana. However, the recent growth in demand and supply of credit cards signifies ascendency of finance and appetite for credit in the economy. The number of credit cards issued has risen by 59.47% between 2016 and 2017 to 14,698. However, only five banks are authorised to issue credit cards in the country, emphasising the paradox of a nation that is under-financed, yet financialising.

MM accounts had been on the rise since the introduction of e-money regulatory reforms in 2013. The growth in MM accounts overtook traditional bank services in 2014, and this preference has persisted during 2017. The number of MM accounts rose from 4,393,721 in 2013 to nearly 24 million in 2017. In 2013, MM accounts were just 57% of bank accounts; by 2017, it was 191.7% of traditional bank accounts. The number of bank accounts increased from 7,361,255 in 2013 to 12,452,734 (figure 40). This accounts for the complex nature of financialisation in Ghana as the formal financial sector is underdeveloped and serves a small proportion of the population.

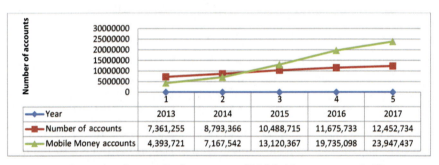

FIGURE 40   Comparison between bank accounts and Mobile Money accounts in Ghana 2013–2017
SOURCE: BANK OF GHANA (2018)

4.2   *The Role of Mobile Money in Financial Inclusion in Ghana*

The traditional banking system (despite the various waves of reforms discussed in chapter 4) failed to provide adequate financial services to a large proportion of the Ghanaian population, especially low-income people, the poor, and those in the rural areas. This financial exclusion is a consequence of banking infrastructure gaps. The recent surge in MM accounts shows how the service has expanded to deliver and facilitate financial services/inclusion in the economy. With the high growth of MM accounts and sizeable geographical coverage areas with access to mobile communication services, MM has the potential to enhance access to financial services than banks and thereby argues to facilitate *financialised* poverty reduction and economic growth.

Several factors have accounted for such unconventional ways of banking in the Ghanaian economy. The demand-side constraints include a lack of trust in the formal financial institutions. This has recently increased due to the collapse of various universal banks and microfinance institutions in the country. The most recent and high-profile cases include the collapse of DKM microfinance, UT Bank, and Capital Bank. The Central Bank in August 2018 also revoked the banking licence of five banks and appointed a receiver over the assets and liabilities of these banks.[7] Interestingly, all these collapsed banks were local banks, and the history of predominantly local banks' failures goes as far back as 2000 after the financial liberalisation (FINSAP). Other demand-side constraints include the bureaucratic and cumbersome documentation needed to open and operate bank accounts and lack of financial knowledge. Besides, inaccessibility due to lack of bank branches and challenges in reaching service points, as well as unaffordability as bank services are often expensive for low-income households have excluded many people from the formal financial institutions.

Table 14 shows that 64.6% of households do not contribute to any savings scheme, while only 35.4% of households have some form of savings bank accounts and are contributing to a saving scheme. The rural population has a higher proportion of no savings account of 78.5% than the urban locality with 46.4%, although rural male individuals are more than twice likely to have a savings account than their female counterparts, with 69.2% and 30.8%, respectively.

In the urban locality, 41.9% of households cited they did not have enough money or income to operate a savings scheme. The proportion is lower in the Greater Accra Metropolitan Area (GAMA), 39.4% than other urban areas of 41.7%. The process of opening a savings account is the least constraint for not having a bank and savings account. A high proportion of females 45.1% and male 42.3% cited lack of money or income as a reason for not having a savings account, while almost 29% of both males and females indicated that irregular income is a constraint for a savings account. For households in the urban locality, 21.7% did not find it necessary to operate a bank account, while 18.4% in the rural areas stated they were not interested. Few individuals surveyed were not aware of savings accounts and found financial institutions too far away with 2.4% and 1.3%, respectively (Table 15).

---

7 These collapsed banks were BIEGE Bank, Sovereign Bank, Construction Bank, UniBank, and Royal Bank. The Central Bank cited insolvency as the main reason for revoking the licenses of these indigenous banks. Deposit and selected assets and liabilities were transferred to a newly established bank- Consolidated Bank Ghana Ltd.

TABLE 14 Households with a bank account or contributing to a saving scheme by locality and gender

Locality	Households with Savings	No savings	Total	Individuals having savings accounts Male	Female	All
Urban	46.4	53.6	100.0	55.2	44.8	75.6
Accra (GAMA)	54.1	45.9	100.0	56.3	43.7	28.2
Other urban	42.9	57.1	100.0	54.5	45.4	52.7
Rural	21.5	78.5	100.0	69.2	30.8	24.4
Rural coastal	22.6	77.4	100.0	70.2	29.8	3.4
Rural forest	23.3	76.7	100.0	67.1	32.9	15.1
Rural savannah	17.6	82.4	100.0	74.0	26.1	5.8
All	35.4	64.6	100.0	58.6	41.4	100.0

SOURCE: GHANA STATISTICAL SERVICE (2013)

The supply-side constraints comprise high costs, bad household credit records, strict regulatory procedures and inappropriate product design. These factors, coupled with the demand-side constraints, deter households from partaking in the formal financial institutions.

Mobile phones and MM have the potential to eliminate most of the barriers to financial inclusion and thereby enable those unbanked and excluded from the financial system to transact business cheaply and securely from their mobile phone. Another potential of MM is the large-scale financial connectedness among distant households. It is easy to connect domestic individuals with their domestic and international counterparts through remittance and transfers. Within the domestic economy, p2p[8] transfer increases money circulation, facilitates economic growth and contributes towards improving the well-being of the poor in the rural areas.

---

8 P2p is the transfer of money on the MM platform from peer-to-peer.

TABLE 15 Reasons for not having a bank account or contributing to a saving scheme by locality and gender

Sex/locality	Reason						
	Not necessary /interested	Not aware of one	Process cumbersome	Financial institution too far away	Don't have enough money or income	Don't have regular income	Other	Total
Male	21.1	2.6	0.9	1.4	42.3	29.1	2.6	100.0
Female	18.9	2.3	0.7	1.2	45.1	29.6	2.3	100.0
Urban	21.7	2.3	0.7	0.4	41.9	29.6	3.5	100.0
Accra (GAMA)	27.7	2.1	1.0	0.7	39.4	21.0	7.9	100.0
Other urban	19.5	2.3	0.6	0.3	42.7	32.7	1.8	100.0
Rural	**18.4**	**2.6**	**0.8**	**2.0**	**45.4**	**29.2**	**1.6**	**100.0**
Rural coastal	22.5	1.8	2.0	1.3	47.4	21.8	3.2	100.0
Rural forest	17.2	2.1	0.7	1.0	44.1	33.3	1.5	100.0
Rural savannah	18.8	3.4	0.7	3.5	46.6	25.9	1.2	100.0
All	**19.9**	**2.4**	**0.8**	**1.3**	**43.8**	**29.4**	**2.4**	**100.0**

SOURCE: GHANA STATISTICAL SERVICE (2013)

Figure 41 illustrates mobile phone ownership and access amongst all demographic groupings. However, there are noticeable similarities amongst females, rural and those below the poverty line, with all below 90% ownership of mobile phones. While nine in ten own a phone – among male, urban, and those above the poverty line groups, only eight in ten own a mobile phone among female, rural, and those below the poverty line category. Thus, poor females, irrespective of the locality and poor males in the rural localities are less likely to have a mobile phone, and therefore excluded from any benefits associated with MM services.

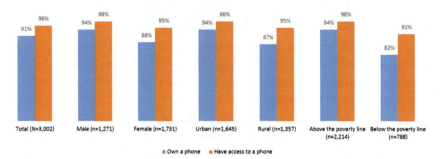

FIGURE 41   Mobile phone ownership and access, by demographic groups (percentage of each demographic group who owns and can access a mobile phone)
SOURCE: INTERMEDIA CGAP GHANA SURVEY (N=3,002, 15+), DECEMBER 2014 -JANUARY 2015

5   Financialisation, Financial Inclusion and Mobile Money

The push for financial inclusion through demonetisation and cashless economy by the Bank of Ghana and the World Bank should be seen as the pinnacle of financialisation in Ghana. As argued by Chandrasekhar and Ghosh (2018), the digitalisation of India's economy, which was facilitated by the USAID, ministry of finance (India), global banks, and FinTech companies, is not intended to alleviate poverty, corruption and black money/market as suggested. They assert that the real purpose is for these FinTech oligopolies to profit directly from household income through the exorbitant fee charges from such digital activities and to make money indirectly from the unbanked, underserved and the poor from the enormous data generated on users. The authors contend that these activities were creating new avenues for private firms to extract profit from the poor, and hence, the privatisation of the payment systems, which José Gabriel Palma (2009) calls *rentiers' delight*. With the help of the state and Central Banks, the reins of the formal payment systems have been given out unreservedly to offer new rents to these FinTech oligopolies and their partners.

Equally, Mader (2015) rejects the claim that financial inclusion has positive effects on the living standards of the poor. He argues that it is more likely growth stimulates financial inclusion than financial inclusion driving growth and development – reigniting the debate of supply leading hypothesis versus demand following theory of financial development discussed in chapter 3. Financial businesses such as FinTech corporations require direct and indirect support from the government and central banks to make it a profitable scheme – a process Hildyard (2016) terms *licenced larceny*. This is best seen as a proxy for how successfully selected few (elites) have created institutions that extract value from the rest of society, especially from the poor. Mader's contribution contests the much-hyped financial inclusion promise that it helps individuals to manage their financial assets safely and efficiently, and hence pro-poor development intervention. He warns that if the financial inclusion agenda is not challenged, it will hand more power to rentier capitalists to extract rents and redesign politics, and subordinate social development to capital markets development.

The concept of mobile money has been one of the most exciting things to happen in the economies of SSA, and in particular Ghana. FinTech companies have enabled cashless systems where mobile phone users can send and receive money over the platform as well as transfer money between bank accounts and MM platforms. These have lessened transaction costs and have made life relatively comfortable for the underserved, unbanked, and the poor in rural areas. Equally, MM has been able to include many Ghanaians who were previously excluded from the formal financial sector into the realms of finance. MM accounts have outpaced the number of traditional bank accounts since 2014 and continue to grow at a faster rate. It provides convenience and reduces the cost of travel and time spent in visiting the few bank branches available. The growth of mobile money agents also provides employment and helps stimulate economic growth. There is no doubt that the investment opportunity provided by the MM platform is an innovative way of enabling the excluded to be inclusive of investment opportunities.

Nevertheless, behind this financial inclusion policy is the cost of transactions to both the sender and the recipient in the chain of these MM transactions. Two key issues arise. Firstly, there is no uniformity in the charges of MM transactions in the country. MTN *Momo* charges are different from *AirtelTigo money*, and Vodafone *cash* charges. One would have expected that the financial inclusion products designed to target the poor and the unbanked would be cheaper than the formal financial products. However, the opposite is what actually happens. Secondly, the double fees paid for a transaction – charges/commission for transferring money, and charges/commission for withdrawing money on the platform make it expensive for the poor users. For example, it costs a user about 1–5% (of the amount transferred) to transfer money from his/her mobile wallet to another. The recipient will also pay about 1% to withdraw the amount received from a vendor/agent/merchant. Part of this two-way transaction costs are paid to vendors as commission, and the rest is shared between the banks and the MMOs (the capitalists in the transactions) as business returns. The amount senders pay for transferring funds depends on the transaction point, that is, whether the transaction took place at an agent's shop or one's own mobile phone, and whether services are C2C, P2P, A2C, or bill payments.[9] Consequently, in most cases, the sender has to send more than the amount required to the recipient to cover the transaction cost incurred by the recipient.

The MM interoperability, which was launched on 10th May 2018, made it possible and more comfortable to transfer mobile money across networks for a fee. Figure 42 explains transaction costs within and across MMOs. For instance, it costs GHc 1 ($0.17) to transfer funds from Vodafone *cash* to MTN *Momo*; however, it costs GHc 1.25 ($0.22) to transfer money the opposite way – from MTN *Momo* to Vodafone *cash*.

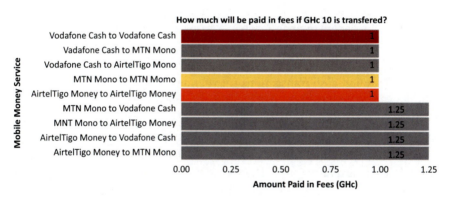

FIGURE 42 The amount (commission) paid in fees for transferring GHc 10
SOURCE: DAVID QUARTEY AIRTELTIGO, MTN, VODAFONE

Mobile money charges are also regressive in structure. Innovations for Poverty Action (IPA) has highlighted the regressive structure of the fees paid by mobile money users. They examined 21 MM services across seven countries[10] and concluded that most MMOs had prices that were regressive in

---

9   C2C is money transfer from merchants/agents to non-mobile money users (5%); P2P is money transfer to a mobile money wallet (0.5%); A2C is money transfer from a mobile wallet to non-mobile money user (3%). Some forms of bill payment services are free of charge, e.g. Electricity and Water bills.
10 These countries were Kenya, Uganda, Tanzania, Pakistan, Nigeria, Bangladesh and India.

structure. The average fee paid falls as the amount of transactions increases. This demonstrates that poor and low-income households, who usually transact lower amounts, pay more fees in percentage terms than middle and high-income segments of society who can transact a higher amount – GHc 1000 ($170) or more. This evidence demonstrates that MM is not designed as a pro-poor policy, but as a way to entangle the unbanked, underserved and poor, who otherwise could not have been reached profitably by the formal financial institutions.

Furthermore, mobile money users do not benefit from all the interests earned on their e-money float balances. Customers only take 80% of the interest earned on their balances, while MMOs and their partners take 20%. The double fees paid for a transaction coupled with little interest earned make MM services and its financial inclusion campaign susceptible to financial expropriation of the poor. This is an extraction of financial profits directly out of the working class, especially the poor layer of the society, who would otherwise have not been able to be exploited profitably by the formal financial systems.

The threat of the MM platform to the profitability of traditional banking was highlighted by PwC in their annual banking survey 2018. MM possesses a threat to the use of banks for transferring a small amount of money in the economy, particularly the payment of bills. This explains why mobile money transactions surpassed all non-cash transactions (in volume) in 2016. If the current trend continues, MM transactions will soon dominate the payment systems with banks struggling to cope with the pace of the volume and value. The threat of MM is not just on the payment side of the transaction but also on the deposit side. The transfers (sending and receiving), deposit and withdrawal, make MM wallets quasi current account. The recent directive from the Bank of Ghana that MMOs must pay monthly interest on the float to customers has attracted deposits to the MM platforms at the expense of the traditional banking system. Other points of sale services such as discounts on items purchased and offers in restaurants make MM wallets appeal to the public. Accordingly, MMOs are now in direct competition with the traditional banks instead of working as partners and service providers in the industry – reminiscent of shadow banking.

However, the MM platform has enabled partner banks in Ghana to enhance the mobilisation of bank deposits. Allotey (2016) contends that MM deposits account for about 30% of total bank deposits in the country. This raises the question as to whether the MM platform is supporting the banking sector's deposit mobilisation efforts or actually competing for it. There is no doubt that the MM platform has provided banks with convenient and cost-effective means of reaching millions of Ghanaians who were excluded from the formal financial systems.

I argue in this book that MM products facilitate shifts towards financialised behaviour for households in the informal sector. The analyses suggest that MM is increasingly associated with financial inclusion, an indirect form of financialisation. However, the outcome is weaker for women and rural segments than men and urban areas. Financial inclusion studies have shown a gender gap in accessing financial products as well as rural-urban divides (see (Demirguc-Kunt and Klapper 2012; Bruhn and Love 2013). Although the gap has narrowed through the MM platform, the trend remains the same with rural and women segments less likely to be financially inclusive than men and urban residents. However, there is evidence to suggest that MM usage is associated with financialisation in the informal financial sector.

Consequently, this book argues that new financial technologies can be leveraged to achieve financialised practices without requiring access to the formal financial system. MM may induce individuals into new financialised behaviours in the informal sector. However, juxtaposed against each other, financialisation in the core countries and SSA has different connotations. In the core countries, financialisation may mean growing dependence on globalised and volatile financial institutions. However, in Ghana, financialisation of households could have positive as well as negative connotations. Financialisation in the informal sector may signify an increased economic security and financial investment in shares and government bonds, as well as savings for future consumption that may improve livelihood. The poor households, the unbanked, and the underserved could have access to financial services – on both the assets and the liabilities' sides of the household balance sheet. They can save and earn interest on their MM float; they can access bank credit without the need to open a bank account. Drawing these people into the realms of finance could improve outcomes by buffering against shocks and expanding their income via interest earned and investments. Thus, MM could induce financialised behaviour of the poor without knowing.

Nevertheless, the exorbitant fees associated with some of the transactions in MM is a reminiscent of financial expropriation similar to financialisation in the core countries. As the World Bank and the IMF gear up to promote financial inclusion, finance and its way of thinking have come to dominate every aspect of the Ghanaian society, and individual well-being is being conceptualised through universal access to financial products. Mader (2015) argues that while many aspects of life in the core countries are already financialised from credit cards and student loans to defined contribution pensions, microfinance and MM are the major vehicles in the periphery lubricating the frontier of financial accumulation. This financial relation extends to every aspect of contemporary life.

The World Bank and the IMF argue that access to finance will enrich the poor to fulfil their potential; this clearly confirms in the literature of neoliberal financialisation that economic and social successes or failures are the consequences of managing finance. Accordingly, social problems are increasingly determined by an individual's inability to access finance, and therefore have nothing to do with politics, economic justice such as unemployment, underemployment, zero-hour contract, low wages, or collective action. This demonstrates Chambers' (1995) point that poverty becomes what has been measured; in this case, new credit relation is required which serves surplus extraction. Since microfinance and MM assume to be speaking the language of empowering the poor, Elyachar (2005) argues that financialisation is associated with accumulation through dispossession. He remarks that since the capitalists can obtain a significant profit on capital by advancing money, there is no need to organise the factors of production to produce goods. This exemplifies Keynes' point that the expansion of finance is due to inappropriate economic policy that has directed investment into financial assets with negative impacts on the real economic sector – *finance mostly finances finance* in the era of financialisation.

6 Conclusion

The theoretical review revealed the weaknesses of the neoclassical theory contributions to household finance. *The LCH and PIH assume that a rational household will smooth out consumption over time by taking on debts. The framework of political economy incorporates the historical and social element that has transformed household financial conduct in the neoliberal era. The political economy approach is more robust to the understanding of the international financial crisis of the last decade, which had household finance at its centre. The framework of political economy does not limit itself to the understanding of household engagement with the financial systems and financial products, but integrates the changing conduct of industrial enterprises and banks; thus, the financialisation of households, albeit class analysis and power asymmetries. The new relation has been conceptualised as *Financial Expropriation* by Lapavitsas (2013). This concept differs from the exploitation of workers in production. Financial expropriation draws on the unequal power relation between financial institutions and households accessing finance.

The failure of the traditional banking system to provide for the needs of all classes in the economy resulted in the financial exclusion of the poor and those in the rural areas. The recent growth in MM accounts has drawn many households into the realms of finance as the government and the World Bank push for financial inclusion. The concept of MM has benefited the demand-side as well as the supply-side of the financial system. Both formal and informal financial institutions can provide bespoke financial services to all segments in the economy, particularly, the underserved, unbanked and the rural poor. The popularity of MM started in 2013 after the e-money regulatory reform by the Bank of Ghana. Since then, the MM account has outpaced the traditional bank account, and the preference continues. However, despite the widespread use of MM, it has been revealed in this book that poor female, irrespective of where they live and poor males in the rural areas, are less likely to have a mobile phone and therefore potentially excluded from any benefits associated with MM.

The push for financial inclusion through MM and the demonetisation and cashless society by the Bank of Ghana has been argued in this book as the prominence of financialisation of households. As presented by Chandrasekhar and Ghosh (2018), the activities have created new avenues for extracting profit, and therefore the privatisation of the payment systems in Ghana. The concept of MM has some benefits to the poor; for example, Ecobank and MTN *TBill4All* provide the opportunity for MM customers to benefit from interest payment. Furthermore, MM services have created jobs for agents and retailers as well as FinTech companies. However, the double fees/commission paid on each transaction and the regressive structure of the fees leads to the poor paying more in proportion. MM account holders are not receiving the full interest earned on their float. The 80:20 split between customers and MMO is reminiscent of financial expropriation discussed in the literature. Thus, financial inclusion financialises poverty and therefore ignores the critical dimensions of poverty. The next chapter summarises the argument presented in this book and offers prospects for the future.

CHAPTER 8

Conclusion

1   Summing Up the Argument

This book has argued that the hegemony of finance has been a distinctive component of contemporary capitalism. The absence of neoclassical theory from the theoretical debate on the growing importance of finance/financialisation should not be seen as a weakness in the assessment but rather the failure of the dominant school of thought in economics to recognise the rising importance of such a defining component of capitalism that emerged in the late 1970s. While orthodox economists are delighted of the exponential growth of finance and its financial actors and motives and reduce the debate of the phenomenon to financial deepening which facilitate trade and investment PwC (2014), heterodox economists are sceptical about the development of financial markets and financial instruments. Heterodox economics warn of its negative consequences on financial stability, income distribution, poverty, employment and productive investment. Thus, the heterodox approach views finance as an axle of economic growth and argue that a large financial sector could at best be a mixed blessing. The advocates of this approach contend that financial markets in neoliberal capitalism are mainly speculative in character, which precipitates financial instability (Gowan 1999; Epstein 2005; Toporowski 2009; Orhangazi 2011; Lapavitsas 2013; Kiely 2018; Storm 2018). Epstein questions the social efficacy of contemporary unregulated financial markets and argues that more resources are being diverted into financial activities that are alien to the production of goods.

Thus, it is erroneous to assume that the development of the financial market somehow funnels investment to the productive sector of the economy and hence, development of the real sector. The trillions of dollars traded on the financial markets could actually aggravate costs on the real sector. Nevertheless, monetary services offered by the financial systems include credit creation, savings, transfer of money across the economy, enabling foreign exchange transactions, and other monetary services. Financial services, on the other hand, include mainly the mobilisation of loanable funds in the economy and its subsequent advance through loans/credits. Besides, financial services include collecting spare money funds across society as well as trading loanable capital in the open markets. However, huge flows of funds into real sector investment in sub-Saharan Africa (SSA) do not pass through the formal financial sector, therefore, financial sector development is alien to the production of goods and services in the region.

It is worth pointing out that the Initial Public Offering (IPO) – the initial sale of shares and bonds to the public to raise funds/capital may or may not be used for the intended purposes of real/productive capital investment. Nevertheless, it is erroneous to assume that the activities on the secondary markets, where the previously traded securities are bought and sold, contribute directly to the real capital investment. As argued by Gowan, investors on this market trade on claims of future value created in future productive activity. Thus, the activities on the secondary markets do not channel any meaningful funds for productive capital investment but establish rights for any future productive royalties. The shares I own in Tesco plc, for instance, is an indirect/direct claim of the future productive value created in Tesco plc. From this discussion, it is not difficult to argue that the activities of global financial markets are not necessarily about supplying funds for productive capital investment, but instead trading in future claims on productive value created in various parts of the world. This sheds light on tensions between the two poles of capitalism presented by Gowan – money-dealing capitalism and productive sector capitalism.

Political economists and other disciplines have captured the exponential rise of finance in the concept of financialisation. In this book, different strands of thoughts were reviewed in their understanding of financialisation – the stagnation in production; French Regulation school theory of financialisation, post-Keynesianism and financialisation, and the trans-nationalisation and liberalisation of finance. All these strands deliberately addressed issues on the global as opposed to national accumulation. However, they failed to examine the changing conduct/behaviour of banks, industrial enterprises and households both within countries and across borders. Like post-Keynesians, Marxists recognise the connection between stagnating production on the one hand and the ascendency of finance on the other in the era of financialisation. However, they differ on the root cause of this financial expansion. While Post-Keynesians argue that the rise of finance is due to inappropriate economic policy, Marxists believe the rise of finance is due to the declining productive sector. Post-Keynesians blame neoliberal policies such as liberalisation and deregulation of financial markets for the emergence of financialisation.

The rise of finance and the financialisation of everything examined the consequences of the shift in financial intermediations from banks and other financial institutions to financial markets. The consequences of this shift are the rising profit of financial assets and the collateralisation of everything that can be collateralised. As financial profit grows, capital then migrates from the real economic sector to financial speculation. The concept of profit upon alienation provides the reasons why so much financial profit is accrued from mortgages, consumption loans to households, and from handling pension and other funds.

The globalisation of finance draws on the internationalisation of the capital markets, which enable domestic and international debtors and creditors to engage in trading. This has reduced the independence of monetary authorities; capital movements tend to disrupt changes in domestic interest rates. The privatisation and deregulations through SAP have created a situation where the domestic bourgeoisie have the freedom to transfer their wealth – both legal and illegal into financial markets outside their countries. The essential vehicles used to transplant financialisation of households in the developing countries have been microfinance and financial inclusion policy under the auspices of the World Bank and the IMF.

The distinctive characteristic of financialisation in Ghana is that the economy is under-financed by international standard measures, yet it is financialising. The underdevelopment of the capital market limits industrial enterprises' access to debt and equity financing. Consequently, firms are more reliant on bank credit as opposed to the core countries where large firms can access a range of sources of finance. Banks continue to lend disproportionately to risk-free government securities, which crowds out the private sector. Numerous neoliberal restructuring, including Structural Adjustment Programme (SAP), privatisation, currency manipulation and trade liberalisation that mainly focused on the economy did not alleviate the fundamental problems but worsened the plight of many citizens, making them poorer than they were before neoliberal restructuring.

The forced liberalisation and the deregulation of the financial sector enabled capital flows and the ascendency of finance in Ghana. However, the initial belief that financial liberalisation will induce capital inflows into the periphery countries was short-lived. As countries opened the capital market, there has been a reverse flow of capital from the periphery to the core countries. Lapavitsas (2013) argues that the accumulation of reserves pioneered by the World Bank and the IMF has been the catalyst for this negative reversal flows of capital to the core countries. Domestic policies to attract more investments and the high interest rates in the periphery countries also contribute to net outflows of capital.

The distinctive characteristic of financialised corporations in Ghana, and the archetypical financialised corporations in the core (for example, the US and UK) is that industrial enterprises in Ghana (large and small) are forced to rely on their non-existing internally generated funds due to contradictions in the political-economic arrangements. The forced liberalisation has resulted in high interest rates and diverted funds away from productive assets to financial assets and government securities. Thus, lack of affordable capital for domestic industrial enterprises in Ghana due to high interest rates charged by moneylenders and demand for high collateral security coupled with limited alternative sources of finance, have resulted in stagnant profit in the productive sector in favour of rising profit in the financial sector. To a large extent, firms in Ghana still rely on the high-cost non-existing bank credit. Subsequently, industrial enterprises make little or no profit from their capital investment, but are burdened with high interest charges and high production costs. The subordinate nature of the Ghanaian economy also impacts costs on firms, resulting in deficient productive capital accumulation. Firms in Ghana are not returning to the undeveloped capital market; banks, however, are not lending to firms, but rather in government securities, which crowds out productive investment and weakens the real economic sector.

Consequently, industrial enterprises are unable to employ many workers as well as pay higher wages. This has resulted in chronic poverty in the country, especially in rural areas. This is consistent with the heterodox economists' view of financialisation discussed above (see, for instance, Krippner 2011; Stockhammer 2012; Kotz 2013; Davis and Kim 2015; Storm 2018).

This thesis presents that the ascendency of financial activities and financial motives on the one hand and the rising poverty headcounts on the other, illustrate that financialisation in Ghana has not improved living standards for the poor, especially the rural population. It is argued in this book that the neoliberal policy has not served Ghana's economy well. Thus, although the incidence of poverty has decreased, there is no improvement in the poverty headcounts, and in some cases, it has worsened.

The argument in this book is that neoliberal policy response to the crisis in Ghana did not succeed in reversing the economic decline permanently. In fact, quite the opposite; rather than undoing the economic decline, the policy prescriptions weakened the country's ability to diversify its economy into industrialisation, particularly manufacturing. Neoliberal policies implemented in the 1980s undermined instead of resolving capital accumulation constraints in the country. This is because the policies intentionally or unintentionally encouraged factors that destabilised the possibility of the real productive assets to earn commensurate returns to facilitate the flow of capital to these sectors to ensure the survival of industrial enterprises. Rising profit in the financial sector incentivised managers to divert funds into financial assets at the expense of productive investment. Thus, the pace of real capital accumulation has been disappointing in the era of neoliberalisation/financialisation due to rising financial profit.

2 The Content of Financialisation in Ghana

2.1 *Banking Sector*

The various waves of financial reforms provided the opportunity for banks to expand their balance sheets on both the assets side and the liabilities side. This thesis found rising profit for the banking industry, and limited lending to industrial enterprises for long-term investment – a feature reminiscent of financialisation in the core. However, what is unique in the context of Ghana is excessive lending to the government. Banks have collaborated with mobile money operators or have devised their mobile applications to engage directly with households. These have enabled banks to extract rising income from households in various ways – from interest income to fee income. The investment (universal) banking status given to commercial banks in 2003 indicates a significant shift in the activities of the banking sector in Ghana. This freedom attracted many foreign banks to the country, together with many different forms of lending to the households and the government. Households hold a more significant proportion of bank debt, and what is worrying is the rate at which banks are increasingly confident to provide unsecured debt. Financial liberalisation did not enhance banking competition and efficiency and did not reduce the cost of capital for long-term productive investment.

2.2 *Industrial Enterprises*

In the context of the Ghanaian economy, this book found no evidence of industrial enterprises increasing access to both debt and equity markets, and therefore do not depend on the domestic banking industry. Primarily, firms in Ghana (both large and small) rely heavily on non-existing bank credit. This could be partly due to the underdevelopment of the domestic capital market in the country. Accordingly, the close relationship between these capitalist agents is contrary to what was expected from the literature of financialisation (see, for instance, (Orhangazi 2008a; Toporowski 2008; Lapavitsas 2011; 2013; Lazonick 2014)). This book, therefore, draws attention to the researchers of financialisation of industrial enterprises to consider the specificities of the location/countries and the development of the capital market. The internal dynamics and domestic institutions should be scrutinised to understand the dynamics of financialisation in each geographical setting fully. In archetypical financialised economies such as the UK and the US, large firms could benefit from the capital markets, transplant the same issue into the periphery where the capital market is underdeveloped, and the outcomes will differ.

However, in line with the heterodox economics understanding of contemporary firms in an era of rising financial profit, banks have lent less to firms and more in financial assets. Industrial enterprises are then forced to rely on their non-existing internally generated funds. Consistent with the theory of financialisation, this research found stagnant and declining profit in the real economic sector and rising profit in the financial sector. However, the reasons for this asymmetry slightly differ from the core countries. Industrial enterprises in Ghana do not have access to varied sources of finance, with high interests in government bonds, which is less risky; banks/investors lend more to the government. Subsequently, banks/investors demand high collateral security from firms coupled with high interest on loans. These obstructive factors, together with other contradictions in the political-economic arrangement, impact high costs on firms and therefore limit their ability to make enough profit resulting in a downward spiral. Declining lending to the agricultural sector that employs the overwhelming majority of the working population has resulted in stagnant wages, inequality and mass unemployment. Consequently, chronic poverty in rural areas has risen.

2.3 Households

The increasing involvement of households with the financial system was demonstrated through the financial inclusion paradigm of the World Bank and the IMF. This engagement resulted in increasing access to short-term loans and some various investment opportunities for households. At the same time, the high-cost fee charges for mobile money transactions, which come from household income, resonates with financial expropriation. The interest made on mobile money float is shared between households and the capitalists involved in the transactions. These arrangements confirm financial expropriation in the literature of financialisation of household income. However, the distinctive characteristics of household debt in Ghana, particularly mortgage and credit card debt, were found to be limited to the top income groups of the population. Few banks are authorised to issue credit cards and provide mortgage services. However, it was found in this study that despite limited coverage in the economy, albeit the underdevelopment of the financial sector, the growth of credit cards is still alarming with almost 60% growth between 2016 and 2017. Even though households' debt is mainly limited to the top income layers, the unbanked, underserved and the poor have all been drawn into the realms of finance through various means, notably mobile money.

The various waves of financial reforms, albeit financial liberalisation to promote financial inclusion to induce microcredit in the formal financial sector failed to expand access. A new form of engagement discovered in this book is the use of mobile money to entangle the unbanked, underserved, and the poor into the formal financial system. However, the experience is not balanced; the poor and the low-income households only have access to the most expensive transaction, resulting in wider income inequality and poverty. Thus, the neoliberal financial liberalisation policy to enhance poverty alleviation and achieve sustainable economic development is a myth. It has financialised poverty by providing the most expensive credit to household and industrial enterprises. The policy failed to address the primary causes of poverty such as unemployment, low wages, vulnerability and the high cost of capital in the economy.

3 Policy Recommendations

The high domestic interest rates adopted by the central bank to reduce inflationary pressures act as a pull factor attracting international capital flows and the subsequent advance of this reserve to buy a foreign government bond, particularly the US government bond.

Capital flight is a huge barrier to economic growth and development in Ghana. The sudden movement of capital destabilises developing economies more than developed economies. The repatriation of MNCs profit from the country contributes to these movements, which negatively impact the domestic currency. Capital flight has been accelerated since neoliberal inception, a period which has been accompanied by huge profits generated from the exploitation of SSA mineral resources. Consequently, capital flight has impeded Africa's economic growth and development by draining off potential investment funds from the continent. This problem could be reduced if not completely controlled by strong institutions and government intervention to control capital movements.

The banking reforms that opened the banking sector to foreign competition did not primarily increase competition and efficiency, but resulted in new forms of lending to households and the government. State-owned banks should not be privatised for the sake of banking reforming. With the right supervision and operating environment, these banks could compete and provide the needed capital for industrial enterprises to perform efficiently. The government can also set up community banks to provide the needed capital to SMEs to ease the credit constraints. Furthermore, universal banks should be encouraged/incentivised to offer medium to long-term financing to industrial enterprises/capitalists at affordable rates and with minimum collateral. Besides, government deficits should be financed from other sources to enable banks to invest in the real sector of the economy. Banks are too reliant on short-term government gilts, which undermine their ability to explore other investment avenues. Good governance and strong institutions allow markets to emerge and can deal with market inefficiencies. As argued by Ang (2016), emerging markets activity may generate problems that require the state to build further stronger institutions to deal with markets' inefficiencies. Good governance will stimulate and preserve market development. This illustrates the significance of government and influential institutions in the fight against poverty. Heavy reliance on neoliberal market-based policies to reduce poverty has been unsuccessful in sub-Saharan.

Ghana can look up to the Asia tigers for inspiration. For instance, reforms to Africa Growth and Opportunity Act (AGOA) that started two decades ago could help boost manufacturing-based employment in many regions and towns where the incidence of poverty has been rising, particularly rural savannah. However, this alone will not be enough; investment in agriculture, a sector that employs the overwhelming majority of the labour force in the country will increase output and income for farmers. Irrigation, useful transport links, storage facilities, training and education of farmers on modern ways of farming could reduce chronic hunger, rural isolation and vulnerability of the rural people. Investment well-tuned to local needs and conditions should be able to benefit the hunger-disease-poverty nexus and set many people free from the bondage of poverty. It is essential that the poor must be involved in decision-making that affects them than has been assumed for them. Previous poverty alleviation programmes have been unsuccessful because organisers have failed to listen to the needs of the local communities who have lived experience.

The fight against poverty and diseases should be a priority than choices about financial inclusion, budget deficit and privatisation. Poverty should not be viewed as a financial problem that requires new credit relations, but should be seen as monetary and non-monetary problems to include dimensions of well-being and indicators of deprivation. To alleviate extreme poverty, Ghana needs to consider a shift in policy from the Washington consensus neoliberalisation market-based policy to active government participation to stimulate industrialisation as seen in some other Asian countries.

Extensive government intervention is needed in periphery countries to speed up growth and development than in core countries. The strategic growth theory advocates some degree of protectionism policies to speed up economic growth and development. Free trade has its benefits to growth and development if it is conducted fairly on the global market. But as presented in this book, this is not the case in the era of neoliberal capitalism. Therefore, combining market-based instruments with strong institutions and government intervention will be vital for successful growth and development. Lessons from the East Asian Miracle show that economic openness has a crucial role in the development of a nation. However, strategic integration into the global economy is better than passive insertion as advocated by neoliberals. SSA should adopt a liberal trade policy for exports but restrictive for imports. Any government policies to attract FDI must be influenced by an industrial strategy in the interest of national development objectives. For effective poverty alleviation strategies, governments in periphery countries need to manage the changing relationship between states and markets and find the correct balance to their respective roles that also evolve in a changing world. The institutional restructuring, modernising the agricultural sector to enhance productivity growth and investment in manufacturing and industry will enable sustained economic development that will improve the standard of living of the people.

References

Abor, Joshua. 2008. 'Determinants of the Capital Structure of Ghanaian Firms'. *African Economic Research Consortium*, Nairobi: AERC Research Paper 176.

Abor, Joshua, and Peter Quartey. 2010. 'Issues in SME Development in Ghana and South Africa'. *International Research Journal of Finance and Economics* 39 (6): 215–28.

Ackah, Charles, and Ernest Aryeetey. 2012. *Globalization, Trade and Poverty in Ghana*. Accra: IDRC.

Adewumi, Funmi. 1997. *Trade Unionism in Nigeria: Challenges for the 21st Century*. Lagos: Friedrich Ebert Foundation.

Adu, George, George Marbuah, and Justice Tei Mensah. 2013. 'Financial Development and Economic Growth in Ghana: Does the Measure of Financial Development Matter?' *Review of Development Finance* 3 (4): 192–203.

Adusei, Michael. 2013. 'Financial Development and Economic Growth: Evidence from Ghana'. *The International Journal of Business and Finance Research* 7 (5): 61–76.

Africa Development Bank. 2012. 'African Economic Outlook 2012'. Africa Development Bank. http://www.africaneconomicoutlook.org/en/countries/west-africa/ghana/.

Africa Development Bank. 2017. 'African Economic Outlook 2017'. Africa Development Bank. https://www.afdb.org/fileadmin/uploads/afdb/Documents/Publications/AEO_2017_Report_Full_English.pdf.

Agbenyega, Christian. 1998. 'Development: The Poverty Alleviation Dilemma'. *Thinking It All over Again*. Accra: Mamattah Rays Enterprise.

Aglietta, M., and A. Rebérioux. 2004. *Dérives Du Capitalisme Financier*, Paris: Albin Michel Economie.

Aglietta, Michel. 2008. Into a New Growth Regime. *New Left Review* 54: 61–74.

Ahiawodzi, Anthony K., and Thomas C. Adade. 2012. 'Access to Credit and Growth of Small and Medium Scale Enterprises in the Ho Municipality of Ghana'. *British Journal of Economics, Finance and Management Sciences* 6 (2): 34–51.

Aitken, Rob. 2013. 'The Financialization of Micro-Credit'. *Development and Change* 44 (3): 473–99.

Akufo-Addo. 2020. 'President Akufo-Addo Addresses Nation on Measures Taken by Government to Combat the Coronavirus Pandemic'. http://presidency.gov.gh/index.php/briefing-room/speeches/1535-president-akufo-addo-addresses-nation-on-measures-taken-by-gov-t-to-combat-the-coronavirus-pandemic.

Allotey, G. 2016. 'Mobile Money' – a Gift to the Banking Industry'. Ghana News. http://citifmonline.com/mobile-money-a-gift-to-the-banking-industry.

Andrianaivo, Mihasonirina, and Charles Amo Yartey. 2010. 'Understanding the Growth of African Financial Markets'. *African Development Review* 22 (3): 394–418.

Ang, James B. 2008. 'A Survey of Recent Developments in the Literature of Finance and Growth'. *Journal of Economic Surveys* 22 (3): 536–76.

Ang, Yuen Yuen. 2016. *How China Escaped the Poverty Trap*. New York: Cornell University Press.

Arestis, Philip, and Panicos Demetriades. 1997. 'Financial Development and Economic Growth: Assessing the Evidence'. *The Economic Journal* 107 (442): 783–99.

Arrighi, Giovanni. 1994. *The Long Twentieth Century: Money, Power, and the Origins of Our Times*. London: verso.

Arrighi, Giovanni. 2002. 'The African Crisis'. *New Left Review* 15: 5.

Arrighi, Giovanni. 2007. *Adam Smith in Beijing: Lineages of the Twenty-First Century*. London: Verso Trade.

Atkinson, A. B. 1987. 'On the Measurement of Poverty'. *Econometrica* 55 (4): 749–64. https://doi.org/10.2307/1911028.

Atta-Boakye, K. 2006. '*Of Nkrumah's Political Ideologies: Communism, Socialism, Nkrumaism. Kwame Nkrumah, Ghana: An Autobiography*'. London: Heinemann, 1957.

Aye, Goodness C. 2013. 'Causality between Financial Deepening, Economic Growth and Poverty in Nigeria'. *The Business & Management Review* 3 (3): 1.

Ayittey, George BN. 2000. 'Combating Corruption in Africa: Analysis and Context'. In *Corruption and Development in Africa*, 104–18. New York: Springer.

Ayyagari, Meghana, Thorsten Beck, and Asli Demirguc-Kunt. 2007. 'Small and Medium Enterprises across the Globe'. *Small Business Economics* 29 (4): 415–34.

Bagehot, Walter. 1873. *Lombard Street: A Description of the Money Market*. London: Scribner, Armstrong & Company.

Baker, Harold Kent, and Gerald S. Martin. 2011. *Capital Structure & Corporate Financing Decisions*. Wiley Online Library.

Bank of Ghana. 2000. 'The State of the Economy'. Accra: Bank of Ghana.

Bank of Ghana. 2015. 'The State of the Economy'. Accra: Bank of Ghana.

Bank of Ghana. 2016. 'The State of the Economy'. Accra: Bank of Ghana.

Bank of Ghana. 2018. 'The State of the Economy'. Accra: Bank of Ghana.

Baran, Paul Alexander. 1957. '*The Political Economy of Growth*, New York: Monthly Review Press.

Baran, Paul Alexander, and Paul Marlor Sweezy. 1968. *Monopoly Capital: An Essay on the American Economic and Social Order*. New York: Monthly Review Press.

Bardhan, Pranab. 2005. 'Globalization, Inequality, and Poverty: An Overview'. Oakland, California: University of California at Berkeley, Mimeo.

Bateman, Milford. 2010. *Why Doesn't Microfinance Work?: The Destructive Rise of Local Neoliberalism*. London: Zed Books Ltd.

Beck, Thorsten, and Asli Demirguc-Kunt. 2006. 'Small and Medium-Size Enterprises: Access to Finance as a Growth Constraint'. *Journal of Banking & Finance* 30 (11): 2931–43.

Beck, Thorsten, Asli Demirgüç-Kunt, and Ross Levine. 2007. 'Finance, Inequality and the Poor'. *Journal of Economic Growth* 12 (1): 27–49.

Becker, Joachim, Johannes Jäger, Bernhard Leubolt, and Rudy Weissenbacher. 2010. 'Peripheral Financialization and Vulnerability to Crisis: A Regulationist Perspective'. *Competition & Change* 14 (3–4): 225–47.

Bencivenga, Valerie R., and Bruce D. Smith. 1991. 'Financial Intermediation and Endogenous Growth'. *The Review of Economic Studies* 58 (2): 195–209.

Boafo-Arthur, Kwame. 1999. 'Ghana: Structural Adjustment, Democratization, and the Politics of Continuity'. *African Studies Review*, 41–72.

Boateng, Agyenim. 2004. 'Determinants of Capital Structure'. *International Journal of Social Economics* 31 (1): 56–66.

Bonefeld, Werner. 2012. 'Freedom and the Strong State: On German Ordoliberalism'. *New Political Economy* 17 (5): 633–56.

Bortz, Pablo G., and Annina Kaltenbrunner. 2018. 'The International Dimension of Financialization in Developing and Emerging Economies'. *Development and Change* 49 (2): 375–93.

Bourguignon, François. 2017. *The Globalization of Inequality*. New Jersey: Princeton University Press.

Boyer, Robert. 2000. 'Is a Finance-Led Growth Regime a Viable Alternative to Fordism? A Preliminary Analysis'. *Economy and Society* 29 (1): 111–45.

Boyer, Robert, and Yves Saillard. 2005. *Régulation Theory: The State of the Art*. Milton Park, Oxfordshire: Routledge.

Braudel, Fernand. 1981. *Civilization and Capitalism. Vol. 1: The Structures of Everyday Life*. London: William Collins Sons & Co.

Brennan, Michael J., and Eduardo S. Schwartz. 1978. 'Corporate Income Taxes, Valuation, and the Problem of Optimal Capital Structure'. *Journal of Business*, 103–14.

Brenner, Robert. 2006. *The Economics of Global Turbulence: The Advanced Capitalist Economies from Long Boom to Long Downturn, 1945–2005*. London: Verso.

Brenner, Robert, and Mark Glick. 1991. 'The Regulation Approach: Theory and History'. *New Left Review* 188 (1).

Britwum, Akua, Kwesi Jonah, and Ferdinand D. Tay. 2001. 'Structural Adjustment Participatory Review Initiative (SAPRI)'. Retrieved March 20: 2016.

Bruhn, Miriam, and Inessa Love. 2013. 'The Economic Impact of Expanding Access to Finance in Mexico'. *Banking the World: Empirical Foundations of Financial Inclusion*, 137–56.

Bunker, N. 2015. 'How Household Debt Affects Economic Growth'. https://www.weforum.org/agenda/2015/10/how-household-debt-affects-economic-growth/.

Capron, C. 2005. *Les Normes Comptables Internationales, Instrument Du Capitalisme Financier*, La Découverte, 27-48.

Centre For Policy Analysis. 2003. 'Policy Building Ghana'. https://cepa.org.gh/aboutus.php.

Chakraborty, Indrani. 2010. 'Capital Structure in an Emerging Stock Market: The Case of India'. *Research in International Business and Finance* 24 (3): 295–314.

Chambers, Robert. 1985. 'The Crisis of Africa's Poor: Perceptions and Priorities'. *IDS Discussion Paper* 201, Brighton.

Chambers, Robert. 1995. 'Poverty and Livelihoods: Whose Reality Counts?' *Environment and Urbanization* 7 (1): 173–204. https://doi.org/10.1177/095624789500700106.

Chandrasekhar, C. P., and Jayati Ghosh. 2002. *The Market That Failed: A Decade of Neoliberal Economic Reforms in India*. Leftword.

Chandrasekhar, C. P., and Jayati Ghosh. 2013. 'The Asian Financial Crisis, Financial Restructuring and the Problem of Contagion'. *The Handbook of the Political Economy of Financial Crises*. New York: Oxford University Press, 311–25.

Chandrasekhar, C. P., and Jayati Ghosh. 2018. 'The Financialization of Finance? Demonetization and the Dubious Push to Cashlessness in India'. *Development and Change* 49 (2): 420–36.

Chang, Ha-Joon. 2010. *Bad Samaritans: The Myth of Free Trade and the Secret History of Capitalism*. New York: Bloomsbury Publishing USA.

Chazan, Naomi. 1982. *Development, Underdevelopment, and the State in Ghana*. Boston: Boston University.

Chemli, Leila. 2014. 'The Nexus among Financial Development and Poverty Reduction: An Application of ARDL Approach from the MENA Region'. *Journal of Life Economics* 1 (2): 133–48.

Chen, Jean J. 2004. 'Determinants of Capital Structure of Chinese-Listed Companies'. *Journal of Business Research* 57 (12): 1341–51.

Chesnais, François. 2001. 'Mundialização: O Capital Financeiro No Comando'. *Revista Outubro* 5 (2).

Chesnais, François. 2006. 'Les Contradictions et Les Antagonismes Propres Au Capitalisme Mondialisé et Leurs Menaces Pour l'humanité'. *Actuel Marx*, no. 2: 71–85.

Clapp, Jennifer, and S. Ryan Isakson. 2018. *Speculative Harvests: Financialization, Food, and Agriculture*. Rugby: Practical Action Pub.

Clarke, George, Robert Cull, Maria Soledad Martinez Peria, and Susana M. Sanchez. 2003. 'Foreign Bank Entry: Experience, Implications for Developing Economies, and Agenda for Further Research'. *The World Bank Research Observer* 18 (1): 25–59.

Cornia, Giovanni Andrea, Rolph Van der Hoeven, P. Thandika Mkandawire, and Macmillan Press. 1992. *Africa's Recovery in the 1990s: From Stagnation and Adjustment to Human Development*. New York: Springer.

Crotty, James. 2005. 'The Neoliberal Paradox: The Impact of Destructive Product Market Competition and 'Modern'Financial Markets on Nonfinancial Corporation Performance in the Neoliberal Era'. *Financialization and the World Economy* 1: 77–110.

Crotty, James. 2011. 'The Realism of Assumptions Does Matter: Why Keynes-Minsky Theory Must Replace Efficient Market Theory as the Guide to Financial Regulation Policy'. Working Paper.

Crotty, James, and Kang-Kook Lee. 2005. '14. The Causes and Consequences of Neoliberal Restructuring in Post-Crisis Korea'. *Financialization and the World Economy*, 334.

Dardot, Pierre, and Christian Laval. 2014. *The New Way of the World: On Neoliberal Society*. London: Verso Trade.

Dauda, Risikat Oladoyin S., and Kayode O. Makinde. 2014. 'Financial Sector Development and Poverty Reduction in Nigeria: A Vector Autoregression Analysis (1980–2010)'. University of Lagos Library Information and Service.

Davis, Gerald F. 2009. *Managed by the Markets: How Finance Re-Shaped America*. Oxford: Oxford University Press.

Davis, Gerald F., and Suntae Kim. 2015. 'Financialization of the Economy'. *Annual Review of Sociology* 41.

DeAngelo, Harry, and Ronald W. Masulis. 1980. 'Optimal Capital Structure under Corporate and Personal Taxation'. *Journal of Financial Economics* 8 (1): 3–29.

Deaton, Angus. 2005. 'Franco Modigliani and the Life Cycle Theory of Consumption'. *Banco Nazionale del Lavoro Quarterly Review*, 58 (233–234): 91–107.

Demirgüç-Kunt, Asli, and Harry Huizinga. 2001. 'The Taxation of Domestic and Foreign Banking'. *Journal of Public Economics* 79 (3): 429–53.

Demirguc-Kunt, Asli, and Leora Klapper. 2012. *Measuring Financial Inclusion: The Global Findex Database*. Washington DC: The World Bank.

Demirgüç-Kunt, Asli, and Ross Levine. 2004. *Financial Structure and Economic Growth: A Cross-Country Comparison of Banks, Markets, and Development*. Cambridge, MA: MIT Press.

Detragiache, Enrica, Thierry Tressel, and Poonam Gupta. 2008. 'Foreign Banks in Poor Countries: Theory and Evidence'. *The Journal of Finance* 63 (5): 2123–60.

Dewi, Sovia, M. Shabri Abd Majid, Aliasuddin Aliasuddin, and Salina Hj Kassim. 2018. 'Dynamics of Financial Development, Economic Growth and Poverty Alleviation: The Indonesian Experience'. *The South East European Journal of Economics and Business* 13 (1): 17–30.

Dhrifi, Abdelhafidh. 2014. 'The Nexus between Financial Crisis and Household Consumption: Evidence from Emerging Countries'. *Journal of Social Economics Research* 1 (8): 169–79.

Diniz, Eduardo, João Porto de Albuquerque, and Adrian Cernev. 2011. 'Mobile Money and Payment: A Literature Review Based on Academic and Practitioner-Oriented

Publications (2001–2011)'. In . Oriented Publications (2001–2011)(December 3, 2011). Proceedings of SIG GlobDev, Fourth Annual Workshop.

Dollar, David, and Aart Kraay. 2002. 'Spreading the Wealth'. *Foreign Affairs* 81 (1): 120. https://doi.org/10.2307/20033007.

Dollar, David, and Aart Kraay. 2004. 'Trade, Growth, and Poverty'. *The Economic Journal* 114 (493): F22–49.

Donkor, Kwabena. 2019. *Structural Adjustment and Mass Poverty in Ghana*. Milton Park: Routledge.

Dos Santos, Paulo. 2009. 'On the Content of Banking in Contemporary Capitalism'. *Historical Materialism* 17 (2): 180–213.

Dos Santos, Paulo L. 2012. 'On the Content of Banking in Contemporary Capitalism'. *Financialization in Crisis*. Chicago: Haymarket, 83–118.

Dos Santos, Paulo L. 2013. 'A Cause for Policy Concern: The Expansion of Household Credit in Middle-Income Economies'. *International Review of Applied Economics* 27 (3): 316–38.

Downward, Paul, and Andrew Mearman. 2007. 'Retroduction as Mixed-Methods Triangulation in Economic Research: Reorienting Economics into Social Science'. *Cambridge Journal of Economics* 31 (1): 77–99.

Duménil, Gérard, and Dominique Lévy. 2004. 'The Real and Financial Components of Profitability (United States, 1952–2000)'. *Review of Radical Political Economics* 36 (1): 82–110.

Economist. 2015. 'Few and Far between. Africans Are Mainly Rich or Poor, but Not Middle Class', 2015. http://www.economist.com/news/middle-east-and-africa/21676774-africans-are-mainly-rich-or-poor-not-middle-class-should-worry.

Eldomiaty, Tarek I. 2007. 'Determinants of Corporate Capital Structure: Evidence from an Emerging Economy'. *International Journal of Commerce and Management*.

Elyachar, Julia. 2005. *Markets of Dispossession: NGOs, Economic Development, and the State in Cairo*. Duke University Press.

Emmanuel, Arghiri. 1972. *Unequal Exchange*. Vol. 1. New York: Monthly Review Press.

Epstein, Gerald A. 2005. *Financialization and the World Economy*. Cheltenham: Edward Elgar Publishing.

Epstein, Gerald A., and Arjun Jayadev. 2005. 'The Rise of Rentier Incomes in OECD Countries: Financialization, Central Bank Policy and Labor Solidarity'. *Financialization and the World Economy* 39: 46–74.

Ernst & Young. 2013. 'Hitting the Sweet Spot: The Growth of the Middle Class in Emerging Markets.' https://www.ey.com/en_gl/inclusive-growth.

Erturk, Ismail, Julie Froud, Sukhdev Johal, Adam Leaver, and Karel Williams. 2007. 'The Democratization of Finance? Promises, Outcomes and Conditions'. *Review of International Political Economy* 14 (4): 553–75.

Esso, Loesse Jacques. 2010. 'Cointegrating and Causal Relationship between Financial Development and Economic Growth in ECOWAS Countries'. *Journal of Economics and International Finance* 2 (4): 036–048.

European Investment Bank. 2013. 'SME Report 2013'. European Investment Bank. https://www.eib.org/attachments/general/reports/fr2013en.pdf.

Feasley, Ashley. 2011. 'SKS Microfinance and For-Profit MFIs, Unscrupulous Predators or Political Prey? Examining the Microfinance Credit Crunch in Andhra Pradesh and Assessing the Applicability of the UN Global Compact" Protect Respect Remedy" Framework'.Cornell University Law Library.

Ferreira, Francisco HG, Shaohua Chen, Andrew Dabalen, Yuri Dikhanov, Nada Hamadeh, Dean Jolliffe, Ambar Narayan, Espen Beer Prydz, Ana Revenga, and Prem Sangraula. 2015. *A Global Count of the Extreme Poor in 2012: Data Issues, Methodology and Initial Results*. Washington DC: The World Bank.

Ferreira, Francisco HG, Julian Messina, Jamele Rigolini, Luis-Felipe López-Calva, Maria Ana Lugo, Renos Vakis, and Luis Felipe Ló. 2012. *Economic Mobility and the Rise of the Latin American Middle Class*. Washington DC: World Bank Publications.

Fine, Ben. 2012. 'Neoliberalism in Retrospect? It's Financialisation, Stupid'. In *Developmental Politics in Transition*, 51–69. New York: Springer.

Fine, Ben, and Alfredo Saad-Filho. 2004. *Marx's Capital, Fourth Edition*, London: Pluto.

Fisher, Irving. 1933. 'The Debt-Deflation Theory of Great Depressions'. *Econometrica: Journal of the Econometric Society*, 337–57.

Foster, John Bellamy. 2014. *The Theory of Monopoly Capitalism*. New York: NYU Press.

Foster, John Bellamy, Robert W. McChesney, and R. Jamil Jonna. 2011. 'The Internationalization of Monopoly Capital'. *Monthly Review* 63 (2): 1.

Foucault, Michel, Arnold I. Davidson, and Graham Burchell. 2008. *The Birth of Biopolitics: Lectures at the Collège de France, 1978–1979*. New York: Springer.

Fouskas, Vassilis, and Bülent Gökay. 2012. *The Fall of the US Empire: Global Fault-Lines and the Shifting Imperial Order*. London: Pluto Press.

Fouskas, Vassilis K. 2018. 'Neo-Liberalism and Ordoliberalism: A Critique of Two Forms of Imperialism and Authoritarianism'. *Politeia-Naučni Časopis Fakulteta Političkih Nauka u Banjoj Luci Za Društvena Pitanja* 8 (16): 149–72.

Fouskas, Vassilis K., and Constantine Dimoulas. 2013. *Greece, Financialization and the EU: The Political Economy of Debt and Destruction*. London: Palgrave Macmillan.

Fouskas, Vassilis K., and Bülent Gökay. 2018. *The Disintegration of Euro-Atlanticism and New Authoritarianism: Global Power-Shift*. New York: Springer.

Frank, Andre Gunder. 1971. *Latin America: Underdevelopment or Revolution: Essays on the Development of Underdevelopment and the Immediate Enemy*. New York: Monthly Review Press.

Friedman, Milton. 1953. 'The Methodology of Positive Economics'. In Friedman, M. (ed.), *Essays In Positive Economics*, Chicago: University of Chicago Press: 3–16 and 30–43.

Friedman, Thomas L. 1999. *The Lexus and the Olive Tree*. New York: Farrar, Straus, Giroux.

Frimpong, Francis. 2020. 'Financialisation and the Myth of Poverty Alleviation in Ghana: A Theoretical and Empirical Investigation of the Impact of Financial Liberalisation on Sustainable Economic Development'. PhD Thesis, University of East London.

Froud, Julie, Colin Haslam, Sukhdev Johal, and Karel Williams. 2000. 'Shareholder Value and Financialization: Consultancy Promises, Management Moves'. *Economy and Society* 29 (1): 80–110.

Gabor, Daniela Veronica. 2012. 'The Road to Financialization in Central and Eastern Europe: The Early Policies and Politics of Stabilizing Transition'. *Review of Political Economy* 24 (2): 227–49.

Gaiha, Raghav. 1993. *Design of Poverty Alleviation Strategy in Rural Areas*. Food & Agriculture Organisation. Economic and Social Development Paper (No.115).

Ghana Statistical Service. 1999. '*Ghana Living Standards Survey. Round 3 Report*'. Accra: Ghana Statistical Service.

Ghana Statistical Service. 2018. '*Ghana Living Standards Survey. Round 7 Report*'. Accra: Ghana Statistical Service.

Goldman Sachs. 2013. *Goldman Sachs Two Decades of Freedom: What South Africa Is Doing with It, and What Now Needs to Be Done*. Goldman Sachs.

Goldsmith, Raymond W. 1969. 'Financial Structure and Development, New Haven, Yale University Press'. Retrieved from http://www.econ.yale.edu/growth_pdf/cdp236.pdf.

Gonzalez, Alvaro, J. Ernesto Lopez-Cordova, and Elio E. Valladares. 2007. *The Incidence of Graft on Developing-Country Firms*. Vol. 4394. Washington DC: World Bank Publications.

Government of Ghana. 1992. '1992 Constitution'. Accra: NDPC.

Government of Ghana. 2009. 'Implementation of the Growth and Poverty Reduction Strategy 2004–2009: 2008 Annual Progress Report'. Accra: NDPC.

Government of Ghana. 2010. 'Medium-Term National Development Policy Framework: Ghana Shared Growth Development Agenda (GSGDA), 2010–2013'. Accra: NDPC.

Gowan, Peter. 1999. *The Global Gamble: Washington's Faustian Bid for World Dominance*. New York: Verso.

Guérin, Isabelle, Solène Morvant-Roux, Magdalena Villarreal, S. Morvant-Roux, and M. Villarreal. 2014. 'Introduction: Microfinance, Debt and Overindebtedness'. *Microfinance, Debt and over-Indebtedness*, 1–23.

Gurley, J. G., and E. S. Shaw. 2002. 'Financial Structure and Economic Development', Economic Development and Cultural Change, 15 (3), April, 257–68'. *International Library of Critical Writings in Economics* 140: 204–15.

Gyimah-Boadi, Emmanuel. 1993. *Ghana under PNDC Rule*. Conseil Pour Le Developement De LA.

Gyimah-Boadi, Emmanuel, and Richard Jeffries. 2000. 'The Political Economy of Reform'. *Economic Reforms in Ghana: The Miracle and the Mirage*, 32–50.

Habitat, U. N. 2011. 'Ghana Housing Profile'. *Nairobi: United Nations Human Settlements Programme*.

Hanson, Emmanuel, John, Baako, and Dickson, Agyekum. 2003. 'The State and Popular Struggles in Ghana, 1982-1986'. *Popular Struggles for Democracy in Africa*. London: Zed Books.

Hall, David. 2009. 'Economic Crisis and Public Services: A Crisis for Public-Private Partnerships (PPPs)?' *Public Services International Research Unit, Note 2*.

Hall, Graham C., Patrick J. Hutchinson, and Nicos Michaelas. 2004. 'Determinants of the Capital Structures of European SMEs'. *Journal of Business Finance & Accounting* 31 (5–6): 711–28.

Hall, Peter A., and David Soskice. 2001. *Varieties of Capitalism: The Institutional Foundations of Comparative Advantage*. Oxford: Oxford University Press.

Harrison, Ann. 2007. *Globalization and Poverty*. Chicago: University of Chicago Press.

Harvey, David. 2005. *A Brief History of Neoliberalism*. Oxford: Oxford University Press.

Harvey, David. 2011. *The Enigma of Capital: And the Crises of Capitalism*. London: Profile Books.

Hayek, Friedrich August. 2014. *The Road to Serfdom: Text and Documents: The Definitive Edition*. Milton Park, Oxfordshire: Routledge.

Hicks, John. 1969. *A Theory of Economic History*. Vol. 9. Oxford: Oxford University Press.

Hildyard, Nicholas. 2016. *Licensed Larceny: Infrastructure, Financial Extraction and the Global South*. Manchester: Manchester University Press.

Hilferding, Rudolf. 1910. *Finance Capital: A Study of the Latest Phase of Capitalist Development*. London: Routledge & Kegan Paul.

Hilferding, Rudolf. 1981. *'Finance Capital: A Study of the Latest Phase of Capitalist Development,* London: Keagan Paul.

Ho, Sin-Yu, and Nicholas M. Odhiambo. 2011. 'Finance and Poverty Reduction in China: An Empirical Investigation'. *International Business & Economics Research Journal (IBER)* 10 (8): 103–14.

Holden, Paul, and Vassili Prokopenko. 2001. 'Financial Development and Poverty Alleviation: Issues and Policy Implications for Developing and Transition Countries'. IMF Working Paper No. WP/01/160.

Husain, Ishrat, and Rashid Faruqee. 1994. *Adjustment in Africa: Lessons from Country Case Studies*. Washington DC: The World Bank.

Hutchful, Eboe. 1989. 'From 'Revolution'to Monetarism: The Economics and Politics of the Adjustment Programme in Ghana'. In *Structural Adjustment in Africa*, 92–131. New York: Springer.

Hutchful, Eboe. 2002. *Ghana's Adjustment Experience: The Paradox of Reform*. Geneva: Unrisd Geneva.

Inoue, Takeshi, and Shigeyuki Hamori. 2012. 'How Has Financial Deepening Affected Poverty Reduction in India? Empirical Analysis Using State-Level Panel Data'. *Applied Financial Economics* 22 (5): 395–408.

International Monetary Fund. 2020a. 'IMF Executive Board Approves a US$1 Billion Disbursement to Ghana to Address the COVID-19 Pandemic." Press Release (13 April 2020'. International Monetary Fund. https://www.imf.org/en/News/Articles/2020/04/13/pr20153-ghana-imf-executiveboard-approves-a-us-1-billion-disbursement-to-ghana-to-address-covid-19.

International Monetary Fund. 2020b. 'World Economic Outlook'. International Monetary Fund. https://www.imf.org/en/Publications/WEO/Issues/2020/06/24/WEOUpdateJune2020.

Isaacs, Julia B., Joanna Young Marks, Timothy M. Smeeding, and Katherine A. Thornton. 2011. 'The New Demography of Poverty: The Wisconsin Poverty Measure and Effects of Federal and State Policies in Wisconsin'. *The Brookings Institution*. 2011. http://www.brookings.edu/research/papers/2011/03/31-wisconsin-poverty-isaacs.

Ismi, Asad. 2004. *Impoverishing a Continent: The World Bank and the IMF in Africa*. Canadian Centre for Policy Alternatives Ottawa.

ISSER. 2013. 'The State of the Ghanaian Economy.' Accra: (ISSER) Institute of Statistical, Social and Economic Research.

Ivanova, Maria N. 2013. 'Marx, Minsky, and the Great Recession'. *Review of Radical Political Economics* 45 (1): 59–75.

Jalilian, Hossein, and Colin Kirkpatrick. 2005. 'Does Financial Development Contribute to Poverty Reduction?' *Journal of Development Studies* 41 (4): 636–56.

Jeanneney, Sylviane Guillaumont, and Kangni R. Kpodar. 2004. 'Développement Financier, Instabilité Financière et Réduction de La Pauvreté'. CERDI *Études et Documents, E.*

Jerven, Morten. 2013. *Poor Numbers: How We Are Misled by African Development Statistics and What to Do about It*. New York: Cornell University Press.

Kabeer, Naila. 1996. 'Agency, Well-Being & Inequality: Reflections on the Gender Dimensions of Poverty'. *IDS Bulletin* 27 (1): 11–21.

Kahler, Miles. 1990. 'Orthodoxy and Its Alternatives: Explaining Approaches to Stabilization and Adjustment'. *Economic Crisis and Policy Choice: The Politics of Adjustment in the Third World*, 33–61.

Kahneman, Daniel, and Amos Tversky. 2013a. 'Choices, Values, and Frames'. In *Handbook of the Fundamentals of Financial Decision Making: Part I*, 269–78. New Jersey: World Scientific.

Kahneman, Daniel, and Amos Tversky. 2013b. 'Prospect Theory: An Analysis of Decision under Risk'. In *Handbook of the Fundamentals of Financial Decision Making: Part I*, 99–127. New Jersey: World Scientific.

Kear, Mark. 2013. 'Governing *Homo Subprimicus:* Beyond Financial Citizenship, Exclusion, and Rights'. *Antipode* 45(4): 926–46.

Keho, Yaya. 2017. 'The Impact of Trade Openness on Economic Growth: The Case of Cote d'Ivoire'. *Cogent Economics & Finance* 5 (1): 1332820.

Kehoe, Timothy J., and David K. Levine. 2001. 'Liquidity Constrained Markets versus Debt Constrained Markets'. *Econometrica* 69 (3): 575–98.

Keucheyan, Razmig. 2017. *Nature Is a Battlefield: Towards a Political Ecology*. New Jersey: John Wiley & Sons.

Keynes, John Maynard. 1936. *The General Theory of Employment, Interest, and Money*. London: Macmillan & Co Ltd.

Keynes, John Maynard. 2018. *The General Theory of Employment, Interest, and Money*. New York: Springer.

Kiely, Ray. 2005. *The Clash of Globalisations: Neo-Liberalism, the Third Way and Anti-Globalisation*. Leiden: Brill.

Kiely, Ray. 2018. *The Neoliberal Paradox*. Cheltenham: Edward Elgar Publishing.

Killick, Tony, and Moazzam Malik. 1992. 'Country Experiences with IMF Programmes in the 1980s'. *World Economy* 15 (5): 599–632.

Killick, Tony, Moazzam Malik, and Marcus Manuel. 1992. 'What Can We Know about the Effects of IMF Programmes?' *World Economy* 15 (5): 575–98.

King, Robert G., and Ross Levine. 1993. *Financial Intermediation and Economic Development*. Vol. 156189. Cambridge: Cambridge University Press.

Kingombe, Christian. 2014. 'Africa's Rising Middle Class amid Plenty and Extreme Poverty'. *European Centre for Development Policy Management Discussion Paper*, no. 167.

Klein, Naomi. 2007. *The Shock Doctrine: The Rise of Disaster Capitalism*. Macmillan.

Kochhar, Rakesh. 2015. 'A Global Middle Class Is More Promise than Reality'. *Pew Research Center's Global Attitudes Project* (blog). 2015. http://www.pewglobal.org/2015/07/08/a-global-middle-class-is-more-promise-than-reality/.

Kose, M. Ayhan, Eswar Prasad, Kenneth Rogoff, and Shang-Jin Wei. 2009. 'Financial Globalization: A Reappraisal'. *IMF Staff Papers* 56 (1): 8–62.

Kotz, David M. 2008. 'Contradictions of Economic Growth in the Neoliberal Era: Accumulation and Crisis in the Contemporary US Economy'. *Review of Radical Political Economics* 40 (2): 174–88.

Kotz, David M. 2010. 'Financialization and Neoliberalism'. *Relations of Global Power: Neoliberal Order and Disorder* 1 (1): 1–18.

Kotz, David M. 2013. 'Changes in the Postwar Global Economy and the Roots of the Financial Crisis'. *The Handbook of the Political Economy of Financial Crises*, 395. Oxford: Oxford University Press.

Kotz, David M. 2015. *3. The Rise of Neoliberal Capitalism. The Rise and Fall of Neoliberal Capitalism.* https://doi.org/10.4159/harvard.9780674735880.c5.

Kotz, David M., and Terrence McDonough. 2010. 'Global Neoliberalism and the Contemporary Social Structure of Accumulation'. *Contemporary Capitalism and Its Crises: Social Structure of Accumulation Theory for the 21st Century*, 93–120.

Krippner, Greta R. 2005. 'The Financialization of the American Economy'. *Socio-Economic Review* 3 (2): 173–208.

Krippner, Greta R. 2011. *Capitalizing on Crisis: The Political Origins of the Rise of Finance*. Cambridge, MA: Harvard University Press.

Kyei, Peter Ohene. 2000. 'Decentralisation and Poverty Alleviation in Rural Ghana'. Ph.D Thesis, Durham University.

Lapavitsas, Costas. 2009a. 'Financialisation Embroils Developing Countries'. *Papeles de Europa* 19: 108–39.

Lapavitsas, Costas. 2009b. 'Financialised Capitalism: Crisis and Financial Expropriation'. *Historical Materialism* 17 (2): 114–48.

Lapavitsas, Costas. 2011. 'Theorizing Financialization'. *Work, Employment and Society* 25 (4): 611–26.

Lapavitsas, Costas. 2013. *Profiting without Producing: How Finance Exploits Us All*. London: Verso Books.

Lapavitsas, Costas, and Paulo L. Dos Santos. 2008. 'Globalization and Contemporary Banking: On the Impact of New Technology'. *Contributions to Political Economy* 27 (1): 31–56.

Lapavitsas, Costas, and Iren Levina. 2010. 'Financial Profit: Profit from Production and Profit upon Alienation'(No.24).

Lavinas, Lena. 2017. 'How Social Developmentalism Reframed Social Policy in Brazil'. *New Political Economy* 22 (6): 628–44.

Lazonick, William. 2010. 'Innovative Business Models and Varieties of Capitalism: Financialization of the US Corporation'. *Business History Review* 84 (4): 675–702.

Lazonick, William. 2012. 'The Financialization of the US Corporation: What Has Been Lost, and How It Can Be Regained'. *Seattle UL Rev.* 36: 857.

Lazonick, William. 2014. ' "Profits Without Prosperity: Stock Buybacks Manipulate the Market and Leave Most Americans Worse Off'. *Harvard Business Review*.

Lazonick, William, and Mary O'Sullivan. 2000. 'Maximizing Shareholder Value: A New Ideology for Corporate Governance'. *Economy and Society* 29 (1): 13–35.

Lemmon, Michael L., and Jaime F. Zender. 2010. 'Debt Capacity and Tests of Capital Structure Theories'. *Journal of Financial and Quantitative Analysis*, 1161–87.

Lenin, Vladimir Il'ich. 1999. *Imperialism: The Highest Stage of Capitalism*. London: Resistance Books.

Levine, Ross. 1997. 'Financial Development and Economic Growth: Views and Agenda'. *Journal of Economic Literature* 35 (2): 688–726.

Levine, Ross. 2002. 'Bank-Based or Market-Based Financial Systems: Which Is Better?' *Journal of Financial Intermediation* 11 (4): 398–428.

Levine, Ross. 2005. 'Finance and Growth: Theory and Evidence'. *Handbook of Economic Growth* 1: 865–934.

Levine, Ross, and Sara Zervos. 1998. 'Stock Markets, Banks, and Economic Growth'. *American Economic Review*, 537–58.

Leyshon, Andrew, and Nigel Thrift. 2007. 'The Capitalization of Almost Everything: The Future of Finance and Capitalism'. *Theory, Culture & Society* 24 (7–8): 97–115.

Logan, Bernard Ikubolajeh. 1995. *Beyond Economic Liberalization in Africa: Structural Adjustment and the Alternatives*. London: Zed Books.

Loizos, Konstantinos. 2006. 'The Financial Repression/Liberalization Debate: A Survey of the Literature'. *Liberalization Debate: A Survey of the Literature (July 1, 2006)*.

Lordon, Frédéric. 2000. *Fonds de Pension, Piége à Cons?: Mirage de La Démocratie Actionnariale*. Raisons d'agir éditions.

Lucas Jr, Robert E. 1988. 'On the Mechanics of Economic Development'. *Journal of Monetary Economics* 22 (1): 3–42.

Lundberg, Mattias, and Lyn Squire. 2003. 'The Simultaneous Evolution of Growth and Inequality'. *The Economic Journal* 113 (487): 326–44.

Luxembourg, R. 1913. *The Accumulation of Capital*, London: Routledge and Keagan Paul.

MacLeavy, Julie. 2011. 'A "New Politics" of Austerity, Workfare and Gender? The UK Coalition Government's Welfare Reform Proposals'. *Cambridge Journal of Regions, Economy and Society* 4 (3): 355–67.

Mader, Philip. 2015. 'The Financialization of Poverty'. In *The Political Economy of Microfinance*, 78–120. New York: Springer.

Mader, Philip, Daniel Mertens, and Natascha Van der Zwan. 2020. *The Routledge International Handbook of Financialization*. Milton Park, Oxfordshire: Routledge.

Magdoff, Harry, and Paul Marlor Sweezy. 1988. *Irreversible Crisis*. New York: NYU Press.

Mandel, Ernest. 1969. *Marx Economic Theory Volume 2*. Vol. 2. New York: NYU Press.

Mandel, Ernest. 2002. *An Introduction to Marxist Economic Theory*. London: Resistance Books.

Marazzi, Christian. 2010. *The Violence of Financial Capitalism*. New York: Semiotext(e).

Marx, K. 1857. *Grundrisse: Outlines of the Critique of Political Economy*. (M Nicolaus, Translated, 1973). London: Penguin.

Marx, Karl. 1867. *Das Kapital: Volume 1*. Vol. 6. New York: William Milner.

Marx, Karl. 2019. *Capital: Volume One*. New York: Courier Dover Publications.
Masoud, Najeb, and Glenn Hardaker. 2012. 'The Impact of Financial Development on Economic Growth: Empirical Analysis of Emerging Market Countries'. *Studies in Economics and Finance*, 29(3), pp.148–173.
Mazzucato, Mariana, and L. Randall Wray. 2015. 'Financing the Capital Development of the Economy: A Keynes-Schumpeter-Minsky Synthesis'. LEM Working Paper Series.
McGregor, Sue. 2005. 'Structural Adjustment Programmes and Human Well-Being'. *International Journal of Consumer Studies* 29 (3): 170–80.
McKinnon, Ronald I. 1973. '*Money and Capital in Economic Development*. Washington DC: Brookings Institution.
McKinnon, Ronald I. 2010. *Money and Capital in Economic Development*. Washington DC: Brookings Institution Press.
McKinsey Global Institute. 1999. 'Lions on the Move: The Progress and Potential of African Economies'. https://www.mckinsey.com/mgi/overview/in-the-news/1999.
McKinsey Global Institute. 2016. 'Lions on the Move: The Progress and Potential of African Economies.' https://www.mckinsey.com/mgi/overview/in-the-news/2016.
Meghir, Costas. 2004. 'A Retrospective on Friedman's Theory of Permanent Income'. *The Economic Journal* 114 (496): F293–306.
Menyah, Nazl, and Wolde-Rufael, Y. (2014). *Financial Development, Trade Openness and Economic Growth in African Countries: New Insights from a Panel Causality Approach, Economic Modelling* 37: 386–94.
Merton, Robert C., and Zvi Bodie. 1995. 'A Conceptual Framework for Analyzing the Financial System'. *The Global Financial System: A Functional Perspective*, 3–31.
Merton, Robert C., and Zvi Bodie. 2004. 'The Design of Financial Systems: Towards a Synthesis of Function and Structure'. National Bureau of Economic Research.
Milanovic, Branko. 2016. *Global Inequality: A New Approach for the Age of Globalization*. Cambridge, MA: Harvard University Press.
Miller, David, and William Dinan. 2008. *A Century of Spin: How Public Relations Became the Cutting Edge of Corporate Power*. London: Pluto Press.
Miller, Merton H. 1988. 'The Modigliani-Miller Propositions after Thirty Years'. *Journal of Economic Perspectives* 2 (4): 99–120.
Miller, Merton H. 1998. 'Financial Markets and Economic Growth'. *Journal of Applied Corporate Finance* 11 (3): 8–15.
Minsky, Hyman P. 1986. *Global Consequences of Financial Deregulation*. Department of Economics, Washington University.
Minsky, Hyman P. 1996. 'Uncertainty and the Institutional Structure of Capitalist Economies: Remarks upon Receiving the Veblen-Commons Award'. *Journal of Economic Issues* 30 (2): 357–68.
Minsky, Hyman P., and Henry Kaufman. 2008. *Stabilizing an Unstable Economy*. Vol. 1. McGraw-Hill New York.

Minton, Bernadette A., and Karen H. Wruck. 2001. 'Financial Conservatism: Evidence on Capital Structure from Low Leverage Firms'. Available at SSRN 269608.

Miotti, Luis, and Dominique Plihon. 2001. 'Libéralisation Financière, Spéculation et Crises Bancaires'. *Économie Internationale*, no. 1: 3–36.

Mishkin, Frederic S. 2006. *The next Great Globalization: How Disadvantaged Nations Can Harness Their Financial Systems to Get Rich*. New Jersey: Princeton University Press.

Mitlin, Diana, and David Satterthwaite. 2013. *Urban Poverty in the Global South: Scale and Nature*. Milton Park, Oxfordshire: Routledge.

Modigliani, Franco, and Richard Brumberg. 1954. 'Utility Analysis and the Consumption Function: An Interpretation of Cross-Section Data'. *Franco Modigliani* 1 (1): 388–436.

Modigliani, Franco, and Merton Miller. 1963. 'Taxes and the Cost of Capital: A Correction'. *American Economic Review* 53 (3): 433–43.

Modigliani, Franco, and Merton H. Miller. 1958. 'The Cost of Capital, Corporation Finance and the Theory of Investment'. *The American Economic Review* 48 (3): 261–97.

Moghalu, Kingsley Chiedu. 2014. *Emerging Africa: How the Global Economy's 'Last Frontier' Can Prosper and Matter*. London: Penguin UK.

Morales, María F. 2003. 'Financial Intermediation in a Model of Growth through Creative Destruction'. *Macroeconomic Dynamics* 7 (3): 363–93.

Mu, Y., P. Phelps, and J. G. Stotsky. 2013. *Bond Markets in Africa. Review of Development Finance, 3 (3),* 121–135.

Mwainyekule, Leah H., and Francis B. Frimpong. 2020. 'The Pandemic and the Economy of Africa: Conflicting Strategies between Tanzania and Ghana'. *Digital Government: Research and Practice* 1 (4): 1–8.

Myers, Stewart C. 2001. 'Capital Structure'. *Journal of Economic Perspectives* 15 (2): 81–102.

Myers, Stewart C., and Nicholas S. Majluf. 1984. 'Corporate Financing and Investment Decisions When Firms Have Information That Investors Do Not Have'. *Journal of Financial Economics* 13 (2): 187–221.

Ndukwe, Ijeoma. 2021. 'Ghana's Farmers Eye Sweet Success from Chocolate'. https://www.bbc.co.uk/news/world-africa-56687427.

Nelson, Julie A. 2018. *Economics for Humans*. Chicago: University of Chicago Press.

Nowak, Maria. 2005. *On Ne Prête Pas Qu'aux Riches*. JC Lattès.

Nsowah-Nuamah, Nicholas, Francis Teal, and Moses Awoonor-Williams. 2012. 'Jobs, Skills and Incomes in Ghana: How Was Poverty Halved?' *Comparative Education* 48 (2): 231–48.

Obeng-Odoom, Franklin. 2012. 'Neoliberalism and the Urban Economy in Ghana: Urban Employment, Inequality, and Poverty'. *Growth & Change* 43 (1): 85–109. https://doi.org/10.1111/j.1468-2257.2011.00578.x.

Odhiambo, Nicholas M. 2009. 'Finance-Growth-Poverty Nexus in South Africa: A Dynamic Causality Linkage'. *The Journal of Socio-Economics* 38 (2): 320–25.

Odhiambo, Nicholas M. 2010a. 'Financial Deepening and Poverty Reduction in Zambia: An Empirical Investigation'. *International Journal of Social Economics*.

Odhiambo, Nicholas M. 2010b. 'Is Financial Development a Spur to Poverty Reduction? Kenya's Experience'. *Journal of Economic Studies*.

OECD. 2011. 'Development Co-Operation Report 2011'. OECD. https://www.oecd-ilibrary.org/development/development-co-operation-report-2011_dcr-2011-en.

Orhangazi, Özgür. 2008. 'Financialisation and Capital Accumulation in the Non-Financial Corporate Sector: A Theoretical and Empirical Investigation on the US Economy: 1973–2003'. *Cambridge Journal of Economics* 32 (6): 863–86.

Orhangazi, Özgür 2008a. "Wall Street vs. the labor movement." In *New Labor Forum*, vol. 17, no. 1, p. 101. California: Sage Publications Ltd.

Orhangazi, Özgür. 2008b. *Financialization and the US Economy*. Cheltenham: Edward Elgar Publishing.

Orhangazi, Özgür. 2011. ' "Financial" vs."Real": An Overview of the Contradictory Role of Finance'. *Revitalizing Marxist Theory for Today's Capitalism*.

Osabu-Kle, Daniel Tetteh. 2000. 'The Politics of One-Sided Adjustment in Africa'. *Journal of Black Studies* 30 (4): 515–33.

Owusi, G., and Paul WK Yankson. 2007. 'Poverty in Ghana Is Basically a Rural Phenomenon": Are We Underestimating Urban Poverty?' *Ghana Journal of Development Studies* 4 (1): 87–105.

OXFAM. 2014. 'Time to End Inequality Report'. OXFAM. https://www.oxfam.org/en/research/time-end-extreme-inequality.

Palley, Thomas I. 2011. 'A Theory of Minsky Super-Cycles and Financial Crises'. *Contributions to Political Economy* 30 (1): 31–46.

Palley, Thomas I. 2013. 'Financialization: What It Is and Why It Matters'. In *Financialization*, 17–40. New York: Springer.

Palma, J. G. 2013. 'How the Full Opening of the Capital Account to Highly Liquid and Unstable Financial Markets Led Latin America to Two and a Half Cycles of 'mania, Panic and Crash' " '. *The Handbook of the Political Economy of Financial Crises*, New York: Oxford University Press.

Palma, José Gabriel. 2009. 'The Revenge of the Market on the Rentiers. Why Neo-Liberal Reports of the End of History Turned out to Be Premature'. *Cambridge Journal of Economics* 33 (4): 829–69.

Panitch, Leo, and Sam Gindin. 2004. 'Global Capitalism and American Empire'. *Socialist Register* 40.

Peck, Jamie, and Nik Theodore. 2007. 'Variegated Capitalism'. *Progress in Human Geography* 31 (6): 731–72.

Piketty, Thomas. 2013. 'Capital in the 21st Century'. Cambridge, MA: President and Fellows, Harvard College.

Powell, Jeff. 2013. 'Subordinate Financialisation: A Study of Mexico and Its Non-Financial Corporations'. PhD Thesis, SOAS, University of London.

Price, R. B. 1974. 'Money and Capital in Economic Development/ Financial Deepening in Economic Development' (Book Review).. *Kyklos,* 27, 187.

Priyadarshee, Anurag, and Asad K. Ghalib. 2011. 'The Andhra Pradesh Microfinance Crisis in India: Manifestation, Causal Analysis, and Regulatory Response'. *Brooks World Poverty Institute Working Paper,* no. 157.

PwC. 2014. 'Anticipating Problems, Finding Solutions: Global Annual Review'. PwC. https://www.pwc.com/gx/en/global-annual-review/assets/pwc-global-annual-review-2014.pdf.

PwC. 2018. 'Ghana Banking Survey: The Future of Banking in Ghana. What Is Next?' The Future of Banking in Ghana. What Is Next? Accra: PwC. http://www.pwc.com/gh/en/assets/pdf/gh-banking-survey-2018.pdf.

Quartey, Peter. 2008. 'Financial Sector Development, Savings Mobilization and Poverty Reduction in Ghana'. In *Financial Development, Institutions, Growth and Poverty Reduction,* 87–119. Springer.

Quartey, Peter, and Frank Prah. 2008. 'Financial Development and Economic Growth in Ghana: Is There a Causal Link?' *African Finance Journal* 10 (1): 28–54.

Ramlall, Indranarain. 2009. 'Bank-Specific, Industry-Specific and Macroeconomic Determinants of Profitability in Taiwanese Banking System: Under Panel Data Estimation'. *International Research Journal of Finance and Economics* 34 (2): 1450–2887.

Ravallion, Martin. 2001. 'Growth, Inequality and Poverty: Looking Beyond Averages'. *World Development* 29 (11): 1803–15. https://doi.org/10.1016/S0305-750X(01)00072-9.

Ravallion, Martin. 2014. 'An Exploration of the International Comparison Program's New Global Economic Landscape'. National Bureau of Economic Research. Working Paper No 20338. Available at www.nber.org/papers/w20338. (Accessed 04/04/2018).

Ravallion, Martin. 2018. 'Inequality and Globalization: A Review Essay'. *Journal of Economic Literature* 56 (2): 620–42.

Ravallion, Martin, Shaohua Chen, and Prem Sangraula. 2009. 'Dollar a Day Revisited'. *The World Bank Economic Review* 23 (2): 163–84.

Reddy, Sanjay G., and Thomas Pogge. 2008. *How Not to Count the Poor.* Oxford: Oxford University Press.

Reed, Larry R., D. S. K. Rao, Sabina Rogers, Camille Rivera, Fabiola Diaz, Sara Gailly, Jesse Marsden, and Xochitl Sanchez. 2015. 'Mapping Pathways out of Poverty. The State of the Microcredit Summit Campaign Report 2015'. Microcredit Summit Campaign, Washington, DC.

Reille, Xavier. 2010. 'SKS IPO Success and Excess'. *CGAP Microfinance Blog.* http://Microfinance.Cgap.Org/2010/08/11/Sks-Ipo-Success-and-Excess/(Accessed March 16, 2011).

Reinhart, Carmen, and Vincent Reinhart. 2009. 'Capital Flow Bonanzas: An Encompassing View of the Past and Present'. In *NBER International Seminar on Macroeconomics 2008*, 9–62. Chicago: University of Chicago Press.

Ricardo, David. 1891. *Principles of Political Economy and Taxation*. G. Bell and Sons.

Robbinson, Joan. 1952. 'The Generalization of the General Theory: The Rate of Interest and Essays'. London: McMillian.

Robinson, Marguerite S. 2001. *The Microfinance Revolution: Sustainable Finance for the Poor*. Washington DC: The World Bank.

Rodrigues Teles Sampaio, Nuno Jorge. 2014. 'Financialisation in South Africa: Examining the Financial Conduct of Non-Financial Enterprises, Banks and Households'. PhD Thesis, SOAS, University of London.

Rojas-Suarez, Liliana. 2016. 'Financial Inclusion in Latin America: Facts and Obstacles'. Center for Global Development Working Paper, no. 439.

Röpke, Wilhelm. 1982. 'The Guiding Principles of the Liberal Programme'. *Standard Texts on the Social Market Economy* 188.

Rosenberg, Justin. 2013. 'The 'Philosophical Premises' of Uneven and Combined Development'. *Review of International Studies*, 569–97.

Roy-Mukherjee, Shampa. 2015. 'Connecting the Dots: The Washington Consensus and the "Arab Spring"'. *Journal of Balkan and Near Eastern Studies* 17 (2): 141–58.

Sachs, Jeffrey D., Andrew Warner, Anders A. Aslund, and Stanley Fischer. 1995. 'Economic Reform and the Process of Global Integration'. *Brookings Papers on Economic Activity* 1995 (1): 1–118.

Salim, Mahfuzah, and Raj Yadav. 2012. 'Capital Structure and Firm Performance: Evidence from Malaysian Listed Companies'. *Procedia-Social and Behavioral Sciences* 65: 156–66.

Samuels, J. M., F. M. Wilkes, and R. E. Brayshaw. 1997. *Management of Company Finance (Ed.)*. London: International Thomson Business Press.

Sayer, Andrew. 1999. *Realism and Social Science*. London: Sage.

Schuman, Michael. 2009. *The Miracle: The Epic Story of Asia's Quest for Wealth*. New York: Harper Collins.

Schumpeter, Joseph. 1911. *The Theory of Economic Development. Harvard Economic Studies. Vol. Xlvi*. Cambridge, MA: Harvard University Press.

Schumpeter, Joseph A. 1982. *The Theory of Economic Development: An Inquiry into Profits, Capital, Credit, Interest, and the Business Cycle (1912/1934)*. New Jersey: Transaction Publishers–January 1: 244.

Seifert, Bruce, and Halit Gonenc. 2008. 'The International Evidence on the Pecking Order Hypothesis'. *Journal of Multinational Financial Management* 18 (3): 244–60.

Seifert, Bruce, and Halit Gonenc. 2010. 'Pecking Order Behavior in Emerging Markets'. *Journal of International Financial Management & Accounting* 21 (1): 1–31.

REFERENCES 261

Shah, Anup. 2013. 'Structural Adjustment – a Major Cause of Poverty'. *Global Issues* 24: 1–24.

Shahbaz, Muhammad, Nanthakumar Loganathan, Aviral Kumar Tiwari, and Reza Sherafatian-Jahromi. 2015. 'Financial Development and Income Inequality: Is There Any Financial Kuznets Curve in Iran?' *Social Indicators Research* 124 (2): 357–82.

Shaw, Edward Stone. 1973. 'Financial Deepening in Economic Development'. Oxford: Oxford University Press.

Sheikh, Nadeem Ahmed, and Zongjun Wang. 2011. 'Determinants of Capital Structure: An Empirical Study of Firms in Manufacturing Industry of Pakistan'. *Managerial Finance.*

Shillington, Kevin. 1992. Ghana and the Rawlings Factor. New York: St. Martin's Press.

Singh, Ajit. 1991. 'The Stock Market and Economic Development: Should Developing Countries Encourage Stock Markets?' MPRA paper published in UNCTAD Review (1 January 1993): pp. 1–74.

Singh, Ajit. 1997. 'Financial Liberalisation, Stockmarkets and Economic Development'. *The Economic Journal* 107 (442): 771–82.

Smith, Adam. 1776. *An Inquiry into the Nature and Causes of the Wealth of Nations: Volume One.* London: printed for W. Strahan; and T. Cadell, 1776.

Smith, Adam. 2006. *An Inquiry into the Nature and Causes of the Wealth of Nations Published in 1776.* Hazleton, PA: PSU-Hazleton.

Smith, Tony. 1979. 'The Underdevelopment of Development Literature: The Case of Dependency Theory'. *World Politics: A Quarterly Journal of International Relations,* 247–88.

Solomon, Ezra. 1963. 'Leverage and the Cost of Capital'. *The Journal of Finance* 18 (2): 273–79.

Sowa, Nii Kwaku. 2002. *An Assessment of Poverty Reducing Policies and Programmes in Ghana.* Accra: Centre for Policy Analysis Citeseer.

Steindl, Josef. 1989. 'Saving and Debt'. In *Money, Credit and Prices in Keynesian Perspective,* 71–78. New York: Springer.

Steuart, James. 1767. *An Inquiry into the Principles of Political Economy: Being an Essay on the Science of Domestic Policy in Free Nations: In Which Are Particularly Considered Population, Agriculture, Trade, Industry, Money, Coin, Interest, Circulation, Banks, Exchange, Public Credit, and Taxes.* Vol. 2. Bristol: A. Millar and T. Cadell.

Stiglitz, Joseph. 2015. *The Great Divide.* London: Penguin UK.

Stiglitz, Joseph E. 2000. 'Capital Market Liberalization, Economic Growth, and Instability'. *World Development* 28 (6): 1075–86.

Stiglitz, Joseph E. 2002. *Globalization and Its Discontents.* Vol. 500. New York: Norton & Co.

Stiglitz, Joseph E. 2006. *Making Globalization Work.* New York: W.W. Norton & Co.

Stockhammer, Engelbert. 2004. 'Financialisation and the Slowdown of Accumulation'. *Cambridge Journal of Economics* 28 (5): 719–41.

Stockhammer, Engelbert. 2010. 'Financialization and the Global Economy'. Political Economy Research Institute Working Paper 242: 40.

Stockhamer, Engelbert. 2012. 'Rising Inequality as a Root Cause of the Present Crisis', Political Economy Research Institute, University of Massachusetts, Amherst, Working Paper.

Stockhammer, Engelbert. 2012a. 'Financialization, Income Distribution and the Crisis'. *Investigación Económica* 71 (279): 39–70.

Stockhammer, Engelbert. 2012b. 'Financialization'. In *Handbook of Critical Issues in Finance*. Cheltenham: Edward Elgar Publishing.

Storey, Andy. 2019. 'Authoritarian Neoliberalism in Europe: The Red Herring of Ordoliberalism'. *Critical Sociology* 45 (7–8): 1035–45.

Storm, Servaas. 2015. 'Structural Change'. *Development and Change* 46 (4): 666–99.

Storm, Servaas. 2018. 'Financialization and Economic Development: A Debate on the Social Efficiency of Modern Finance'. *Development and Change* 49 (2): 302–29.

Strebulaev, Ilya A. 2007. 'Do Tests of Capital Structure Theory Mean What They Say?' *The Journal of Finance* 62 (4): 1747–87.

Sum, Ngai-Ling, and Bob Jessop. 2013. *Towards a Cultural Political Economy: Putting Culture in Its Place in Political Economy*. Cheltenham: Edward Elgar Publishing.

Sweezy, Paul M. 1994. 'The Triumph of Financial Capital'. *Monthly Review* 46 (2): 1–11.

Symbiotics. 2017. 'Symbiotics MIV Survey'. https://symbioticsgroup.com/wp-con-tent/uploads/2017/09/Symbiotics-2017-MIV-Survey.pdf.

Tabb, William K. 2013. 'The International Spread of Financialization'. *The Handbook of the Political Economy of Financial Crises*, 526–39. New York: Oxford University Press.

Tandon, Yashpal. 1999. *Globalization and Africa's Options* (issue 2). Indiana: International South Group Network.

Teye, Joseph Kofi, Isaac Teye, and Maxine Ohenewa Asiedu. 2015. 'Financing Housing in Ghana: Challenges to the Development of Formal Mortgage System'. *Journal of Housing and the Built Environment* 30 (1): 1–16.

Tickell, Adam, and Jamie Peck. 2003. 'Making Global Rules: Globalization or Neoliberalization'. *Remaking the Global Economy: Economic-Geographical Perspectives*, 163–82.

Tobin, James. 1965. 'The Monetary Interpretation of History'. *The American Economic Review* 55 (3): 464–85.

Toporowski, Jan. 2008. 'Excess Capital and Liquidity Management'. Levy Economics Institute Working Papers No.549.

Toporowski, Jan. 2009. 'The Economics and Culture of Financial Inflation'. *Competition & Change* 13 (2): 145–56.

Toporowski, Jan. 2010. 'The Transnational Company after Globalisation'. *Futures* 42 (9): 920–25.

Townsend, Peter. 1962. 'The Meaning of Poverty'. *The British Journal of Sociology* 13 (3): 210–27. https://doi.org/10.2307/587266.

Townsend, Peter. 2010. 'The Meaning of Poverty'. *The British Journal of Sociology* 61: 85–102.

Townsend, Peter. 2014. *International Analysis Poverty*. Milton Park, Oxfordshire: Routledge.

Trotsky, Leon. 2010. *The Permanent Revolution & Results and Prospects*. Seattle: Red Letter Press.

Uddin, Gazi Salah, Muhammad Shahbaz, Mohamed Arouri, and Frédéric Teulon. 2014. 'Financial Development and Poverty Reduction Nexus: A Cointegration and Causality Analysis in Bangladesh'. *Economic Modelling* 36: 405–12.

Udeogu, Ejike. 2018. *Financialisation, Capital Accumulation and Economic Development in Nigeria: A Critical Perspective*. Newcastle Upon Tyne: Cambridge Scholars Publishing.

UNCTAD. 2011. 'Trade and Development Report (2011). Price Formation in Financialized Commodity Markets'. United Nations. http://unctad.org/en/docs/gds20111_en.pdf.

UNCTAD. 2018. 'World Investment Report: Investment and New Industrial Policy'. https://unctad.org/en/PublicationsLibrary/wir2018_en.pdf.

UNCTAD. 2020. 'World Investment Report 2020: International Production Beyond the Pandemic'. https://unctad.org/webflyer/world-investment-report-2020.

UNDP. 2010. 'The Real Wealth of Nations: Pathways to Human Development'. http://hdr.undp.org/sites/default/files/reports/270/hdr_2010_en_complete_reprint.pdf.

Valdez, Stephen, and Philip Molyneux. 2015. *An Introduction to Global Financial Markets*. London: Macmillan International Higher Education.

Van der Zwan, Natascha. 2014. 'Making Sense of Financialization'. *Socio-Economic Review* 12 (1): 99–129.

Warnock, Veronica Cacdac, and Francis E. Warnock. 2008. 'Markets and Housing Finance'. *Journal of Housing Economics* 17 (3): 239–51.

Weeks, John. 2014. *Capital and Exploitation*. Vol. 332. New Jersey: Princeton University Press.

Wolf, Martin. 2014. *The Shifts and the Shocks: What We've Learned–and Have Still to Learn–from the Financial Crisis*. London: Penguin UK.

Wolfson, Martin H., and Gerald A. Epstein. 2013. *The Handbook of the Political Economy of Financial Crises*. New York: Oxford University Press.

Woodruff, David M. 2016. 'Governing by Panic: The Politics of the Eurozone Crisis'. *Politics & Society* 44 (1): 81–116.

World Bank. 1990. 'World Development Report 1990: Poverty'. Oxford University Press: World Bank.

World Bank. 1993. 'The World Bank Annual Report 1993'. Washington DC: World Bank.

World Bank. 1997. 'The World Bank Annual Report 1997'. Washington DC: World Bank.

World Bank. 2010. 'The World Bank Annual Report'. Washington DC: World Bank.

World Bank. 2013. 'The World Bank Annual Report 2013'. Washington DC: World Bank.

World Bank. 2018. *Poverty and Shared Prosperity 2018: Piecing Together the Poverty Puzzle*. Washington DC: The World Bank.

World Bank. 2020. 'Commodity Markets Outlook, April 2020'. World Bank. https://documents.worldbank.org/en/publication/documents-reports/documentdetail/543311587659880031/commodity-markets-outlook-april-2020.

World Bank Enterprise Survey. 2013. 'Business Environment in Ghana'. World Bank Enterprise Survey. https://www.enterprisesurveys.org/data/exploreeconomies/2013/ghana.

World Bank Group. 2016. *World Development Report 2016: Digital Dividends*. Washington DC: World Bank Publications.

World Trade Organisation. 2018. 'World Trade Statistical Review'. World Trade Organisation. https://www.wto.org/english/res_e/statis_e/wts2018_e/wts2018_e.pdf.

Wray, L. Randall. 2011. 'Minsky's Money Manager Capitalism and the Global Financial Crisis'. *International Journal of Political Economy* 40 (2): 5–20.

Yunus, Muhammad. 2007. *Banker to the Poor: Micro-Lending and the Battle against World Poverty*. New York: PublicAffairs.

Index

Absolute poverty   173, 189, 192, 197
Accumulation of reserves   236
Africa Development Bank   81, 94, 122, 196
Africa Growth and Opportunity Act (AGOA)   16, 241
Arrighi   1n1, 35, 36, 36n15, 37, 46, 58, 61, 244

Behavioural economics   211, 211n2
Bretton Woods system   21, 21n4, 23, 24, 27, 30, 53
British colonial rule   164
British industrialisation   71

Capital accumulation   3, 15, 34, 45, 67, 68, 68n8, 70, 71, 72, 76, 78, 79, 110, 145, 149, 151, 152, 170, 171, 215, 237
Capital market   31n12, 46, 69, 72, 76, 118, 121, 135, 146, 228, 236, 238
Capital structure   5, 7, 10, 12, 14, 15, 144, 145, 146, 147, 148, 153, 169, 171
Capitalism   8, 13, 16, 18, 19, 19n2, 20, 21, 22, 22n5, 23, 25, 26, 27, 28, 29, 30, 32, 33, 34, 35, 37, 38, 39, 39n17, 41, 42, 43, 44, 48, 49, 51, 53, 54, 55, 56, 57, 58, 62, 65, 67, 68, 69, 70, 71, 71n11, 76, 99, 106, 112, 133, 134, 146, 162, 177, 194, 205, 212, 213, 215, 216, 234, 235, 241
Capitalist accumulation   7, 32, 34, 57, 65
Chambers, Robert   181, 182, 183, 193, 194, 232
Consumer credit   51, 58, 158
Core-Periphery   ix, 9n11, 10, 45
Corruption   1n1, 11, 100, 105, 165, 227
COVID-19   14, 83, 84, 85, 86, 87, 88, 89, 202
Credit money   50, 216

Demonetisation   16, 227, 233
Depreciation   90, 96, 104, 113, 114, 141, 166, 167

East Asian Miracle   2, 108
Economic crisis   22, 89, 94, 98
Extreme poverty   6, 20, 84, 92, 110, 172, 173, 176, 177, 178, 179, 184, 186, 187, 196, 197, 199, 206, 207, 241

Fictitious money   51
Finance capital   56, 57, 58
Finance Capital   58
Financial accumulation   38, 65, 66, 91, 231
Financial asset   3, 14, 23, 44, 55, 59, 64, 66, 67, 72, 91, 134, 137, 141, 148, 149, 169, 170, 212, 228, 232, 235, 237, 239
Financial crisis   15, 69, 70, 74, 75, 145
Financial development   4, 54, 70, 75, 76, 78, 79, 80, 81, 82, 91, 228
Financial expropriation   64, 214, 215, 230, 231, 233, 239
Financial inclusion   7n7, 13, 15, 16, 40, 48, 49, 50, 52, 53, 59, 63, 186, 187, 194, 208, 209, 217, 221, 223, 225, 227, 228, 230, 231, 233, 236, 239, 241
Financial Instability Hypothesis   xvi, 41n19
Financial liberalisation   2, 3, 5, 45, 69, 73, 74, 118, 143, 158, 204, 205, 211, 213, 224, 236, 239, 240
Financial market   6, 7, 23n8, 31, 39, 44, 46, 48, 49, 51, 59, 60, 68, 70, 71, 73, 74, 74n13, 75, 79, 122, 126, 130, 131, 137, 143, 212, 216, 234
Financial profit   x, 3, 14, 36, 37, 43, 44, 47, 50, 54, 55, 57, 61, 63, 64, 66, 67, 91, 132, 149, 215, 235, 236, 237, 238
Financial sector   3, 4, 5, 6, 7, 11, 12, 14, 15, 20, 23, 25, 28, 30, 31, 33, 40, 43, 48, 53, 56, 67, 69, 69n9, 70, 72, 73, 74, 75, 78, 79, 80, 81, 82, 86, 91, 93, 98, 113, 116, 117, 118, 119, 121, 122, 124, 126, 127, 128, 129, 133, 134, 135, 142, 144, 148, 149, 152, 155, 178, 212, 216, 221, 223, 228, 231, 234, 235, 236, 237, 239
Financial Sector Adjustment Programme   6
Financial system   3, 4, 24, 25, 31n11, 41, 49, 59, 65, 66, 68, 69, 73, 74, 76, 76n15, 77, 78, 79, 82, 91, 92, 115, 118, 119, 121, 122, 134, 152, 164, 212, 214, 219, 221, 225, 231, 233, 239
Financial/fictitious accumulation   65, 66, 91
Fordism   38, 40

Foreign Direct Investment   xv, xvi, 7, 69, 89, 137, 140t5, 149n2, 194
French Regulation   38, 53
French Regulation school   13, 18, 235

Ghana Living Standard Survey   xvi, 179
Ghanaian economy   6, 7, 9, 11, 12, 14, 84, 87, 88, 90, 93, 103, 104, 118, 134, 135, 141, 167, 170, 204, 208, 224, 237, 238
Global financial crisis   26, 69, 116, 133, 139
Globalisation   2, 3, 14, 15, 18, 24, 31, 31n12, 31n12, 45, 46, 47, 56, 70, 83, 88, 90, 110, 131, 171, 180, 200, 201, 202, 203, 204, 205, 206, 207, 208, 236
Golden Age of Capitalism   20, 21n4
Gowan, Peter   68, 69, 135, 216, 234, 235

Harvey, David   19, 22, 22n6, 23, 24, 25, 29, 47, 48, 58, 66, 74n13, 111n8, 134, 203
Hegemony   16, 18, 36, 36n15, 37, 61, 234
Heterodox economics   69, 169, 170, 212n3, 234, 238
Hilferding, Rudolf   56, 57, 58, 149
Household credit   158, 162, 225
Human Development Index   193

Indian crisis   132
Inequality   2, 6, 6n6, 10, 11, 20, 44, 44n20, 49, 75, 80, 84, 92, 134, 142, 171, 179, 195, 199, 200, 201, 204, 205, 215, 239, 240
Inflation   19, 21, 39, 40, 44, 47, 96, 97, 102, 104, 106, 107, 113, 114, 115, 118, 137, 141, 157, 158, 180
Informal sector   5, 83, 85, 113, 117, 134, 163, 166, 217, 231
Interest rates   6, 7, 39, 41, 45, 46, 47, 52, 73, 96, 97, 108, 114, 116, 118, 119, 134, 136, 137, 141, 143, 152, 155, 157, 158, 170, 207, 236, 237, 240
International market   47, 86, 108, 111, 112, 205
International Monetary Fund   xvi, 2n2, 6, 21, 81, 84, 85
International Poverty Line   xvi, 84, 176
International trade   27, 90, 101, 108, 136, 201, 203, 204, 205

Keynes, John Maynard   4, 27, 33, 42, 46, 70, 72, 109, 149, 150, 232

Life Cycle Hypothesis   209

Marx, Karl   4, 14, 32, 55, 57, 62, 62n6, 63, 64, 65, 65n7, 71n11, 149, 150, 214, 215
Marxist Political Economy   30, 35, 62
Marx's profit   14, 55
McKinnon, Ronald   6, 8, 8n8, 70, 72, 73
McKinsey Global Institute   79, 198
Microfinance   13, 48, 49, 50, 51, 52, 53, 132, 224, 231, 232, 236
Millennium Development Goals   81, 178
Mobile Money   xiv, xv, xvi, 7, 16, 58, 58n2, 209, 210, 217, 218, 218f38, 218n5, 220t12, 221f39, 223f40, 243
Modigliani, Franco and Miller, Merton   4, 4n3, 145, 146, 147, 169
Monetary policy   xiii, 97, 157f23
Monopoly Capital   32, 33, 34, 35, 56
Monthly Review   32n13, 33, 34, 35
Multinational Corporations   xvi, 2, 34, 56

Neoliberalism   9n10, 14, 15, 18, 19, 20, 22, 26, 27, 28, 29, 33, 50, 55, 75, 93, 97, 102, 134, 144, 180, 195, 205, 213
Nkrumah, Kwame   98, 99, 99n4, 100, 244

Ordoliberalism   28, 28n10, 29
Oxfam   171

Pecking-order   147, 148
Periphery countries   6, 8, 9, 10n12, 10n13, 14, 15, 16, 24, 25, 36, 37, 39, 45, 46, 47, 48, 53, 64, 69, 73, 74, 77, 79, 82, 100, 101, 103, 107, 112, 121, 130, 131, 135, 136, 137, 141, 143, 144, 148, 151, 162, 172, 178, 180, 192, 203, 204, 205, 206, 207, 236, 241, 242
Permanent Income Hypothesis   210
Ponzi finance   41
Post-Keynesian   13, 18, 30, 40, 42
Poverty alleviation   8, 13, 17, 22, 48, 49, 50, 52, 53, 61, 80, 81, 82, 83, 89, 92, 109, 113, 170, 178, 180, 183, 187, 201, 203, 204, 205, 206, 207, 209, 240, 241, 242
Poverty headcount   75, 173, 178, 184
Poverty measurement   178, 179, 180, 181, 193
Primary sector   204
Private sector   20, 25, 26, 48, 80, 96, 97, 98, 99, 102, 107, 113, 117, 118, 120, 122, 124, 142, 157, 158, 198, 199, 236
Public sector   2, 6, 15, 107, 111, 144

INDEX

Reagan, Ronald   19
Real capital investment   65, 80, 157, 235
Real commodity accumulation   14, 54, 55, 65, 66, 91
Regulated Capitalism   20
Relative poverty   15, 171, 193
Return on Equity   xiii, 132, 133, 133f16, 133n15

Schumpeter, Joseph   4
Securitisation   24, 50, 51, 119, 120, 212, 213
Shareholder Value Orientation   42
Stiglitz, Joseph   47, 107, 108, 171, 172, 204, 206, 207
Stockhammer, Engelbert   4, 9n9, 31, 43, 44, 45, 47, 67, 70, 130, 170, 237
Structural Adjustment Programme   xvi, 14, 47, 48, 93, 98, 178, 187, 236
Structural Adjustment Programmes   6, 45
Subordinate/Inferior Financialisation   10, 12, 37, 101, 134, 135, 144
Sub-Saharan Africa   ix, x, xiii, xvi, 1, 5, 13, 15, 22, 37, 37n16, 42, 45, 46, 84, 121, 165f24, 173, 194, 199, 200, 234
Surplus-value   32, 35, 39, 62, 63, 65, 214

Thatcher, Margaret   19, 25

Trade liberalisation   99, 102, 110, 111, 136, 166, 201, 208, 236
Trade-off theory   147, 148, 169

UNCTAD   xvi, 11n15, 89, 137, 203, 204
Under-financed   14, 93, 122, 125, 129, 134, 142, 223, 236
Unequal exchange   110, 111, 112
United Nations   xvi, 11n15, 21, 83, 178, 198
Universal banks   16, 114, 119, 121, 122, 137, 163, 219, 224, 240

Volker, Paul   19

Washington Consensus   2, 2n2, 6, 99
Working capital   152, 154, 154n4, 155
World Bank   xiii, xiv, 2n2, 6, 11n15, 15, 21, 22, 27, 40, 47, 48, 50, 53, 61, 63, 75, 80, 81, 84, 85, 86, 87, 94, 97n3, 100, 102, 108, 109, 110, 111, 112, 113, 128, 135, 136, 141, 143, 151, 151n3, 152, 153, 153f18, 154f19, 155f20, 156f21, 156f22, 162, 164, 165f24, 165n6, 168t8, 172, 172f26, 174f27, 174f28, 175f30, 176, 177, 177f31, 178, 181, 187, 193, 194, 197, 207, 209, 217, 221, 227, 231, 232, 233, 236, 239